THE ANDERSON HOUSE COOKBOOK

**Ida Hoffman Anderson and Mahala Hoffman Cook
exchanging recipes**

The Anderson House Cookbook

Jeanne M. Hall
and John Hall

Pelican Publishing Company
Gretna 1986

Also by Jeanne Hall

*500 Recipes By Request From Mother Anderson's Famous
Dutch Kitchens*

500 More Recipes By Request

Also by Jeanne and John Hall

Bread and Breakfasts

Sketch of Anderson House by Ron Cook
Artwork on pgs. 37, 57, 76, 105, 138, 147, 171, 223, 255, 265, 267, 293, 297, 375,
    and 380 by Lauren Cunningham Tucker
All other artwork by La Verne Ford Taylor

Library of Congress Cataloging-in-Publication Data

Hall, Jeanne.
    The Anderson House cookbook.

    Includes index.
    1. Cookery, American. 2. Anderson House (Wabasha, Minn.)
I. Hall, John, 1944-   . II. Title.
TX715.H178 1986   641.5'09776'13   85-31040
ISBN 0-88389-475-7

Manufactured in the United States of America
Published by Pelican Publishing Company, Inc.
1101 Monroe Street, Gretna, Louisiana 70053

Dedication

This book is warmly dedicated to the family:

To Gayla Broadwater Hall, John Shields Hall III, Joseph Hall, Elizabeth Anne Hall, Ann McCaffrey, Margaret Kappa, Chris and Nick Kappa, Johanna Shields Hall, and Hal Hall.

To all parts of the Anderson family tree, all contributors to the cookbook, and all descendants of Ida Hoffman Anderson who established the Anderson House in 1896.

Contents

Preface

As the Pennsylvania Dutch would say...the book is all! Finally it is ready to go to the printer, and all of the last minute worries begin. Did we include *all* the recipes our guests have been requesting? Did we include too much? Leave out too much? Is the book too large? or too small? Most of all, will it be as well received as the previous books? Surely we must learn from each book!

Our first book was a collection of recipes Grandma Anderson had used in her time, and we literally struggled through many, many notebooks with her favorite recipes carefully written down. The second book included more of Grandma's recipes, as well as recipes we have developed in our test kitchen and recipes sent to us from guests.

This book is a collection of recipes from our guests now used in the dining rooms and recipes we developed ourselves in the test kitchen. There are some from the places where we have worked as well.

Each book seems to me to be better than the preceding one. All the while (six months actually) that I was working on this one I kept thinking that the recipes were more unusual, different, and not too expensive to make.

The last books brought many guests to the Anderson House...we didn't expect that bonus! We hope this one will do the same. Remember, if you're heading for the Mayo Clinic, we are only 45 minutes away, and if you are taking that incredibly beautiful ride on Highway 61 along the Mississippi, we are right there in Wabasha, overlooking the river and ready to extend our finest hospitality your way.

Acknowledgments

Another Anderson House cookbook is going out into the world, and it is somewhat more informal than the preceding books. Our guests come from all over the world. We are located only 45 minutes from the Mayo Clinic in Rochester, Minnesota, and visitors to the clinic are directed here by clinic personnel and others who know us well. Guests have become friends, and they have contributed many wonderful recipes sent to us from every part of the universe.

The recipe for our wonderful and famous Double Dutch Fudge Pie came that way, as did the recipe for Grandma Anderson's Famous Lemon Elegance Pie. We try every recipe that comes our way in our test kitchen and many of them are instantly incorporated into our food service.

We have selected the recipes most in demand, being careful not to duplicate recipes from our first books, with a few exceptions. For example, our recipe for plain, ordinary Rhubarb Pie was in an earlier cookbook, but we feel it is so special that it belongs in this one as well.

The bread sections in our books are always large because we serve ten to twenty kinds of bread or rolls every day, and we keep trying and testing to add still more. Because we specialize in desserts, the dessert section is also large.

Now is our chance to thank all our wonderful guests for their recipes, their unflagging interest in the Anderson House, and all the nice things they do for us. Many a new guest is happily referred to us by others. We are grateful, and we hope you like the book, for it is really your book too!

THE ANDERSON HOUSE COOKBOOK

Soups

Grandma Anderson said you could make soup out of anything, and Grandpa Anderson said he didn't want any soup that didn't stick to his ribs. I like the story about the tramp who came to somebody's back door and asked for a bit of soup. The lady of the house informed him she had nothing with which to make soup. He lifted a shiny nail out of his pocket and informed her he could make the best nail soup in the world. Fascinated, she agreed to let him try. He placed the nail in a pot of water and watched it begin to boil. After a few minutes he said this would be perfect soup if he could just have a few celery tops and a big, old carrot. The lady immediately produced them. As the aroma began to fill the kitchen, he sniffed appreciatively and said he sure wished he could find an onion or two. They were instantly provided. The woman began to be quite interested in the soup and said she thought maybe he could make nail soup after all. A moment later he ventured to say that a bit of cabbage would really polish things off, and if he could find a potato or two, it would probably be the best nail soup he had ever made. They were delivered at once. As the soup cooked merrily, the tramp spied four tomatoes in the window. He quickly grabbed them and sliced them into the soup. By this time the aroma was intense, and the lady of the house kept peeking into the soup pot. Sometime later, the tramp mentioned that all it lacked was a bit of barley to make it the king of all soups. After the barley cooked for a half hour, the tramp pronounced the soup completed. He was given a big bowl and his nail returned. The lady of the house devoured two bowls, then acclaimed the nail soup as being the best soup she had ever had and wondered where she could find a nail.

So much for the nail soup. We don't have that at the Anderson House but we have some good ones. Anderson House Chicken Noodle Soup is on our menu every day, and Pennsylvania Dutch Corn Chowder is another delight. There are more and more strange soups appearing. I once went to a luncheon and was served Cream of Deviled Egg Soup. I have to say I was horrified, but I HAD to eat it. And I wasn't all that thrilled with the cooks who made Minnesota Wild Rice Soup, and Chicken Giblet Soup, Shorty Piotter's specialty. Now, I'd walk a mile for both! These soup recipes and more are here. We hope you like them!

ANN'S BACON
AND POTATO CHOWDER

6 medium potatoes, diced
2 medium onions, diced
1 green pepper, diced
½ pound bacon, diced

1 to 1½ quarts milk
2 cups Medium White
  Sauce (see index)

Cover the potatoes, onions, and green pepper with water and cook until tender in a covered pan. Cover the bacon with water and simmer. Stir the white sauce into the cooked vegetables and whatever water remains after cooking. Add the simmered bacon. Slowly pour in the milk and cook an additional ten minutes, taking care not to burn. Serves eight.

SENATE BEAN SOUP

When we asked several of our friends in the Washington area to send us the recipe for Senate Bean Soup, we received four different recipes. To add to our confusion, we found still another version in a Sunday paper. We liked the first one we received, and made it most often.

1½ cups navy beans
1 large smoked ham hock
2 cups diced celery
1 cup grated carrots
1 large clove garlic,
  finely minced
2½ quarts water

½ cup diced green peppers
2 teaspoons salt
¼ teaspoon white pepper
½ teaspoon dry mustard
1 bunch green onions,
  chopped (use only some
  of the tops)

Wash beans, cover with cold water, and soak overnight. Drain beans. Combine remaining ingredients except the green onions. Bring to a boil, reduce the heat, and simmer for 2½ hours. Remove the ham hock. Discard fat, cut meat into bite-sized pieces, and return to soup. Add green onions and cook about 20 more minutes. Serves eight.

CREAM OF BROCCOLI SOUP

½ cup chopped onion
2 ribs celery,
   finely chopped
4 tablespoons butter
2 bunches broccoli,
   cleaned and trimmed

1 quart beef bouillon
1½ teaspoons salt
½ teaspoon Tabasco
1½ cups half-and-half
Fresh parsley (garnish)

Sauté onion and celery in butter in heavy saucepan. Cut broccoli into 2-inch to 3-inch pieces. Add broccoli, bouillon, salt, and Tabasco to onion and celery. Simmer 20 minutes over medium heat. Puree in blender. Before serving, stir in half-and-half. Heat gently. Garnish with sprig of fresh parsley. Makes about 2 quarts. Serves eight.

CABBAGE SOUP SAN JUAN

½ cup butter
1 medium head of
   cabbage, chopped
1 head cauliflower,
   coarsely chopped
8 cups chicken broth

1 2-ounce jar pimiento
¼ cup or 2 ounces
   Roquefort cheese
1 cup heavy cream
Salt and pepper
Popcorn (garnish)

Melt butter in large saucepan. Add cabbage and stir so that it is well coated with butter. Cook over low heat until soft, then add cauliflower and chicken broth. Bring to a boil, then reduce heat, cover, and simmer about 45 minutes, stirring occasionally. Add pimiento. Mix cheese and cream in a blender. Slowly stir the cheese and cream mixture into soup and season to taste. Serve with popcorn floating on top. Serves eight.

Note: This recipe was given to us by the owner of a small hotel on the square in Castañer, Puerto Rico.

THE CAPTAIN'S CHOWDER

When I was growing up, the Mayo doctors kept their yacht, the *North Star*, tied up in Wabasha. I'm sure it was the largest yacht on the Mississippi. In later years, one of their longtime crewmen retired and elected to live at the Anderson House. He came from Norway, had no family left there, and had no desire to return, so the Anderson House suited him well. After a year of inactivity, he decided to work for us when one of our clerks left. He was a great addition to our staff and regaled our guests with past adventures in many countries. Fred could also cook, although he hid that talent well for many years. One night, he was supposed to bring an offering to a Coon Feed he was attending, and he took along a gallon of The Captain's Chowder. We got leftovers when he came back, and though we didn't think his offering went with roast coon, we thought it went great with our appetites. As best we could reconstruct (Fred never measured), here it is.

1 pound fresh mushrooms	**1 cup heavy cream**
2 tablespoons butter	**1 pint fresh oysters,**
1 onion, minced	**drained**
1 quart chicken broth	**1 teaspoon seasoning salt**
½ cup butter, softened	**White pepper to taste**
½ cup flour	**Minced parsley (garnish)**
3 cups whole milk	

Sauté mushrooms in the 2 tablespoons butter. In a saucepan, simmer the onion in broth about 30 minutes. Melt the ½ cup butter in skillet, add flour, and stir until blended. Heat milk separately and add to flour mixture, stirring constantly until the sauce is thick and smooth. Add cream. Add oysters and mushrooms. Mix in blender. Return the mixture to the saucepan and season with salt and pepper to taste. Sprinkle lightly with parsley before serving. Serves eight.

Note: Fred said a captain of the North Star *showed him how to make this, and we are glad he did!*

ANDERSON HOUSE
BEER AND CHEESE SOUP

½ cup butter
1 cup flour
½ teaspoon salt
1½ pints milk
7 ounces american or
  cheddar cheese
¼ cup finely diced
  celery
¼ cup finely diced
  onions

¼ cup finely diced
  peppers
¼ cup finely chopped
  carrots
1 pint chicken stock
Paprika to color
8 ounces stale beer
Popcorn (garnish)

Melt butter and blend in flour, salt, and milk. Cook until thickened. Melt cheese in double boiler, parboil vegetables in chicken stock, and then combine all ingredients, except stale beer and popcorn. Bring to a boil, stirring constantly. Remove from heat; add beer. Do not bring to boil after adding beer, as this will cause curdling. Float 5 or 6 pieces of popcorn on top and serve at once, piping hot. Generously serves eight to ten.

CHEESE AND SPINACH SOUP

3 cups milk
1 cup grated cheese
1 cup spinach pulp
2 tablespoons butter
1½ tablespoons flour

1 teaspoon grated onion
Salt and pepper to taste
Whipped cream (garnish)
Parsley (garnish)

In a saucepan, heat the milk, then add the cheese and spinach pulp. Melt the butter, then add the flour. Thicken soup mixture with the flour and butter and season with grated onion, salt, and pepper. Serve with a tablespoon of whipped cream on top and sprinkle with dried parsley or fresh parsley if available. Serves four.

CHEESEBURGER CHOWDER

1 pound ground beef
½ cup finely chopped
  celery
¼ cup chopped onion
2 tablespoons chopped
  green pepper
3 tablespoons all-purpose
  flour
½ teaspoon salt
4 cups milk
1 cup pitted California
  ripe olives, halved
1 tablespoon beef-flavored
  gravy base
1 cup shredded sharp
  cheddar cheese

In large skillet, brown beef over medium heat. Drain off fat. Add celery, onion, and green pepper; cook till vegetables are tender but not brown. Blend in flour and salt; add milk, olives, and gravy base. Cook and stir over low heat until mixture thickens and bubbles, about 10 to 15 minutes. Add cheese and stir until it melts. Serves four to six.

CHICKEN-CORN SOUP

1 4-pound chicken
2 teaspoons salt
¼ teaspoon saffron
2 cups noodles
2 cups corn
1 teaspoon chopped parsley
1/8 teaspoon pepper
2 hard-cooked eggs,
  chopped

Cut chicken into pieces; place in soup kettle. Cover with water; add salt and saffron. Over medium heat, simmer until chicken is tender, then remove it from stock and let it cool. Remove skin; cut chicken into small pieces. Return chicken to stock; add noodles and corn. Bring to a boil and let simmer until noodles are tender. Stir in parsley, pepper, and eggs; serve immediately. Serves six.

CHICKEN DUMPLING SOUP

1 chicken
2 bay leaves
1 onion, chopped
Dash garlic powder
Poultry seasoning to taste
Salt and pepper to taste

2 large carrots,
    thinly sliced
2 ribs celery,
    thinly sliced
Dumplings (below)

In a soup kettle, cover the chicken with water. Add bay leaves, onion, garlic powder, and poultry seasoning, and boil. Add salt and pepper to taste. Simmer until the chicken is tender. Remove chicken and add carrots and celery; cook until the vegetables are tender. Remove meat from bones and add to broth. Top with Dumplings. Serves six.

DUMPLINGS

5 eggs, beaten
¼ cup milk
pinch salt

dash poultry seasoning
2 cups sifted flour

Mix all of the ingredients together, and beat until smooth. Drop by teaspoons into boiling broth. Cook about 15 minutes.

SHORTY PIOTTER'S CHICKEN GIBLET SOUP

This is an interesting variation of the usual chicken soup.

4 cups chicken stock
4 tablespoons chopped
    celery
4 tablespoons chopped
    onion
4 tablespoons butter

Salt to taste
3 cups milk
1 egg yolk, beaten
¾ cup cooked ground
    chicken giblets
    (precooked for 2½ hrs.)

Combine chicken stock, celery, and onion, and cook until vegetables are tender; strain. Make a white sauce of the butter, flour, salt, and milk, and combine with the chicken stock. Add giblets. Cook 30 minutes at low heat. Add beaten egg yolk just before serving. Serves six.

Note: This recipe comes from Shorty Piotter, the chef for many years of our Athearn Hotel in Oshkosh, Wisconsin. The Athearn was a 150-room Victorian dazzler with seven dining rooms and two bars. The dining rooms were busy every day, and many of the recipes developed by Chef Piotter found their way over to our Anderson House. This one has lasted through the years and is a prime favorite.

DUTCH CHOWDER 'N' DUMPLINGS

1½ cups ham strips
¼ cup chopped onion
2 tablespoons butter
  or margarine
2 11¼-ounce cans
  condensed celery soup
1½ cans water
1 10-ounce package
  frozen mixed vegetables,
  cooked and drained
¼ teaspoon ground nutmeg
Dash of salt
½ cup biscuit mix
2 teaspoons chopped
  parsley
3 tablespoons milk

In saucepan, brown ham and cook onion in butter until it is tender. Add soup and gradually blend in water. Add vegetables, nutmeg, and salt. Bring to a boil. Combine biscuit mix, parsley, and milk; drop by teaspoonsful into simmering soup. Simmer for 5 minutes; cover, and cook 5 minutes more or until the dumplings are tender. Serves four.

ANDERSON HOUSE
CHICKEN NOODLE SOUP

1 3½- to 4-pound
  chicken, quartered
2 quarts water
2 medium carrots, shaved

2 tablespoons finely
  chopped fresh or dried
  parsley
Noodles (below)

Place chicken in water and bring to a boil. Reduce heat after boiling stage and cook at medium heat for 1 hour. Add carrots and parsley to the chicken broth. Remove chicken. Skin chicken and chop coarsely; return to the pot. Cook 20 minutes more, then add noodles. Cook uncovered for 10 more minutes. Serves six.

NOODLES

2 beaten eggs
4 tablespoons milk

1 teaspoon salt
2 cups all-purpose flour

Combine the eggs, milk, and salt. Add flour and make a stiff dough. (Flours vary. You may have to add a little more flour to make dough the right consistency.) Flour a flat surface and roll dough very thin. Let stand for about 30 minutes. Roll up in loose roll and slice ¼ inch wide. Spread noodles out on flat surface and let them dry for about 2 to 2½ hours. After noodles are dried, drop them in the boiling chicken stock. Makes about 6 cups of cooked noodles.

Note: We sprinkle ¼ teaspoon of parsley on each serving. Also, after the chicken is cooked, we use only the chicken breast and upper thigh for the soup and save the remainder for chicken salad or chicken velvet soup.

BILOXI CHOWDER

½ cup butter
2 ribs celery, chopped
1 medium onion, chopped
2 10-ounce packages
frozen spinach, thawed
and chopped
1 cup whole milk
1 6-ounce can tiny shrimp
1½ quarts oysters and juice

2 cups heavy whipping
cream
1 teaspoon Worcestershire
sauce
½ teaspoon garlic salt
Salt and pepper to taste
Whipped cream (garnish)
Paprika (garnish)
Parsley (garnish)

Melt butter in a heavy kettle or Dutch oven. Sauté the celery and onion until the onion is transparent. Add spinach and milk. Bring to a boil and simmer for about 10 minutes. Add shrimp, oysters, and juice, and cook covered until oysters begin to curl at the edges. Place this mixture in your blender, and liquefy in batches. Return to the kettle and stir in cream, Worcestershire sauce, garlic salt, and salt and pepper. When serving, put a dollop of whipped cream on each serving with a light dusting of paprika or finely chopped parsley flakes. Serves twelve.

Note: This recipe came from Biloxi, Mississippi, where you never run out of shrimp, oysters, crabs, or other creatures of the deep. The first time we ever went to Florida, we went to New Orleans first. We stayed a week instead of two days, then started for Florida along the coast and never made it past Biloxi. We stayed at the Biloxi Hotel and went wild with joy when we were sent down to manage it 12 years later. I consider Biloxi the real South.

PENNSYLVANIA DUTCH
CORN CHOWDER

1 bunch celery
1 cup cubed raw potatoes
1 small onion,
  finely chopped
½ teaspoon salt
1 cup fresh chopped
  tomatoes

1 cup creamed corn
1 tablespoon green pepper,
  chopped
1/8 teaspoon baking soda
1 pint hot milk
1 cup cream
2 tablespoons dried parsley

Cook tops of celery in water for 30 minutes. Strain and save 1½ cups of the water. Into the water put raw potatoes, onion, and salt. Simmer over low heat until potatoes are tender. Meanwhile, cook tomatoes, canned corn, and green pepper a few minutes and then add to potato mixture. Add soda and combine with 1 pint of hot milk. Add cream and dried parsley. Check seasonings. Serves four.

CORN SOUP WITH RIVELS

1 No. 2½ can corn
2 quarts water
1 cup light cream
1-1/3 cups flour
1 egg

3 tablespoons butter
1½ teaspoons salt
Pinch pepper
Chopped parsley (garnish)

Heat corn and water to boiling. Make batter from cream, flour, and egg. Pour this batter through a colander into boiling corn. Add butter, salt, and pepper. Cook slowly for 3 minutes. Add chopped parsley. Serve hot. Serves six.

CREAM SOUP BASE

½ cup butter
½ cup flour
1½ teaspoons salt

¼ teaspoon white pepper
3 cups milk
1½ cups half-and-half

Melt butter in saucepan. Add flour, salt, and pepper. Remove from heat and mix well. Place back on heat and add 1 cup milk. Stir constantly until smooth. Stir in the rest of the milk and cream. Stir constantly until it begins to thicken. Serves four to six.

Note: You can use this base for fresh mushroom soup, broccoli and cheese soup, cream of tomato, cream of celery, and, best of all, vegetable soup, which is made by adding your vegetable leftovers together, spinning them in the blender just half a second and adding to this base. To look really fancy, add a tablespoon of whipped cream to top of this soup with finely chopped parsley or a dusting of paprika.

GREEN ONION AND
POTATO SOUP

1 bunch green onions,
  minced (bulbs only)
1 small onion, minced
2 tablespoons butter
1 quart water
2 teaspoons salt
4 potatoes, minced

2 cups hot milk
2 teaspoons dried parsley
  or 4 teaspoons finely
  chopped fresh parsley
2 tablespoons
  Parmesan cheese

Cook green onions and onion slowly with 1 tablespoon butter in saucepan until they are soft. Do not brown. Add water, salt, and potatoes. Continue cooking slowly for about 40 minutes. Add milk and 1 tablespoon of butter. Serve with a piece of French bread that has been dried in oven, floating on top with parsley and Parmesan cheese. Serves six.

GAZPACHO

2 cloves garlic, crushed
2 pounds medium
  tomatoes (about 6),
  peeled and chopped
1 medium cucumber,
  pared and cut in chunks
1 large green pepper,
  chopped
2 slices white bread,
  trimmed and crumbled
  (1 cup)
¼ cup red wine vinegar
2 cups tomato juice

1 cup water
¼ cup olive or
  vegetable oil
½ teaspoon salt
¼ teaspoon freshly ground
  black pepper
Cucumber slices (optional)
½ cup green onions,
  chopped
½ cup packaged
  garlic croutons
½ cup green pepper,
  chopped

Combine garlic, tomatoes, cucumber, green pepper, bread, and vinegar in container of electric blender; mix until smooth. Press mixture through sieve, discarding the solids. Add tomato juice, water, oil, salt, and pepper to the tomato liquid; chill well. Serve in chilled bowls; garnish with cucumber, green onions, croutons, and green pepper. Serves six.

MUSHROOM-BARLEY SOUP

3½ ounces onions, chopped
3½ ounces celery, chopped
1 clove garlic, minced
4 tablespoons butter
2½ ounces barley

2 quarts chicken stock
13 ounces fresh
  mushrooms, sautéed
  in ¼ cup butter

Sauté onions, celery, and garlic in butter until tender. Add dry barley and sauté 10 more minutes, until barley gets thick. Add chicken stock and mushrooms. Boil and simmer until barley is tender, about ½ hour to 45 minutes. Serves six.

DICK BURGE'S BILOXI, MISSISSIPPI, GUMBO

1 cup bacon drippings
1 cup all-purpose flour
8 stalks celery, chopped
3 large yellow onions, chopped
1 bunch green onions, chopped
1 green pepper, chopped
2 cloves garlic, minced
½ cup chopped parsley
1 pound okra, sliced
2 tablespoons shortening
2 quarts chicken stock
2 quarts water
½ cup Worcestershire sauce
Tabasco sauce to taste
½ cup catsup
1 16-ounce can whole tomatoes
2 tablespoons salt
2 bay leaves
¼ teaspoon thyme
¼ teaspoon rosemary
2 cups chopped cooked chicken
1 pound claw crabmeat
3 to 4 pounds boiled shrimp
1 pint oysters (optional)
1 teaspoon brown sugar
Lemon juice to taste

In a large pot, heat bacon drippings over medium heat, add flour slowly, and stir constantly until roux is a chocolate-like brown. This takes a long time, about 30 to 45 minutes. Add celery, onions, green pepper, garlic, and parsley and simmer 45 minutes to 1 hour, stirring occasionally. Fry okra in shortening until slightly browned. Add to pot and stir well for a few minutes. Add chicken stock, water, Worcestershire sauce, Tabasco sauce, catsup, tomatoes with juice, salt, bay leaves, thyme, and rosemary. Simmer 2½ hours. Add chicken, crabmeat, and shrimp, and simmer 30 minutes more. (If using oysters, add with seafood.) Add brown sugar and lemon juice. Serve in bowls over hot rice. Well worth the time! Serves twenty.

Note: Dick Burge was a bachelor officer at Keesler Air Force Base in Biloxi. He belonged to a progressive dinner club. His two offerings were fried chicken and gumbo, both of which won much acclaim among the other club members and their ladies.

CREAM OF ONION SOUP

3 large sweet Spanish
   onions, thinly sliced
3 cups chicken broth
2 medium potatoes, sliced
1½ tablespoons butter
1 cup chopped sweet
   Spanish onion
1 tablespoon flour

1 cup heavy cream
1 cup milk
1½ teaspoons salt
¼ teaspoon pepper
Chopped parsley or
   toasted croutons
   (garnish)

Boil onion slices in broth over high heat, stirring constantly, for 20 minutes. Add potatoes and cook 15 minutes longer or until potatoes are tender. Puree in blender or mash with potato masher. Melt butter in saucepan. Add chopped onion and sauté until tender and golden. Blend in flour. Add cream and milk; cook until slightly thickened. Add to pureed mixture and bring to boil. Season with salt and pepper. Top each serving with parsley or croutons. Serves eight.

OXTAIL SOUP

3 oxtails
1 cup pearl barley
½ cup split peas
1 medium onion, chopped
1 cup chopped celery
Pinch powdered bay leaves

¾ cup chopped parsley
   (the more the better)
1 clove garlic, pressed
2 tablespoons vinegar
Salt and pepper to taste
About 4 peppercorns

Put all ingredients in a very large kettle, cover with water, and let simmer over medium heat 2 or 3 hours or until everything is soft. If necessary, add more water (the barley swells). That's it! Just taste for flavoring before serving. This served with hot bread and a salad is a meal in itself. Serves six to eight.

PEA SOUP ANDERSON HOUSE

This pea soup is a company dish that can be made in a jiffy, assuming you freeze any chicken broth you don't use.

2 cups chicken broth
3 cups frozen green peas
½ cup half-and-half
1 ounce pimiento, minced
2 tablespoons sherry

Salt and pepper to taste
½ cup whipping cream,
    whipped (garnish)
Paprika or parsley (garnish)

Boil peas and chicken broth together for 15 minutes in a covered saucepan. Puree in blender. Put back into pot over low heat, being careful not to boil. Add half-and-half, pimiento, and sherry. Season to taste. Serves four.

Note: We serve a tablespoon of whipped cream over this with a light dusting of paprika or chopped parsley.

SPLIT PEA SOUP

1 cup split peas
5 cups cold water
1 cup diced celery
1 carrot
1 onion
1/8 teaspoon thyme
1/8 teaspoon marjoram

1/8 teaspoon pepper
Dash cayenne pepper
½ bay leaf
2 teaspoons salt
2 teaspoons butter or fat
Ham bone or 1 ham hock

Put all ingredients in soup kettle and cook slowly for 2 hours. If you use ham bone or hock, omit salt and butter or fat. Strain. Serves six.

CREAM OF PEANUT SOUP

¼ cup butter
1 medium onion, chopped
2 ribs celery, chopped
1 tablespoon flour
2 quarts chicken stock
  or beef broth

2 cups smooth
  peanut butter
1¼ cups half-and-half
12 rounded teaspoons
  chopped roasted peanuts

In a 4-quart soup kettle, melt butter. Add onion and celery. Sauté over medium heat until onions are soft but not brown. Stir in flour until well blended. Add chicken stock, stirring constantly. Bring to a boil. Remove from heat. Pour through sieve if smooth soup is desired. Add peanut butter and cream, stirring to blend thoroughly. Return to low heat until heated thoroughly, about 5 minutes; do not boil. Serve in small bowls. Drop about 1 rounded teaspoonful peanuts into each bowl. Serves twelve.

Note: This soup is also good served chilled.

BASQUE POTATO SOUP

1 pound chorizo or Italian
  sausage, sliced
½ cup chopped onion
2 16-ounce cans tomatoes
4 Idaho potatoes (6 cups),
  pared and diced
¼ cup chopped parsley
1 cup diagonally sliced
  celery

2 tablespoons chopped
  celery leaves
1½ cups water
2 beef bouillon cubes
1 bay leaf
1 tablespoon salt
½ teaspoon dried thyme
¼ teaspoon pepper
1 tablespoon lemon juice

In large saucepan or kettle, brown sausage over medium heat. Add onion and cook 5 minutes. Add remaining ingredients. Bring to a boil, reduce heat, and simmer uncovered 40 minutes, or until potatoes are tender. Serves six.

POTATO AND BEAN SOUP

1½ pounds green beans,
   coarsely chopped
¼ cup butter
2 cups peeled, thinly
   sliced potatoes
1 quart beef stock
Parsley
1 sprig thyme
1 clove

1 bay leaf
Salt and pepper
2 cups undiluted
   evaporated milk or
   light cream, scalded
2 egg yolks, beaten
2 tablespoons sweet butter
   (optional)
Croutons (garnish)

Put beans in saucepan with enough water to cover. Cook 5 minutes. Drain. Heat butter, add beans and potatoes. Cook for 5 minutes, stirring to prevent browning. Put into soup kettle with stock, herbs, and seasonings. Bring to a boil and let simmer for 30 minutes. Pour through a sieve. Return to heat, bring to a boil, and stir in evaporated milk, alternating with egg yolks. If desired, add butter, a little at a time, before serving. Serve with croutons. Serves six.

PUMPKIN SOUP

½ of a small pumpkin
3 tablespoons butter
1 teaspoon sugar
1 teaspoon salt

¼ teaspoon white pepper
3 cups milk, heated
Croutons (garnish)

Cut pumpkin into wedges, and remove seeds and outer skin. Chop into pieces and cook in boiling salted water until tender. Drain the pumpkin pulp and press through a sieve. You should be left with about 2 cups of pumpkin puree. Combine the puree with butter, sugar, salt, and white pepper. Cook over a low heat for about 10 minutes. Stir in milk and simmer soup for 10 more minutes. Serve hot with croutons. Serves four to six.

WELCOME ANDERSON'S SAUERKRAUT SOUP

Welcome Anderson liked soup and hot pie for breakfast, and that's what he had every morning of his life as far as I know. In Grandma's handwritten cookbooks she called this his "harvest soup." We make it often for the after-ski crowds.

1½ pounds short ribs
  of beef
1 cup chopped onion
¼ cup peanut oil
1 #303 can sauerkraut
6 cups beef broth

1 16-ounce can stewed
  tomatoes
6 peppercorns
1 large bay leaf
¼ cup chopped green
  peppers (optional)

Remove fat from short ribs. Leave meat on. In a large saucepan or soup kettle, brown meat and onion in oil. Add sauerkraut. Add the rest of the ingredients and bring to a boil. Simmer for 1 hour. Remove bones, peppercorns, and bay leaf. Strip the bones of meat, cut into bite-sized pieces, and add to soup. Taste for seasonings, then serve at once. You may add ¼ cup chopped green peppers if you like that flavor. Serves eight.

SHORT RIB SOUP

5½ cups water
2 pounds short ribs of beef,
  cut in 2-inch pieces
5 beef bouillon cubes
2 tablespoons
  onion powder
¾ teaspoon garlic powder
½ teaspoon ground ginger
¼ teaspoon salt

1/8 teaspoon ground
  red pepper
¼ pound fresh spinach,
  torn into bite-sized pieces
1 carrot, slivered
4 green onions, cut in
  2-inch pieces
1 egg, beaten

In a large saucepan, combine water and short ribs. Bring to a boil; skim off foam. Add bouillon cubes. Cover and simmer until meat is tender, 1½ to 2 hours. Stir in onion and garlic powders, ginger, salt, and red pepper. Add spinach, carrot, and green onions; simmer 5 minutes. Bring to a boil; stir in egg. Remove from heat and serve. Serves four.

REUBEN SOUP

½ cup beef broth
½ cup chicken broth
¼ cup coarsely chopped celery
½ cup coarsely chopped onion
½ cup coarsely chopped green pepper
¼ cup pimiento
¼ pound shredded cooked corn beef
1 cup chopped Swiss cheese

¾ cup sauerkraut, drained, rinsed, and squeezed dry
½ stick butter
2 cups half-and-half
1 tablespoon cornstarch dissolved in 2 tablespoons water
Salt and fresh ground pepper to taste
1 tablespoon finely chopped parsley
Paprika

Place broths, celery, onion, green pepper, and pimiento in a heavy 2-quart saucepan, with water to cover. Bring to boiling point. Reduce heat and simmer until vegetables are tender but still slightly crisp, about five minutes. Remove from heat. Add the beef, cheese, and sauerkraut.

Melt butter in top of double boiler set over gently simmering water. Blend in half-and-half. Blend in cornstarch. Add soup and stir until smooth and completely heated. Do not boil. Season with salt and pepper, and stir in chopped parsley. Dust lightly with paprika. Serve at once. Serves eight.

Note: We have Catherine Bastian, the soup cook at the Jacksonville, Florida, Hospitality Inn, to thank for this one. A popular soup there, it has been a smash hit at the Anderson House.

RED CABBAGE AND SAUSAGE SOUP

4 tablespoons butter
1 medium onion, chopped
2 cloves garlic, minced
1 #2½ can pickled beets, julienne cut (reserve liquid)
2 14-ounce cans beef broth, undiluted
1 small head red cabbage (about 1 pound), finely shredded
1 pound Kielbase (Polish sausage), cut in ½-inch slices
1 tart apple, peeled and chopped
Sour cream (garnish)

In a Dutch oven or 4-quart heavy saucepan, melt butter and sauté onion and garlic until golden. Add beet liquid, broth, and cabbage to saucepan. Bring to a boil, cover, and simmer for 1 hour and 15 minutes. Add beets, sausage, and apple to saucepan. Return to boiling and simmer 15 minutes more, or until apple pieces are tender. Skim and discard fat. Serve hot and offer sour cream to spoon over individual portions. Serves four.

MINNESOTA WILD RICE SOUP

1 medium onion, thinly sliced and quartered
4 ounces fresh mushrooms, sliced or chopped
3 tablespoons butter
¼ cup flour
4 cups chicken stock
1½ cups cooked wild rice
1 cup half-and-half
¼ cup dry sherry
Chopped parsley (garnish)

Cook onion and mushrooms in butter until onion is transparent. Add flour and cook for 15 minutes, stirring occasionally. Add chicken stock and cook approximately 10 minutes, stirring until smooth. Add wild rice, half-and-half, and sherry, stirring until heated throughout. Garnish with parsley. Serves six to eight.

WELCOME ANDERSON'S
COUNTRY SOUP

Welcome Anderson was my grandfather's brother. He lived to be 101 years old, and he was more interested in good food than anything else in the world, an interest that continued until the day he died. Fresh breads, soups, and stews were held in high regard, and this soup was one of his favorites that he often made himself.

½ cup butter
2 oxtails, cut in 1-inch
 pieces
12 cups water
½ cup barley
2 teaspoons salt
1 tablespoon butter
1 clove garlic, crushed

1 cup diced carrot
1 cup diced celery
Flour
2 teaspoons Worcestershire
 sauce
3 tablespoons chopped
 parsley
2 ounces sherry or wine

Melt butter. Brown oxtails. Drain off fat. Add water, barley, and salt. Simmer for two hours. Heat the tablespoon of butter and garlic in a large skillet over low heat for about 5 minutes. Add vegetables. Brown lightly, dust with flour, and brown another 10 minutes. Add 1 cup of soup broth to skillet and bring to a boil. Add vegetables to soup and cook 1 hour. Just before serving, add the Worcestershire sauce, parsley, and sherry or wine (preferably sherry). Serves eight.

SQUASH-APPLE BISQUE

4 cups chicken stock
1 medium butternut
   squash, unpeeled,
   seeded, and chopped
2 large tart apples,
   peeled and chopped
1 small onion,
   peeled and chopped

1/8 teaspoon rosemary
6 tablespoons butter
6 tablespoons flour
¾ cup whipping cream
   or half-and-half
Salt and pepper to taste
Raw apples, diced
   (garnish)

Combine stock, squash, apples, onion, and rosemary in a 4-quart saucepan. Cover and simmer over low heat until squash is tender, about 10 to 15 minutes. Puree in blender or food processor and return to pan. Melt butter in a 1-quart saucepan. Stir in flour and cook 2 to 3 minutes over medium heat, stirring constantly. Stir into squash puree; simmer, uncovered, 15 minutes over low heat. Add cream and season with salt and pepper. Pour into serving bowls and sprinkle with diced apple, if desired. Serves six to eight.

AMSTERDAM TOMATO SOUP

Beef soup bones to make
   1½ quarts good beef
   stock (about 3 pounds
   beef knuckles)
1 can tomatoes (not whole)
1 large onion,
   finely chopped

4 half-ribs celery,
   with leaves on
1 bay leaf
8 peppercorns
¼ cup minced parsley
1 tomato, sliced

Make a stock from the soup bones. Remove bones. You should have 1 to 1½ quarts of stock. Add all the other ingredients, except fresh tomato. Put over medium heat. Bring to a boil and cook 30 minutes. Strain. Place a very thin slice of tomato in the soup bowl and fill with soup. Serves four.

Salads

Senors & Senoras...
YOU'LL LOVE
PEPE'S wonderful
POOL SIDE SALAD!

In Grandma Anderson's day a crew of men braved the below-zero weather and cut enough ice out of the Mississippi to last the Anderson House until the next year. It was stacked on flatbed trucks and hurried to our backyard ice house where it was buried in sawdust from floor to ceiling. It was cut into fifty-pound blocks, which fit nicely into the iceboxes in the big, old-fashioned kitchen complete with two enormous wood- and coal-burning stoves.

In those days salads hadn't reached the popularity they now have, and of course there weren't as many recipes. Cole slaw was popular—the cooks devised hundreds of ways to make and serve it. The Pennsylvania Dutch favorite in days past was wilted lettuce served with crumbled bacon, sweet-and-sour dressing, or sometimes just plain melted butter.

There was one rule in Grandma's kitchen that couldn't be broken. Hot salads had to be hot and cold salads had to be chilled well. One of the hot salads we still serve often is most popular—the Old-Fashioned Potato Salad. Grandma served it with slices of home-cured ham or sausages that Will Anderson stuffed himself.

At our little inn, our house salad is a blend of romaine, watercress, lettuce, and fresh spinach. We serve it with our house dressing, which is a marvelous dressing with a bit of blue cheese. Our fruit salad is served in a lettuce cup with dusted paprika edges and filled with wonderful fresh fruit when available. We serve Honey Dressing with this one.

Surely tomatoes have to be the most popular of all salad vegetables. We raise as many of our own tomatoes as three small garden plots will hold, and it's still not enough. We have enormous steak tomatoes, yellow tomatoes, Italian tomatoes, cherry tomatoes, and miniature tomatoes in both yellow and red. When winter comes and all we can serve are hothouse tomatoes, it is a time for mourning!

Our favorite non-green salad is King's Ransom Salad. We serve it for almost every wedding luncheon or dinner and for very festive parties. The dressing is as delightful as the salad. We recommend it for when you want to serve a very special salad.

We hope you will enjoy the salads in this section. For special dressings, be sure to look in the next section.

AVOCADO MOLD

1 cup water
2 envelopes (2 tablespoons)
  unflavored gelatin
3 cups diced avocados
  (about 2 medium)
2 tablespoons lime juice

1 cup yogurt
2 tablespoons honey
1 teaspoon salt
¼ teaspoon Tabasco
Spinach leaves
2 cups diced pineapple

Sprinkle gelatin over ½ cup of the water; set aside to soften. Bring remaining water to boil; stir in gelatin mixture, and dissolve completely. Toss avocados with lime juice; set aside 1 cup. Place remaining avocado, gelatin mixture, yogurt, honey, salt, and Tabasco in blender. Blend until smooth, scraping sides as needed. Stir in reserved avocado cubes. Pour into 4- to 5-cup mold. Chill until firm, about 3 hours. Unmold onto spinach-lined plate; surround with pineapple. Serves six to eight.

FROZEN BANANA SALAD

2 3-ounce packages
  cream cheese
1 teaspoon salt
½ cup mayonnaise
Juice of 1 lemon
½ cup crushed pineapple
  with juice
2 medium bananas, sliced

½ cup chopped walnuts
½ cup maraschino
  cherries, chopped
1 cup whipping cream,
  whipped and sweetened
  with 1 teaspoon sugar
Crisp lettuce leaves

Mix cream cheese with salt, mayonnaise, and lemon juice; then add pineapple, bananas, nuts, and cherries. Fold into whipped cream and pour into tray to freeze. Freeze 24 hours. Cut into squares, place on crisp lettuce leaves on chilled plates, and serve. Serves six.

APRICOT SALAD

1/3 cup finely chopped
  celery
5 dates, pitted and finely
  chopped
8 walnut halves
Apricot Dressing (below)

1 head romaine lettuce
8 canned apricot halves
  (reserve syrup)
8 tablespoons pistachio
  nuts or green coconut,
  finely chopped

Combine celery, dates, and walnut halves. Add enough Apricot Dressing to bind ingredients together. Place romaine leaves on 4 salad plates, and top with celery-date-walnut mixture. Place 2 apricot halves on each plate, and spoon more dressing over salads. Sprinkle with the pistachio nuts or green coconut. Serves four.

APRICOT DRESSING

¼ cup syrup from canned
  apricots
1 tablespoon lemon juice
1/8 teaspoon paprika
Few grains salt

1 egg yolk
2 tablespoons sugar
1 egg white, stiffly beaten,
  or 1/3 cup cream, beaten
  until light

Mix apricot syrup, lemon juice, paprika, and salt in top of double boiler. Bring to boiling point and pour over egg yolk mixed with sugar. Return to double boiler and stir until thickened. Turn onto beaten egg white or cool and fold in cream.

NORA HOFFMAN'S
BEET AND EGG SALAD

In Grandma's house back in Pennsylvania there were always hard-boiled eggs pickled in beet juice. She said her mother often made Beet and Red Egg Salad. At the Anderson House, the boarders soon grew to like it and to expect it. Whenever she served potatoes and onions, she also served the salad.

½ cup cider vinegar
½ teaspoon salt
2 tablespoons sugar
1 teaspoon dried mustard

¼ teaspoon allspice
1 16-ounce can small beets
4 hard-cooked eggs
Shredded lettuce

Combine vinegar, salt, sugar, mustard, and allspice. Cook to boiling point and pour over well-drained beets. Cool. After completely cooked, add the hard-cooked, shelled eggs, and store in refrigerator for a day. Move eggs occasionally so all sides are exposed to juice and they color evenly. Serve beets on shredded lettuce and quartered eggs as a garnish. Serves four.

BEET AND APPLE SALAD

This recipe is a specialty of the Calumet Country Inn at Pipestone, Minnesota. If you go to the Black Hills, check your map and plan to stay at the Calumet overnight. It's worth the few miles out of your way, and one of the national monuments in the United States is at Pipestone, so it's an extra bonus for you. The rooms are beautiful in this restored country inn. The inn has magnificent antique furniture, walls of natural stone, and superb food. Don't miss it!

1 16-ounce jar pickled
   beets
2 medium tart apples,
   peeled and diced
2 tablespoons mayonnaise
1 tablespoon sugar

Dash salt
Pepper to taste
Iceberg or Romaine lettuce
2 tablespoons dried or
   fresh parsley (garnish)

Drain beets. Cut into julienne strips ½ inch thick. Mix beets, apples, mayonnaise, sugar, salt, and pepper. Toss lightly together. Serve in lettuce cup or with chopped romaine. Garnish with parsley. Serves six.

ANN'S BEET MOLD

1 16-ounce can cubed beets
Water
1 onion, chopped
½ bay leaf
½ teaspoon salt
Pepper to taste
1 package lemon-flavored
  gelatin

1 teaspoon tarragon
  vinegar
1 tablespoon cider vinegar
Chicory or lettuce (garnish)
French dressing or
  mayonnaise

Drain one can of cubed beets. Save juice. Place beets in well-greased 9-inch square pan. Add enough water to juice to make 2 cups. Simmer liquid 2 minutes in covered saucepan with onion, bay leaf, salt, and pepper. Remove bay leaf. Add package of gelatin and tarragon and cider vinegars. Cool. Pour over beets. Chill until firm. Serve unmolded on bed of chicory or lettuce with French dressing or mayonnaise. Serves six.

BEER CABBAGE SLAW

1 medium head green
  cabbage (about 2 pounds),
  shredded
1 large green pepper,
  shredded
1 to 2 tablespoons celery
  seed

1 teaspoon salt
¼ teaspoon pepper
1 teaspoon minced onion
2 ounces pimiento
1 cup mayonnaise
½ cup light beer

Combine cabbage and green pepper in large bowl with celery seed, salt, pepper, onion, and pimiento. In small bowl, combine mayonnaise and beer; blend well. Add to cabbage mixture; toss until well blended. Refrigerate, covered, until well chilled, at least 3 hours. Serves six.

JELLIED
BLACK CHERRY SALAD

1 package lemon-flavored
  gelatin
2 cups grape juice
1 tablespoon lemon juice

1 #2 can black cherries
½ cup pecans
Banana Dressing (below)
Lettuce

Dissolve gelatin with 1 cup hot grape juice. Add lemon juice and cold grape juice. Pit cherries and stuff with pecans, then add to partially congealed gelatin mixture. Pour into individual molds and chill until set. Serve on lettuce with Banana Dressing or any other preferred dressing. Serves eight to ten.

BANANA DRESSING

2 ripe bananas
2 tablespoons strained
  honey

1 tablespoon lemon juice
½ cup whipped cream

Crush bananas with fork but do not work until smooth. Add honey and lemon juice. Fold in whipped cream.

ANN'S CABBAGE SLAW

1 head cabbage, grated
1 carrot, grated
1 small onion, grated
1½ tablespoons salad oil
¾ cup mayonnaise
½ cup sugar

2 tablespoons cider vinegar
½ teaspoon celery seed
1½ teaspoons prepared
  mustard
¼ teaspoon salt

Toss cabbage, carrot, onion, and salad oil together until cabbage is coated. Combine remaining ingredients with cabbage mixture; toss and chill. Serves eight to ten.

BERMUDA SALAD BOWL

1 small head cauliflower,
  separated into buds
1 small head lettuce,
  shredded
¼ large Bermuda onion,
  peeled and thinly sliced
¾ cup French dressing

½ cup stuffed olives, sliced
2 cups watercress
1¼ ounces Roquefort
  cheese
India Relish Dressing
  (below)

Toss ingredients together with India Relish Dressing. Serves twelve.

INDIA RELISH DRESSING

½ teaspoon salt
½ teaspoon sugar
½ teaspoon paprika
3 tablespoons India relish

½ cup olive oil
¼ cup cider vinegar
Few drops Worcestershire
  sauce

Beat with a rotary beater.

JELLIED CANTALOUPE SALAD

1 package lime-flavored
  gelatin
¾ cup boiling water
2½ cups cantaloupe balls

¼ teaspoon salt
¾ cup mayonnaise
½ cup evaporated milk,
  chilled

Dissolve gelatin in water. Chill until mixture begins to thicken. Fold in the cantaloupe balls, salt, and mayonnaise. Whip the evaporated milk until stiff, and fold it into cantaloupe mixture. Pour into 8-inch square pan or a ring mold and chill until firm. Unmold on lettuce leaves. Serves six.

CAESAR SALAD

This popular salad, like so many other classics, owes its birthright to that greatest of all mothers, necessity. Caesar Cardini, a restaurateur in Tijuana, Mexico, in the 1920s, found himself with a crowd of unexpected patrons and an almost empty pantry. Empty, except for a case of romaine lettuce, eggs, and some less-than-fresh bread. Using creativity and showmanship, he created the salad that now bears his name.

1 clove garlic, peeled and sliced
½ cup olive oil
1 cup French bread cubes, crust removed
1 large head romaine lettuce, washed and drained
2 tablespoons wine vinegar
1/8 teaspoon Worcestershire sauce
¼ teaspoon dry mustard
Salt and pepper to taste
3 tablespoons grated Parmesan cheese
1 egg
2 tablespoons lemon juice

Combine garlic and olive oil in jar with tight-fitting lid. Let stand several hours or overnight. Remove garlic. In medium frying pan, cook bread cubes in 2 tablespoons garlic oil until golden brown on all sides. Set aside. Tear romaine into bite-sized pieces and place in large salad bowl. To remaining garlic oil, add vinegar, Worcestershire sauce, mustard, salt, and pepper. Shake well. Pour over lettuce. Sprinkle with cheese. Toss until lettuce is coated. Break egg over center of salad. Pour lemon juice directly over egg. Toss well. Sprinkle with bread cubes. Toss lightly. Serve immediately on chilled dinner plates. Serves four to six.

Note: 1 cup packaged croutons may be substituted for French bread cubes. Omit cooking cubes in garlic-oil mixture.

CHICKEN AND SWEETBREAD SALAD

2 pair sweetbreads
1 teaspoon celery seed
2 teaspoons tarragon
 vinegar
2 cloves garlic, halved
5 pounds boiled chicken,
 diced
¼ cup grated onion

1 teaspoon salt
1 cup heavy cream
1 cup mayonnaise
2 heads lettuce
8 ounces blanched almonds,
 finely chopped
1 cup pine nuts
Ripe olives (garnish)

Wash sweetbreads, cover with boiling water, and simmer 1 hour. Cool quickly, then pull apart. Tear sweetbreads into small pieces. Sprinkle with celery seed and vinegar. Put in bowl with garlic to stand overnight. At serving time lift sweetbreads from garlic. Mix with chicken. Sprinkle with grated onion and salt. Mix in pine nuts. Whip cream, fold into mayonnaise at last moment, and mix half with chicken. Line plates with lettuce, and spoon salad onto lettuce. Spoon remaining whipped cream–mayonnaise mixture over tops of salads. Garnish with ripe olives and almonds. Serves eight.

BLEU CHEESE COLESLAW

6 cups shredded cabbage
1½ cups diagonally sliced
 celery
1 cup sliced radishes
½ cup chopped green
 pepper
¼ cup minced parsley
3 green onions, thinly
 sliced
1 cup sour cream

½ cup mayonnaise
3 tablespoons wine vinegar
1 tablespoon sugar
1½ teaspoons salt
½ teaspoon ground white
 pepper
2 ounces crumbled bleu
 cheese
Cherry tomatoes (optional)

Put prepared vegetables in large bowl. Blend sour cream, mayonnaise, wine vinegar, sugar, salt, and pepper. Toss dressing with vegetables and bleu cheese. Chill to blend flavors. Garnish with cherry tomatoes, if desired. Serves eight to ten.

CHEESE AND PINEAPPLE SALAD

This recipe is so old, we just assume everyone has it. However, requests have come in every time we serve it, so we have decided to include it here.

2 tablespoons unflavored gelatin	**8 ounces American cheese, grated**
½ cup cold water	**1 cup whipping cream, whipped**
2 cups crushed pineapple	**Nut Dressing (below)**
Juice of 1 lemon	
1 cup sugar	

Stir gelatin into water and set aside to dissolve. Heat pineapple, lemon juice, and sugar. Mix the heated pineapple and gelatin thoroughly and place in refrigerator until mixture begins to congeal. Stir grated cheese into mixture and thoroughly fold in whipped cream. Pour the mixture into a 9-inch square pan or individual molds and place in refrigerator until firm. Serve with Nut Dressing. Serves twelve.

NUT DRESSING

1 cup mayonnaise	**4 tablespoons finely chopped nuts**
4 tablespoons finely chopped celery	
2 tablespoons finely chopped green pepper	

Blend all ingredients together and serve with Cheese and Pineapple Salad.

PENNSYLVANIA DUTCH
GO-TO-MEETING HOT SLAW

2 tablespoons butter
½ head large cabbage
Dressing (below)

3 slices bacon, cooked,
drained, and crumbled
1 ounce pimiento

Melt butter in heavy skillet. Cut cabbage in two, place cut side down on bread board and slice down entire length of cabbage so it falls in fine shreds. Place cabbage in skillet with butter and steam gently while making dressing. Pour dressing over cabbage. Add bacon and pimiento. Cook over low heat a few seconds until wilted and serve at once. Serves four.

DRESSING

½ teaspoon salt
1/8 teaspoon white pepper
1 teaspoon mustard
2 heaping tablespoons
sugar

1 heaping teaspoon flour
1 egg, beaten
½ cup vinegar
½ cup water

Mix first 5 ingredients in blender to be sure all lumps are removed. Add egg, vinegar, and water. Place in pan and cook slowly until thick.

STUFFED CUCUMBER RINGS

3 medium firm cucumbers
8 ounces cream cheese,
softened
3 tablespoons chopped nuts
2 ounces chopped pimiento
1/16 teaspoon onion
powder

1/16 teaspoon white pepper
Dash garlic powder
1 teaspoon paprika
½ pint cherry tomatoes

Wash cucumbers in warm water to remove wax coating if necessary. Wipe dry. Remove centers with an apple corer. Chill until firm. Combine cream cheese, nuts, pimiento, onion powder, pepper and garlic powder. Stuff cavities of cucumber, packing firmly. Wrap in waxed paper and chill until stuffing is firm. Cut into slices 1/8 inch thick. Dust lightly with paprika. Arrange on trays with alternate slices of cherry tomatoes. Serves six.

STUFFED DILL PICKLES

Unusual and tangy stuffed dill pickle slices.

2 large dill pickles
1 tablespoon butter
1 tablespoon minced onion
1 tablespoon minced parsley

¼ pound smoked Braunschweiger sausage

Cut off ends of dill pickles and cut in half crosswise. Remove centers with a large apple corer. Reserve centers. Melt butter and sauté onion and parsley until onion is soft. Add Braunschweiger and continue cooking for 2 minutes until thoroughly warmed and well blended. Cool. Add chopped centers. Stuff pickles. Seal well in plastic wrap and refrigerate. Before serving, slice in 1/3-inch slices and arrange on platter. Makes about 12 slices.

SUMMER GINGER ALE SALAD

2 3-ounce packages lemon-
  flavored gelatin
1 cup boiling water
1 6-ounce can frozen
  lemonade concentrate

2 cups ginger ale
2 cups cantaloupe balls
  or watermelon balls
2 bananas, sliced
1 cup green grapes, halved

Dissolve gelatin in boiling water, then add lemonade concentrate. Stir until dissolved. Carefully add ginger ale. Chill until slightly thickened. Fold in the fruit. Pour into 9 x 13 inch pan and chill until firm. Serves sixteen.

HOSPITALITY INN
SALAD

1 pound fresh spinach
1 clove garlic, cut in half
1 medium red onion, diced
½ pound fresh mushrooms,
  sliced
1 large tomato, peeled
  and diced

1 red or green pepper,
  diced
3 tablespoons oil
¼ cup Parmesan cheese
3 cups garlic croutons
Salt and pepper to taste

Wash, re-wash, and destem spinach. Toss spinach, onion, mushrooms, tomato, and pepper in a large bowl rubbed with garlic. Add oil, cheese, and croutons. Add salt and pepper. Place in a warm oven for 5 to 7 minutes. (Long enough to wilt slightly.) You may serve with thinly sliced red onions over the top and additional cheese. Serves four.

KING'S RANSOM SALAD

Almost every wedding dinner we've ever had at the Anderson House features King's Ransom Salad, and we've given the recipe to guests year after year. Now it's finally in a book, and we hope everyone likes it as well as our brides.

1 3-ounce package lemon-
flavored gelatin
½ cup hot water
1 8-ounce package
cream cheese
1 10¾-ounce can tomato
soup
1 cup mayonnaise
1 2-ounce jar pimiento,
finely chopped

½ cup finely chopped
celery
½ cup chopped green
pepper
6 fresh green onions
(the bulb and 2 inches
of tops), finely chopped
Mayonnaise Dressing
(below)

Dissolve gelatin in hot water. Add cream cheese and tomato soup. Blend until smooth. Stir in mayonnaise until smooth. Add pimiento, celery, green pepper, and green onions. Put in individual molds or a 9-inch square pan. Serve with Mayonnaise Dressing. Serves eight.

MAYONNAISE DRESSING

1 cup mayonnaise
¼ cup cream

8 green onion tops,
finely chopped

Mix together and serve on salad.

PENNSYLVANIA DUTCH
WILTED LETTUCE SALAD

1 clove garlic, mashed
1 head lettuce
3 tablespoons finely
 chopped celery
3 tablespoons finely
 chopped green onion
3 tablespoons finely
 chopped green pepper

3 radishes, finely chopped
1 tablespoon finely
 chopped parsley
8 slices crisply fried bacon
Hot Salad Dressing (below)

Rub sides and bottom of large salad bowl with mashed garlic. Break lettuce into bite-sized pieces. Place lettuce and remaining ingredients (except dressing) in bowl. Pour Hot Salad Dressing over salad and toss lightly. Serve at once. Serves six.

HOT SALAD DRESSING

8 slices crisply fried bacon,
 cut in small pieces
 (keep warm until needed)
2 teaspoons dry mustard
2 tablespoons
 Worcestershire sauce

1 tablespoon flour
1 tablespoon horseradish
1 teaspoon paprika
1 teaspoon salt
½ cup vinegar

Mix these ingredients together and let boil for 10 minutes.

MANDARIN ORANGE
SHERBET SALAD

2 8-ounce packages
 cream cheese
1 tablespoon light cream
2 large packages orange-
 flavored gelatin

2 cups boiling water
1 pint orange sherbet,
 softened
2 cans mandarin oranges,
 well drained

Soften cream cheese with 1 tablespoon of cream until it is almost liquified. Dissolve gelatin in water. Stir until completely dissolved. Add a little of the sherbet and liquefy in blender. Add the cream cheese and liquify. Fold mixture into remaining sherbet. Pour into a 9 x 9 inch pan or individual molds. Chill until partially set, then add mandarin oranges. Chill until firm. Serves eight.

Note: This is certainly not an Anderson original. We include it because we have so many requests for it.

PASTA PRIMAVERA

6¼ ounces white wine vinegar
1/8 cup fresh lemon juice
1 tablespoon Dijon mustard
3 cloves garlic, minced
2 teaspoons salt
¾ teaspoon crumbled dried leaf oregano
½ teaspoon pepper
¼ teaspoon sugar
1¼ cups vegetable oil

16 ounces uncooked spiral pasta (rotini)
20 ounces cherry tomatoes, halved
12 ounces julienne-cut zucchini
1½ cups shredded carrots
8 ounces broccoli flowers, blanched 1 to 2 minutes
¾ cup chopped scallions

Combine first eight ingredients in large bowl. Gradually stir in oil and set aside. Cook pasta until tender. Drain and add to vinaigrette. Combine vegetables. Add to vinaigrette and pasta. Toss gently. Chill several hours or overnight. Serve cold. Serve on romaine, fresh spinach, or red-tipped lettuce. Serves twelve.

Note: This is Chef Eustace Bennett's recipe from the Hospitality Inn in Jacksonville, Florida. It was a smash hit there and when we began serving it at the Anderson House we just couldn't make enough. For a variation add 4 cups of cubed white chicken meat to make it an entrée.

BELLE EBNER'S SPECIAL
LUNCHEON SALAD

1 3-ounce package lemon-
flavored gelatin
1 cup boiling water
1 cup evaporated milk
1 cup mayonnaise
¼ cup finely minced onions
½ cup finely chopped
celery
2 tablespoons finely
chopped green pepper

1 17-ounce can peas,
drained
1 cup grated mild
cheddar cheese
1 tablespoon chopped
pimiento
Lettuce

Dissolve gelatin in boiling water. Combine evaporated milk and mayonnaise. Stir into gelatin. Chill until mixture begins to thicken. Fold in remaining ingredients, and blend well. Turn into 8 to 10 individual molds. Chill until firm, at least 2 hours. Unmold on lettuce cup. Serve with mayonnaise or cucumber dressing if you like the combination. Serves eight to ten.

PICKLED EGGS

1 cup juice from pickled
beets
1 cup vinegar
4 cups water
1 clove garlic
1 medium bay leaf

2 teaspoons mixed
pickling spice
½ teaspoon salt
12 hard-cooked eggs
1 small onion, sliced and
separated into rings

Place beet juice, vinegar, and water in large bowl; add garlic, bay leaf, pickling spice, and salt; mix well. Add eggs and onion rings; cover and refrigerate for several days. Serve whole, or slice and use with pickled beets and greens for a festive salad. Makes 1 dozen pickled eggs.

PEAR SALAD WITH WATERMELON ICE

**2 cups crushed ripe
watermelon**
2 tablespoons lemon juice
**3 to 4 tablespoons sugar,
or to taste**
**1 cup lemon-lime
carbonated beverage**

Red food coloring (optional)
6 fresh Bartlett pears
Salad greens
Mint Dressing (below)

Cut ripe red pieces of watermelon from rind, discard seeds, and blend melon in electric blender. Combine crushed watermelon with lemon juice, sugar, and carbonated beverage. Add food coloring. Freeze until slightly mushy; take out of freezer and beat with mixer or rotary beater. Return to freezer until firm. When time to serve, halve and core pears; pare, if desired. For each serving, arrange 2 pear halves on salad greens with scoop of watermelon ice. Serve with Mint Dressing. Serves six.

MINT DRESSING

**1 teaspoon chopped
fresh mint, or
½ teaspoon crumbled
dry mint**

1/3 cup mayonnaise
1/3 cup sour cream

Combine all ingredients. Chill in refrigerator so that flavor can develop.

BACON POTATO SALAD

6 cups hot diced cooked
  potatoes
1/3 cup finely chopped
  mild onion
9 slices bacon, diced
3 tablespoons bacon
  drippings
1/3 cup vinegar
1 tablespoon sugar

¾ cup boiling water
1½ tablespoons prepared
  mustard
1 cup sour cream
1 tablespoon finely minced
  parsley
Salt and pepper to taste
Salad greens (garnish)
Cherry tomatoes (garnish)

Combine potatoes and onion. Cook bacon until crisp and remove from skillet with a slotted spoon. Drain on unglazed paper. Pour off all but 3 tablespoons of drippings. Add vinegar, sugar, water, and mustard to the 3 tablespoons of drippings and stir until the sugar is dissolved. Add hot mixture to potatoes and toss gently until most of the moisture is absorbed. Fold in sour cream, parsley, bacon, salt, and pepper until the mixture is well blended. Serve warm or well chilled with a garnish of greens and cherry tomatoes. Serves six.

OLD-FASHIONED
POTATO SALAD

2 tablespoons sugar
1 tablespoon cornstarch
¾ teaspoon salt
¼ teaspoon pepper
1 teaspoon dry mustard
1/3 cup vinegar
1 egg, slightly beaten
¾ cup evaporated milk
6 cups cubed or sliced
  cooked potatoes (4 or 5
  large)

1 cup chopped celery
½ cup finely chopped
  onion
½ cup finely chopped
  parsley (optional)
Lettuce
3 hard-cooked eggs
  (garnish)

Combine sugar, cornstarch, salt, pepper, mustard, and vinegar in a heavy saucepan. Cook, stirring constantly, over low heat until the mixture is smooth and thickened. Remove from the heat. Slowly stir cooked mixture into the beaten egg in a bowl. Return mixture to saucepan and cook and stir 1 minute longer. Cool. Gradually blend in milk, stirring until smooth. Combine potatoes, celery, onion, and parsley in a bowl. Add the liquid mixture and toss lightly to coat the ingredients. Chill until ready to serve, then serve in a lettuce-lined bowl or in crisp lettuce cups for individual servings. Garnish with slices or wedges of hard-cooked egg, if desired. Serves ten.

KATIE HALL'S RASPBERRY SALAD

1 3-ounce package
  raspberry-flavored gelatin
1 cup boiling water
1 10-ounce package
  frozen raspberries

1¾ cups raspberry ice
  cream (you may use
  vanilla), softened

Dissolve gelatin in water. Stir in frozen berries. Fold ice cream in gelatin mixture. Pour into 9-inch square pan and refrigerate until set. Serve in squares on shredded romaine as a salad or cut in squares and place on meringue shells; pour raspberry syrup over it and top with whipped cream to use as a dessert. Serves nine.

SALMON SALAD TROPICALE

1 pound canned salmon
2 pineapples
4 ounces seedless
   green grapes
12 ounces mandarin
   oranges
8 ounces melon balls,
   in season

8 ounces litchi fruit
2 ounces macadamia nuts,
   chopped
2 cups Island Spice
   Dressing (below)
Orchids for garnish
   (optional)

Drain and flake canned salmon. Cut pineapple in half. Core and remove fruit. Cut into bite-sized pieces. Combine all fruit. Fill pineapple "boats" with fruit medley. Mound 4 ounces of salmon on top of fruit. Sprinkle with macadamia nuts. Serve with Island Spice Dressing. Garnish with an orchid. Serves four.

ISLAND SPICE DRESSING

¾ cup heavy cream
½ teaspoon ground ginger

½ cup mayonnaise

Whip heavy cream with ground ginger until it holds soft peaks; fold in mayonnaise.

STRAWBERRY SALAD

2 packages strawberry-
   flavored gelatin
1½ cups boiling water
1 12-ounce package
   frozen strawberries

1 cup crushed pineapple
½ cup pecans
1 cup sour cream

Dissolve gelatin in water. Add strawberries. Chill until slightly congealed. Add pineapple and nuts; mix. Put half the mixture into greased 9-inch square pan. Chill until firm. When set, mix the other half with sour cream. Gently pour into mold and chill until ready to serve. Serves six.

MADAME'S ROQUEFORT MOLD

This recipe came from one of the estates where I have worked. The estate was beautiful, and the food we served was sensational.

½ pound Roquefort cheese
2 cups heavy whipping
  cream

2 tablespoons dried or
  fresh parsley
Salt and pepper to taste

Let cheese sit at room temperature for 45 minutes. Then cream the cheese so that it is smooth and easy to stir. Whip cream until it holds points. Carefully fold into the cheese. Add parsley, salt, and pepper to taste. Freeze in ice-cube trays. Serve as garnish with roast beef, putting a small sprig of parsley on top. Or, it can be served as a dessert or salad garnished with cucumber sticks. Serves eight.

COLE SLAW-STUFFED TOMATO

6 medium-sized ripe
  tomatoes

Cole slaw (see index)
Lettuce, shredded (garnish)

Dip the tomatoes in boiling water for 1 minute. Drain. Peel and chill. Hollow out a large center and fill tomatoes with cole slaw. Chill until serving time and serve on a bed of freshly shredded lettuce. Serves six.

SWEETBREAD SALAD

1 pair sweetbreads
3 hard-cooked eggs
1 rib celery, finely sliced
3 green onions, bulb and
    one inch of stalk finely
    chopped
1 ounce pimiento

¼ tablespoon green
    pepper, finely minced
1 10-ounce package frozen
    peas, cooked and cooled
2/3 cup mayonnaise
2 tomatoes, quartered

Soak sweetbreads in salt water (about 1 teaspoon salt) about 1 hour, then parboil, remove skin, and let cool. Dice sweetbreads, then mix with hard-cooked eggs, celery, green onions, pimiento, green pepper, and peas. Mix gently with mayonnaise. Garnish with tomatoes. Serves four.

VEGETABLE-BEEF SALAD

2 heads iceberg lettuce
1½ cups sliced zucchini
2 cups julienne-cut cooked
    beef (about ¾ pound)
1/3 cup corn oil

3 tablespoons vinegar
1 teaspoon onion salt
½ teaspoon coarsely
    ground black pepper

Core, rinse, and drain lettuce thoroughly. Refrigerate in plastic bag or crisper. Cook zucchini in boiling salted water 5 to 8 minutes just until tender-crisp; drain. Place zucchini and beef in shallow dish. Mix corn oil, vinegar, onion salt, and pepper; pour over zucchini and beef. Marinate 1 hour or longer. Cut lettuce lengthwise into halves. Place cut-sides down on board; cut into bite-sized chunks to make 2 quarts. Place lettuce chunks in six individual salad bowls. Spoon zucchini, beef, and marinade over lettuce. Serves six.

Sauces and
Salad Dressings

Grandma truly believed that any man could be caught by a good cook, and she so admonished every young girl who worked for her. She based it all on the great victory of Effie Mae Higginbottom.

Effie Mae was a good, plain girl who took care of her ill mother and father until they died. It meant she didn't have much time for fun like other girls, and it gave her plenty of time in the kitchen. When she took her offerings to the bake sales at the church, her pies, cakes, or cookies were spoken for before she ever got there. After her mother and father died, Effie kept living on at the big old Victorian home place. Ebeneezer Carpenter, who actually was a carpenter, said she took the little den downstairs and ripped out the walls and made a great, big kitchen there. She had tile shipped from Italy and was the first one in town to use barn siding inside a house. She had two stoves, two iceboxes, and enough skillets, pots, and pans to stock an army. Along about this time, the church decided to have another box lunch social during which you bid on the box lunches.

Dr. Dave Galloway was new in town—and single. All mothers within thirty miles were in a fret parading their daughters into his clinic with imagined ills and ails.

Along came the box social, and Effie Mae's box was a perky red basket with a red and white checked napkin sticking out, and it looked as though it were wrapped around a bottle of champagne. There were some hisses and raised eyebrows in the congregation that Sunday afternoon. Old Tyson Hobart always bid for Effie Mae's boxes in the past because he knew they were stuffed with vittles prepared with a lavish and loving hand. However, Dr. Galloway fancied the basket, so he kept bidding until the bidding reached twenty dollars, a small fortune in those days.

After the feast, he looked for the basket's owner, and someone took him to Effie Mae. "Imagine chicken salad in croissants!" he said. "Imagine home-cured ham, sliced thin and rolled around cream cheese and chopped ripe olives, imagine stuffed cucumbers and a chocolate cake to make you want more! Do you do this very often?" He smiled, and everyone knew he really wanted to know.

That was the start of it. Effie Mae bloomed like a June rose. Her sun-kissed, flawless skin, lightly tanned from all her outside gardening, and her naturally curly sun-streaked hair made her almost a beauty.

After the first supper in her cozy kitchen, the young Dr. Galloway was lost, Grandma said. She served him cream of broccoli soup, stuffed chicken breasts with fresh mushroom sauce, sweet potato balls, a molded cream of tomato salad, and a lemon pie with a four-inch meringue.

He was mesmerized.

Then she started to go on house calls with him and always packed a lunch so they could stop by the river on the way home. Then they started to go to church together, and finally, in the fall, they married. He moved into her house—she didn't want to leave her kitchen and move into his!

So, Grandma used the story of Effie Mae Higginbottom to prove that good cookin' lasts, and that it's a mighty fine bait to net a good catch.

BARBECUE SAUCE

1 14-ounce bottle catsup
½ bottle Heinz-57 steak
  sauce
½ bottle Worcestershire
  sauce
1 tablespoon Tabasco
1 tablespoon prepared
  mustard

2 tablespoons vinegar
2/3 cup dark brown sugar
1 tablespoon butter or
  margarine
1 small onion diced small
1 clove garlic
Dash salt and pepper

Mix all ingredients in a small saucepan and bring to a fast boil. Then let cook slowly for 30 minutes. Makes about 1 quart.

SAUCE MOUTARDE

1½ quarts mayonnaise
2 cups sour cream
½ cup tarragon vinegar
3 tablespoons sugar

3 tablespoons Dijon mustard
3 tablespoons dill weed, chopped

Blend all ingredients until smooth in texture. Season to taste with salt. Cover and refrigerate. Makes 2 quarts.

MAHALA'S MUSTARD SAUCE

Ham, in its various forms, is much used by the Pennsylvania Dutch, at least in our family. Everyone tried every conceivable accompaniment to impress others at box socials, family dinners, picnics, and other similar affairs. Mahala was a sauce expert, and everyone loved her Mustard Sauce.

1 cup whipping cream
½ cup mayonnaise
2 teaspoons lemon juice
1 teaspoon Dijon mustard
½ teaspoon dry mustard

Salt and white pepper to taste
1 teaspoon dried or minced fresh parsley

Whip cream until stiff. Fold in mayonnaise, lemon juice, mustards, salt, pepper, and parsley. Refrigerate at least 1 hour before using. Makes 1¾ cups.

POLONAISE SAUCE

Unlike many sauces in which eggs are used as a thickener, this one adds hard-cooked eggs for color and texture. In the 19th century, A. Careme, a famous French chef, published a version of Polonaise that was similar, but included horseradish. This Polonaise is well suited to fish and vegetable dishes.

¼ cup butter
3 tablespoons minced
   parsley
1 tablespoon lemon juice
1½ teaspoons dried
   minced onion

Dash salt
Dash pepper
2 tablespoons fine dry
   bread crumbs
2 hard-cooked egg yolks,
   finely chopped or sieved

In small saucepan melt butter over medium heat. Stir in parsley, lemon juice, onion, salt, and pepper. Cook, stirring occasionally, about 1 minute. Stir in bread crumbs and egg yolks. Makes ½ cup.

SAUCE VERTE

1 quart mayonnaise
1 cup chopped parsley
½ cup chopped watercress
½ cup chopped chives

¼ cup lemon juice
1½ tablespoons sugar
½ teaspoon white pepper
Salt to taste

Blend all ingredients except salt until smooth in texture. Season to taste with salt. Cover and refrigerate. Makes 1½ quarts.

SOUR CREAM-CUCUMBER SAUCE

1 cup sour cream
2 tablespoons capers, drained
1 teaspoon Dijon mustard

¼ teaspoon salt
½ cup diced seeded cucumber

In a saucepan over medium heat combine sour cream, capers, mustard, and salt, and bring to a boil while stirring constantly. Stir in cucumber. Serve cold. Makes approximately 1½ cups.

COTTAGE CREAM DRESSING

1 cup cottage cheese
½ cup sour cream
2/3 cup cooked, crumbled bacon (about 8 slices)

¼ cup milk
2 tablespoons sliced green onions
¼ teaspoon salt

In a mixing bowl beat together cottage cheese and sour cream until fairly smooth. Add bacon, milk, onions, and salt. Cover and chill. Makes approximately 2 cups.

CUCUMBER DRESSING

2 cups mayonnaise
1 large, peeled, chopped cucumber

¼ cup finely diced onion
¼ cup dried parsley flakes or fresh minced parsley

Blend all ingredients together. If too thick, add 2 tablespoons cream. Makes 3 cups.

CREAMY PEPPER DRESSING

2 cups mayonnaise
½ cup half-and-half
¼ cup water
2 tablespoons Parmesan
cheese
1 tablespoon freshly
ground pepper
1 tablespoon cider vinegar

1 teaspoon fresh lemon
juice
1 tablespoon finely
minced onion
1 teaspoon garlic salt
1 ounce pimiento
Dash Worcestershire sauce

Blend all ingredients together until well mixed. Chill for 4 hours before using. Makes about 1 quart.

CREOLE MUSTARD DRESSING

I always stayed at the Monteleone Hotel in New Orleans because it is in the French Quarter and because it was across from the Solari grocery store, which was enormous. It was always my last stop before heading back to Minnesota. My baggage was always way overweight because of the goodies I used to pick up there, especially Creole mustard, which is just different from any other kind. When I went back one time and found the Solari store closed, I almost went into mourning. Then I stayed at the Royal Orleans Hotel in the French Quarter because it was across from the Four Seasons, a pastry shop, so you can see how my mind works! I am probably the only person in the world to totter into a plane loaded down with twelve boxes of pastries! Anyway, here's a dressing we like to make with that wonderful Creole mustard.

1 cup olive oil
2 tablespoons white wine

1 teaspoon salt
¼ cup Creole mustard

Blend all ingredients until smooth and creamy. I use it over shredded romaine and lettuce. Sometimes I put hard-cooked eggs through the ricer over the top. Makes 1½ cups.

HONEST-TO-GOODNESS DIETERS' DRESSING

1 cup water
2 tablespoons flour
¼ cup vinegar
¼ cup catsup
1 teaspoon horseradish
1 teaspoon dry mustard

½ teaspoon paprika
½ teaspoon Worcestershire
sauce
1/8 teaspoon artificial
sweetener
1 clove garlic, cut in half

Mix together water and flour. Cook until thick, then beat smooth. Add vinegar, catsup, horseradish, mustard, paprika, Worcestershire sauce, artificial sweetener, and garlic. Mix and shake well. Remove garlic before serving. Makes 1¾ cups.

DILL DRESSING

¼ cup sour cream
2 tablespoons salad oil
1 tablespoon cider vinegar
½ tablespoon finely grated
onion (pulp and juice)

¼ teaspoon salt
½ teaspoon dill seed
¼ teaspoon paprika
1/8 teaspoon pepper

Whisk together all the ingredients; cover tightly and chill overnight to allow flavors to blend. Makes ½ cup.

MISSISSIPPI FIG AND FRUIT MEDLEY

1 lemon, sliced (unpeeled)
1 orange, sliced
  (unpeeled)
2 cups dried, pitted prunes,
  soaked in water for
  2 hours
4 cups ripe figs, peeled
1 #2 can crushed
  pineapple, drained
½ teaspoon salt
2 tablespoons light
  molasses

1½ cups white or golden
  raisins
4 cups sugar
1 teaspoon whole cloves
2 sticks cinnamon
1½ teaspoons Tabasco
1 16-ounce can whole-berry
  cranberry sauce
1 cup chopped pecans
4 ounces rum

Chop lemon and orange in blender. Put all ingredients except pecans and rum in a large pot and cook over medium heat until thick. Stir frequently so mixture doesn't stick to pan. It should cook for about 1 hour. Add pecans about 10 minutes before removing from the stove. Add rum. Remove cinnamon sticks. Stir briskly. Makes about 2 quarts.

Note: This can be poured into sterilized jars and sealed. We use it so fast that we keep it in a crock in our refrigerator. We de-bone hams and stuff with this mixture. We also use it as a glaze with some thinning or as a meat accompaniment. And we have been known to add a cup or so to our barbecue sauce. We were given the recipe from a fellow tourist at the Cornstalk Hotel in New Orleans who owned a fig orchard in Poplarville, Mississippi.

THE ANDERSON HOUSE
SPECIAL FRENCH DRESSING

2 cups sugar
1 quart sunflower oil
3 cups catsup
2 tablespoons onion juice

1 cup vinegar
Juice of 2 lemons
2 teaspoons salt

Blend all ingredients together. Shake well before serving. Will keep weeks in refrigerator.

GREEN GODDESS DRESSING

1 to 1¼ cups mayonnaise
4 large sprigs parsley,
  snipped
2 green onions, minced
2 tablespoons lemon juice
  or wine vinegar

1 tablespoon anchovy paste
½ clove garlic, crushed
  and minced
½ teaspoon salt
Dash pepper
½ cup sour cream

Blend together all ingredients. Or prepare in blender: Place all ingredients except sour cream in blender container. Blend at high speed just until parsley and onions are finely chopped. If necessary, turn off blender occasionally and clean sides with rubber spatula. Add sour cream. Blend at medium speed just until combined. Chill thoroughly. Makes about 2 cups.

BASIC WHITE SAUCE

	Butter	*Flour*	*Milk*
Heavy	3 tablespoons	3 tablespoons	1 cup
Medium	2 tablespoons	2 tablespoons	1 cup
Light	1 tablespoon	1 tablespoon	1 cup

Cream butter and flour. Add milk, stirring constantly over medium heat until it thickens. Add seasonings to taste.

HERB DRESSING

2 cups buttermilk
1 cup sour cream
1 cup peanut oil (or other vegetable oil)
2 tablespoons vinegar
1 clove garlic, chopped
½ cup diced onion
4 teaspoons dried sweet basil
¼ cup chopped parsley
½ cup chopped scallions
1 teaspoon sugar
½ cup cream
Salt and white pepper to taste

Mix buttermilk and sour cream until smooth. While whipping mixture constantly, very slowly pour in oil, vinegar, garlic, onion, basil, parsley, scallions, sugar, and cream. Adjust seasonings with salt and pepper. Serves ten to fifteen. Makes 5 cups.

HONEY DRESSING

2-2/3 cups sugar
4 teaspoons dry mustard
4 teaspoons paprika
1 teaspoon salt
1¼ cups vinegar
4 teaspoons grated onion
4 teaspoons celery seed
1-1/3 cups honey
4 tablespoons lemon juice
3 to 3½ cups salad oil

Mix in blender all ingredients except oil. Add oil very slowly, continuing to mix. Store in covered jar in refrigerator. If mixture separates, shake jar. Serve over fresh fruit. Makes 1½ quarts.

MUSHROOM SAUCE

12 ounces fresh mushrooms
2 tablespoons butter
2 tablespoons butter,
  melted
¼ cup flour
1 cup milk

Salt to taste
Onion juice to taste
1 teaspoon vinegar
Worcestershire sauce to
  taste

Sauté mushrooms in 2 tablespoons butter and set aside. Combine remaining melted butter and flour and cook several minutes. Add milk and stir until thickened. Stir in seasonings and mushrooms. Thin sauce with mushroom liquid left over from first step, if desired. Makes about 1¾ cups.

PEANUT SAUCE

18 ounces creamy peanut
  butter
6 cups water

1 cup soy sauce
1 cup lemon juice
¾ teaspoon garlic powder

Cook peanut butter and water over low heat, stirring constantly, until smooth. Stir in soy sauce, lemon juice, and garlic powder. Heat to boiling; remove from heat and cool. Makes 2¼ quarts.

DILL BUTTER

½ cup butter
1 tablespoon minced onion
1 tablespoon fresh lemon
  juice

1 teaspoon Dijon mustard
1 teaspoon dill weed
1/3 cup cocktail peanut
  halves

Over low heat melt butter in a saucepan and stir in onion, lemon juice, mustard, and dill weed. Continue to heat the mixture until onion is cooked; stir in peanuts. Serve hot. Makes approximately 2/3 cup.

POLYNESIAN SALAD DRESSING

7 egg yolks
½ cup fresh lemon juice
1 tablespoon black pepper
1 tablespoon ground
  mustard
2 tablespoons Maggi
  seasoning
½ tablespoon salt
½ cup white wine

1 teaspoon Worcestershire
  sauce
½ teaspoon garlic powder
1 quart salad oil
2 tablespoons chopped
  dried chives
2 tablespoons diced
  sweet red pepper
Tabasco to taste

Mix all ingredients except oil, chives, pepper, and Tabasco on high speed for 10 minutes. Turn mixer to low and slowly add oil, then chives, pepper and Tabasco. Store, covered, in refrigerator. Makes 1½ quarts.

SALT PORK CREAM GRAVY

1 pound salt pork, cut in
  small cubes
3 tablespoons cornmeal
5 tablespoons flour
1 tablespoon butter

1 tablespoon lard
2 cups whole milk
½ teaspoon salt
¼ teaspoon white pepper

Cover salt pork cubes with boiling water. Let stand 5 minutes. Drain well. Dip cubes in mixture of cornmeal and 3 tablespoons of flour. Melt butter and lard in heavy skillet. Add pork cubes and cook over low heat until crispy and brown on all sides. Drain cubes on paper toweling. Pour off all but 5 tablespoons of fat from the skillet. Stir in remaining 2 tablespoons of flour, gradually add the milk, cooking and stirring until smooth and thickened. Add salt, pepper, and pork cubes. Serve with corn fritters, boiled new potatoes, rice, or mashed potatoes. Makes 2½ cups.

Note: The greatest delight you could serve an old-fashioned man lost in the memories of the good old days in Pennsylvania, or anywhere else!

THICK WHITE SAUCE

¼ cup butter or margarine   Few grains of pepper
¼ cup flour   1-1/3 cups milk
1 teaspoon salt

In small saucepan, melt butter or margarine; blend in flour, salt, and pepper. Stir in milk until smooth. Cook and stir until mixture thickens and boils. Remove from heat. Makes about 1½ cups.

Fish and Seafood

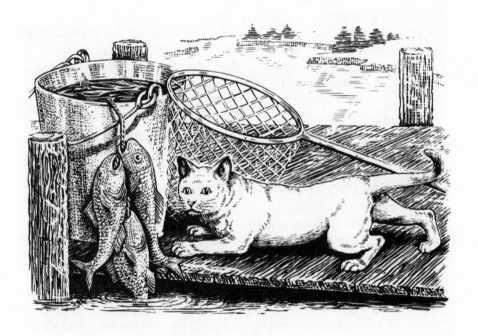

When you check into the Anderson House and look out of your window at the Mississippi running through the Hiawatha Valley, you just know the fishing has to be great, and it is. The wingdams, the little backwater bayous, and the many islands through the river are all great places for fish to linger. Although there are many species of fish here, Wabasha has been called the home of the small-mouth bass.

When pike is on the menu, many guests assume they come from the river and were caught that morning. In Grandma's day, there were fewer federal stipulations about such things, and the fish we served actually did come from the Mississippi or the Chippewa. The days of fish fresh from the river in front of the hotel are gone, unless a guest brings his private catch to us to cook the way he wants. However, air transportation brings fish from both coasts daily to our area, and fish from the Gulf of Mexico comes our way as well.

Grandma did everything that could possibly be done with fish. She cooked them in cream, stuffed them, broiled them, wrapped them in foil and cooked them outdoors, smoked them, dried them, pickled them, and actually canned them. The only restriction was that if a fish smelled like a fish, it wasn't fit to cook; everything Grandma served was absolutely fresh.

Maybe because of my college diet of creamed tuna fish and McCaffrey Spaghetti, I turned a cold eye on anything that swam and could be scaled. Not Grandma! Her scalloped crabmeat brought tears to displaced Easterners, and her stuffed shrimp with whipped tomato cream sauce was a joy to behold, and an even greater joy to devour. Most of the time her pike or bass was rolled in corn meal, fried in butter, and served with cucumber sauce. Lobster tails were broiled, and the meat removed from the shell and added to cream sauce that had been simmering a long time, rich with mushrooms and delicacies. This wonderful concoction was served in a pastry shell better than any available in stores.

You will find fish in this chapter, but you'll find it in the soup and salad chapters as well. We think our fish and seafood dishes are sensational, and we think you will too!

DR. CRISCUOLO'S CLAM SPAGHETTI

"Chris" lives the good life in Palm Springs, California, most of the time. When he comes to the Anderson House, we run up to the office and look for the recipes he likes best. This one keeps him smiling in between many trips to our local library. (Chris takes a vacation to read and unwind.)

¼ cup plus 1 tablespoon butter
¼ cup plus 1 tablespoon olive oil
1 cup chopped fresh green onions, including some tops
1 tablespoon chopped parsley
½ teaspoon oregano
½ teaspoon basil

2 cloves garlic, crushed
1 tomato, peeled and chopped
Salt and pepper to taste
2 7½-ounce cans clams, chopped (reserve juice)
1 16-ounce package spaghetti
¼ cup parmesan cheese
2 ounces chopped pimiento

In a saucepan, heat ¼ cup butter and ¼ cup oil. Add onions and sauté. Add parsley, oregano, basil, garlic, tomato, salt, pepper, and juice drained from clams. Simmer for 10 minutes. Add clams and turn heat to lowest point. Boil spaghetti, drain and return to pan. Add 1 tablespoon melted butter and 1 tablespoon olive oil. Mix and add parmesan cheese and pimiento. Mix gently. Add half of the spaghetti sauce and toss together. Divide spaghetti among 4 plates; additional sauce can be added as desired. If sauce is thinner than you like, thicken with a small amount of cornstarch. Serve with additional parmesan cheese. Serves four.

ALASKAN KING CRAB GOURMET SANDWICH

3 ounces Alaskan king crab
½ ounce brandy
2 ounces cream cheese
1 tablespoon mayonnaise
1 tablespoon heavy
  cream
2 bread slices

2 lettuce leaves
2 tomato slices
1 ounce mushroom slices
1 ounce grated Swiss
  cheese
¼ avocado, sliced (garnish)
Olives (garnish)

If frozen, thaw crab and drain thoroughly. Place in bowl and sprinkle with brandy. Set aside. Place softened cream cheese in mixing bowl and whip. Add mayonnaise and heavy cream and continue to whip until mixture is well aerated and increased in volume. Blend in crab and brandy. Lightly toast bread. Place lettuce leaf and tomato on each slice. Spread mixture evenly over slices. Add sliced mushrooms and top with grated cheese. Place under broiler until cheese is melted. Serve open-faced. Garnish with sliced avocado and ripe olives. Makes 1 sandwich.

CRAB CASSEROLE DELUXE

4 teaspoons salt
2½ cups (8 ounces) small
  macaroni shells
2 6½-ounce cans or
  1 pound fresh crabmeat
2 10½-ounce cans cream
  of celery soup
1⅓ cups liquid (crab
  liquid and milk)
1 teaspoon Worcestershire
  sauce
½ cup blanched almonds,
  slivered

2 hard-cooked eggs,
  chopped
4 tablespoons finely
  chopped parsley
4 tablespoons fine dry
  bread crumbs
1 tablespoon melted butter
4 tablespoons grated
  romano or parmesan
  cheese

Add salt and macaroni to 5 cups boiling water. Boil rapidly, stirring constantly for 2 minutes. Cover, remove from heat and let stand 10 minutes. Drain liquid from crabmeat into measuring cup, remove cartilage from crabmeat, and separate into bite-sized pieces. Place soup in mixing bowl; add liquid and milk and Worcestershire sauce and blend well. Fold in almonds, eggs, parsley, and crabmeat. Drain and rinse macaroni with warm water and turn into a greased 2-quart casserole. Pour soup and crabmeat mixture over macaroni and mix lightly. Blend crumbs with butter and cheese and sprinkle over top of casserole. Bake at 375 degrees for 30 minutes. Serves eight to ten.

BAKED RED SNAPPER CREOLE

3 pounds red snapper
Salt and freshly ground
  pepper
½ cup margarine, softened
2 tablespoons flour
2 cups chopped onions
1 cup chopped celery
½ cup chopped green
  pepper

1 32-ounce can tomatoes,
  chopped
½ teaspoon thyme
¼ teaspoon Creole
  seasoning
1 tablespoon
  Worcestershire sauce

Salt and pepper fish and rub inside and out with margarine. Sprinkle with flour and place in buttered baking dish in 375-degree oven. Sauté onions in skillet until lightly browned with celery and green pepper. Add tomatoes, seasonings, and Worcestershire sauce, and simmer for 5 minutes. Pour over fish and continue baking, basting with sauce occasionally, until fish flakes easily with fork, about 20 to 25 minutes. Serves six.

CRABMEAT PUFFS

These miniature cream puffs are said to have become popular as appetizers during Prohibition. At that time, the quality of the drinks might have been uncertain, but these puffs, with various fillings, always drew raves. They still make a hit at parties.

1 cup water
½ cup butter
1 cup all-purpose flour
¼ teaspoon salt
1 cup (4 ounces) shredded
   cheddar cheese

2 tablespoons chopped
   chives
4 eggs
Crabmeat filling (below)

In a medium saucepan bring water and butter to boil, stirring until butter melts. Remove from heat. Add flour and salt, stirring vigorously until mixture forms a ball, 1 to 2 minutes. Add cheese and chives, stirring until cheese melts. Add eggs, one at a time, beating well after each. Drop batter by slightly rounded tablespoons onto greased cookie sheets, allowing 2 inches of space between each. Bake in preheated 400-degree oven until lightly browned, 18 to 20 minutes. For firmer puffs, pierce each side with tip of sharp knife and bake 5 minutes longer. Cool on wire racks. Cut off tops and fill each with 2 tablespoons Crabmeat Filling. Replace tops. Chill before serving, if desired. Makes 3 dozen.

CRABMEAT FILLING

6 hard-cooked eggs,
   finely chopped
1 6½-ounce can crabmeat,
   drained

1 cup finely chopped celery
½ cup mayonnaise
½ teaspoon salt
½ teaspoon dry mustard

Mix all ingredients thoroughly. Set aside until ready to use.

MISSISSIPPI SCALLOPED
CRAB CASSEROLE

In Biloxi, Mississippi, crab is easily come by. You put on your old clothes, grab your net and some old pieces of meat or bones, and trot down to the pier—there are many of them there. Tie string to an old bone and hang it over the edge of the pier while you dry your hair, read a magazine, or just absorb the marvelous Gulf Coast sun. Now and then reach over and give your string a little tug. If it seems heavy, slowly raise it, and when you see a fine blue-point crab hanging on, grab your net and scoop him up. It used to take us only an hour to fill a bushel basket—most days, that is.

½ cup finely chopped onion
½ cup butter
¼ cup finely chopped green peppers
¼ cup finely chopped green onions
8 ounces mild cheddar cheese, grated
White Sauce (see index)
2 eggs, well beaten

8 ounces medium-dry noodles
½ cup finely grated fresh carrots
1 2-ounce jar pimiento
1 pound fresh crabmeat
½ cup chopped parsley
1 cup finely crushed potato chips
Parsley (garnish)
Paprika

Braise onions, green peppers, and green onions together in butter for about 10 minutes over medium heat. Stir occasionally. Add cheese to warm White Sauce. Add eggs to 1 cup of the White Sauce, stir well, and return to the pan of White Sauce. Cook noodles, drain, and add to White Sauce. Add lightly braised vegetables, carrots, pimiento, and crabmeat to the White Sauce. Pour into a 2-quart casserole, cover with potato chips, sprinkle with parsley, dust with paprika, and cover and bake 1 hour at 350 degrees. Serves six.

SECRET FISH BATTER

Almost everybody knows that the secret of good fried fish is the batter. We offer herewith Gloria Pitzer's Secret Fish Batter. Any recipe that comes from the Pitzer household (where the entire family is involved in cooking) is bound to be a five-star recipe. We include the recipe for Secret Tartar Sauce as well.

**2 to 3 pounds fish fillets
  (firm white fish)**
Milk (enough to cover fish)
**2 tablespoons lemon juice,
  or 1 lemon, sliced**
2 cups all-purpose flour

1 teaspoon sweet basil
1 teaspoon pepper
½ teaspoon garlic salt
2½ to 3 cups pancake mix
1 quart club soda
3 cups vegetable oil

Cut fillets in half. Place in shallow pan and cover with milk and lemon juice or sliced lemon. Refrigerate 3 to 4 hours to remove fishy taste and odor. Drain off milk. Dip to coat each piece lightly in flour. Let dry on cookie sheet. Do not let pieces touch each other. Heat oil to 425 degrees in heavy saucepan or electric fry pan; use enough to keep oil 2½ to 3 inches deep. Combine basil, pepper, garlic salt, and pancake mix. Stir in enough soda (about 2 cups) to make thin batter, about the consistency of buttermilk. Do not overcoat. Dip floured pieces quickly into batter and drop 3 or 4 at a time into hot oil. Pieces will drop to bottom of pan and float to top to brown in about 4 to 5 minutes. Remove to cookie sheet and keep warm in 250-degree oven until all pieces have been fried. Serves six to eight.

Note: Batter could be spicier, so double or triple seasonings if desired.

SECRET TARTAR SAUCE

⅓ cup mayonnaise (not
   salad dressing)
⅓ cup creamy horseradish
   sauce
⅓ cup sour cream
¼ teaspoon dried
   celery leaves, crushed

1 teaspoon dill seed
Dash pepper
1 teaspoon sugar
2 to 3 drops hot pepper
   sauce

Combine all ingredients and mix thoroughly. Refrigerate; keeps about one week, chilled. Makes about 1 cup.

HEAVENLY SCALLOPS
(From Grandma Anderson's *Primer for Brides*)

¼ cup butter
2 pounds scallops
Flour
1 large clove garlic,
   finely chopped

3 tablespoons dried or
   fresh parsley
Salt and pepper to taste
1 lemon, quartered

Melt butter in skillet. Dust scallops lightly with flour and pan-fry for about 5 minutes. Slide pan back and forth over heat. Add garlic and parsley, and slide pan 1 minute longer. Remove to hot plate and serve at once. Season with salt and pepper, and serve with wedge of lemon and additional parsley sprinkled over the scallops. Serves 4.

MUSHROOM-STUFFED FISH ROLLS

1 pound fresh mushrooms
6 tablespoons butter
2 pounds fish fillets
Salt and ground pepper
  to taste
½ cup dry white wine
  or water

2 tablespoons lemon juice
2 tablespoons flour
½ cup light cream or milk
Minced parsley (garnish)

Rinse, pat dry, and slice half the mushrooms; chop remaining mushrooms. Heat 2 tablespoons butter in a skillet. Add sliced mushrooms and sauté until golden; remove and reserve. Heat 2 tablespoons butter in same skillet; add chopped mushrooms. Sauté until golden. Sprinkle fish with salt, pepper, and chopped mushrooms. Roll up, jelly-roll fashion; arrange in a 9 x 9 or 9 x 12 inch greased casserole. Pour wine and lemon juice over fish; dot with 2 tablespoons butter. Cover with foil. Bake in preheated 350-degree oven for 45 minutes. Pour off fish stock from casserole; set aside. In small saucepan blend flour with 1 tablespoon fish stock. Gradually stir in remaining stock; cook and stir until thickened. Remove from heat, stir in cream and reserved sliced mushrooms; heat, but do not boil. Pour sauce over fish. Sprinkle with parsley if desired. Serves six.

SALMON IMPERIAL

1 head lettuce
1 1-pound can salmon
1 egg, beaten
¼ cup fine dry bread
  crumbs
¼ cup milk

¼ teaspoon dry mustard
½ teaspoon onion salt
Dash pepper
Imperial Sauce (below)
Parsley (garnish)

Core, rinse, and thoroughly drain lettuce. Remove 5 large outside leaves; chill remaining head in plastic bag for later use. Pour boiling water over reserved lettuce leaves; drain immediately. Discard bones and skin from salmon. Mix salmon, egg, crumbs, milk, mustard, onion salt, and pepper. Form into 5 logs each about 3 inches long, and place each on a softened lettuce leaf. Roll the leaf around the salmon and secure with toothpick. Place lettuce rolls in buttered baking dish, cover and bake at 350 degrees for 25 minutes. Transfer to warm platter; spoon Imperial Sauce over logs. Garnish with parsley. Serves five.

IMPERIAL SAUCE

¼ cup butter or margarine
¼ cup flour
½ teaspoon salt

1½ cups light cream or
 half-and-half
¼ cup sauterne or water

Melt butter in small saucepan; blend in flour and salt. Add cream; cook, stirring, until thickened. Remove from heat. Stir in sauterne or water. Keep warm until ready to use.

SCALLOPS RUMAKI

4 tablespoons soy sauce
1 cup dry white wine
24 scallops

24 slices bacon
24 whole water chestnuts
 (optional)

Make a marinade of soy sauce and wine. Soak scallops in marinade for several hours. Cut bacon slices in half. Remove scallops from marinade and wrap ½ slice of bacon around each scallop and water chestnut. Secure with a toothpick. Place in 350-degree oven until bacon is cooked, about 5 to 10 minutes.

SHRIMP SQUARES WITH FRESH MUSHROOM SAUCE

1 dozen eggs, beaten
¼ cup butter
1 cup flour
2 teaspoons baking powder
Salt and white pepper
  to taste
2 cups cottage cheese
1 pound grated Monterey
  Jack cheese
1 4-ounce can green
  chiles, chopped

1 6-ounce can small shrimp
  or 6 ounces fresh shrimp,
  boiled and peeled
¼ cup finely diced onions
4 ounces fresh mushrooms,
  sauteed
Fresh Mushroom Sauce
  (below)

Melt butter and add flour and baking powder. Mix eggs in thoroughly and add remaining ingredients. Pour into a well-greased 3-quart baking dish (not round) and bake 1 hour at 350 degrees. Serve at once, cut in squares, with Fresh Mushroom Sauce. Serves six.

FRESH MUSHROOM SAUCE

1 pound fresh mushrooms,
  washed, patted dry,
  and sliced
½ cup butter

Medium White Sauce
  (see index)
Salt and pepper to taste

Melt butter. Add mushrooms and sauté. Add to White Sauce. Season.

THIRTY-DAY TUNA FISH

When I went to the University of Minnesota money was getting tight, and my father had two other daughters to educate—one at St. Benedict's in northern Minnesota, and one at Cornell in Ithaca, New York. I was sent thirty dollars a month for food, which didn't leave much room for banana splits, malted milks, or any of those goodies that college students cherish. My roommate, Mary Pendergast, and I often thanked God for tuna fish. We used to buy a case of the cheapest tuna fish we could buy (around seventeen cents a can), and we knew every second-day bread store in Minneapolis. Most of the time we ate creamed tuna on toast, but when we had company, we aspired to greater delights.

1 10¾-ounce can cream
　of mushroom soup
1 can milk
2 eggs, well beaten
1 6-ounce can tuna fish,
　packed in water
4 ounces cheddar cheese,
　cubed
½ cup minced green pepper

1 2-ounce jar pimiento,
　minced
¼ cup dried or ½ cup
　fresh parsley
Salt and white pepper
　to taste
1 8-ounce package medium-
　sized dry noodles
1 cup crushed potato chips

Place soup and milk in large mixing bowl and add eggs, tuna fish, cheese, green pepper, pimiento, parsley flakes, salt, and white pepper. Cook noodles until done and drain well. Add to tuna mixture. Cover with crushed potato chips and bake 1 hour at 350 degrees. Serves four.

ALASKAN SNOW CRAB
MONTE CRISTO DECKER

3 teaspoons butter
3 slices bread
2 1-ounce slices Swiss
cheese
1 ounce ham slice

1 tablespoon Thousand
Island dressing
2 ounces Alaskan Snow
crabmeat
1 egg, beaten

Spread 1 teaspoon butter on each slice of bread. Cover one slice of bread with slice of Swiss cheese and slice of ham. Add second slice of buttered bread, spread with Thousand Island dressing and cover with crabmeat and another slice of Swiss cheese. Top with third slice of buttered bread. Dip sandwich in beaten egg. Grill until browned. Place into 425-degree oven for 5 minutes. Cut diagonally and secure with toothpicks. Serves one.

TUNA CLUB LOAF

2 6-ounce packages wide
noodles
6 hard-cooked eggs,
quartered
1 13-ounce can tuna fish,
coarsely flaked
2 tablespoons grated onion
2 tablespoons minced
green pepper or parsley
2 tablespoons diced
pimiento
¼ pound fresh mushrooms,
sliced, or 1 4-ounce can
mushrooms, drained

½ cup butter or margarine
½ cup flour
½ teaspoon salt
½ teaspoon celery salt
1/8 teaspoon pepper
2 cups chicken broth
2 cups milk
1 teaspoon Worcestershire
sauce
1 5-ounce package potato
chips, crushed, or 3 cups
bread crumbs

In a large saucepan boil noodles in large amount of salted water until tender. Drain and return to saucepan. Add eggs, tuna, onion, green pepper or parsley, pimiento, and mushrooms. (If fresh mushrooms are used, sauté in 2 tablespoons shortening about 5 minutes.) Melt butter in another saucepan. Add flour and blend in seasonings; then stir in chicken broth, milk, and Worcestershire sauce, stirring until smooth and thick. Add to noodle and tuna mixture, and toss well until mixed but not mashed. Grease a 9-inch square baking pan and spread a thin layer of potato chips or crumbs on the bottom. Put in half of tuna mixture and repeat. Bake about 1 hour in 350-degree oven. Serves twelve to fifteen.

TUNA PUFFS

2 cups cooked rice
1 9½-ounce can tuna fish
⅓ cup minced onion
1 cup grated cheddar
  cheese

1 teaspoon salt
¼ teaspoon pepper
3 eggs, well beaten
⅓ cup half-and-half
Mushroom Sauce (below)

Combine rice, tuna, onion, cheese, and seasonings. Blend eggs and half-and-half. Pour over rice mixture and mix well. Spoon into 12 greased custard cups or muffin tins. Bake at 350 degrees for 30 minutes. Serve with Mushroom Sauce. Serves six.

MUSHROOM SAUCE

1 10¾-ounce can cream
  of mushroom soup

2 tablespoons diced
  pimiento

Heat mushroom soup, undiluted. Add pimiento. Keep warm until ready to use.

RAINBOW TROUT WITH ORANGE STUFFING

6 whole fresh or frozen
  rainbow trout, cleaned
2 teaspoons salt
1 cup chopped celery
  (with leaves)
¼ cup chopped onion
¼ cup melted fat or oil
¾ cup water
¼ cup orange juice

2 tablespoons lemon juice
1 tablespoon grated
  orange rind
¾ teaspoon salt
1 cup cooked rice
½ cup chopped peanuts
2 tablespoons melted fat
  or oil
2 tablespoons orange juice

Thaw trout if frozen. Sprinkle inside and out with salt. Cook celery and onion in fat or oil until tender. Add water, juices, orange rind, and salt; bring to a boil. Add rice and stir to moisten. Cover and remove from heat. Let stand 5 minutes. Add peanuts and mix thoroughly. Stuff fish. Close opening with small skewers or toothpicks. Place fish in a well-greased 14 x 11 x 1 inch baking pan. Combine fat and 2 table-spoons orange juice. Brush fish with fat mixture. Bake in a preheated 350-degree oven for 25 to 35 minutes, turning once, or until fish flakes easily when tested with a fork. Baste occasionally with fat mixture. Remove skewers. Serves six.

SWEET 'N' SOUR TROUT

6 small whole dressed
rainbow trout (fresh or
frozen)
1 clove garlic, crushed
1 tablespoon vegetable oil
1 6-ounce can pineapple
juice
½ cup water
¼ cup light brown sugar
(firmly packed)
2 tablespoons white vinegar
2 tablespoons soy sauce
2 tablespoons watermelon
pickle juice
2 tablespoons chopped
watermelon pickles (or
2 tablespoons sweet
pickle juice and 2
tablespoons chopped
sweet pickles)

2 tablespoons cornstarch
¼ cup water
¾ cup crinkle-cut carrots
(3 small)
½ green pepper, cut in
julienne strips
1 cup halved cherry
tomatoes
2 7¾-ounce packages
bean threads
Cornstarch or flour
2 eggs, beaten
Sesame oil
Cooked rice

Thaw trout if frozen; wash and dry. To make sauce, sauté garlic in oil in small saucepan. Stir in pineapple juice, water, brown sugar, vinegar, and soy sauce. Add pickle juice and chopped pickles. Combine 2 tablespoons cornstarch and water and stir into sauce. Place saucepan over medium heat and bring to a boil while stirring constantly. Continue to boil for 2 minutes. Cook carrots and green pepper in separate saucepan in water until tender; drain and add to sauce along with tomatoes. Keep sauce warm while frying trout. To fry trout, blend bean threads in a blender until coarsely ground. Dip trout in cornstarch or flour to coat, then in beaten egg, and then in ground bean threads. Fry in skillet in sesame oil until golden and fish flakes easily when tested with a fork. Do not overcook. Serve trout with Sweet 'n' Sour Sauce and rice. Serves six.

Meat

Because Grandma Anderson's relatives lived long, full, healthy lives, I guess I thought I had all the time in the world to learn from her and foolishly took my time learning. This Easter I decided to make the Pennsylvania Dutch eggs she used to make for me, and I realized I had no idea how to proceed. I knew the eggs were colored by hard-boiling them in onion skins, but my memory stopped right there. The eggs she made came out as beautiful, soft dappled shades of butterscotch, tan, and brown; occasionally she put adhesive strips around them to make stripes. (At least I *think* it was adhesive tape.)

I tried. I peeled the loose outer leaves from red onions and thought that would be it. Alas, the eggs came out all one color, sort of burnt umber. Why didn't I listen? Fortunately a newly found notebook revealed the recipe!

And why didn't I pay more attention to what she did with bacon? She used to put brown sugar on both sides of her bacon strips and then bake them in the oven—a strange, wonderful dish, but I have never been able to duplicate it. She used to buy fat Dutch weiners, 3 or 4 to a pound, slit them down the middle, fill them with the most heavenly stuffing, wind a strip of bacon around each, and bake them in the oven. These weiners were usually served with shredded cabbage fried in butter. Mine *never* taste like hers.

Grandma said you could catch any man if you knew how to cook. Once I asked her what she considered the perfect meal to use as bait. I was only 13 at the time, and the world's greatest wallflower, so I cherished and remembered every word she said. "Take two sixteen-ounce strip steaks," she said. "Marinate them in our special marinade all night long. Get some enormous potatoes (there are some that weigh almost as much as the steaks). Scrub them, butter the skins and bake for an hour. Don't wrap them in foil—that steams them. Cook some fresh asparagus so that it is still crunchy and sprinkle with garlic-flavored buttered crumbs. Your salad should be fresh spinach with bacon and vinegar and sugar dressing or serve with wilted lettuce, which is typically Dutch. Make baking powder biscuits light as air, and finish off with a steamed chocolate pudding with foamy Bourbon sauce. The trick is the steak. Instead of serving the meat like steak, slice crosswise about one-half inch thick. Roll in flour, and put into a skillet with melted butter. Cook slowly, turning occasionally and browning. This will not take long. Remove from pan and add one cup of water to the pan drippings. Stir and work pan scrapings into the gravy. Put steak strips on plate, cover with gravy, season to taste, add potato cut crosswise and pushed up from either side, add asparagus, serve the salad, and watch him fall into your arms."

I have used that menu more times than I would like to admit, and it was always a success.

Another trick of Grandma's was to take the bone out of ham and stuff it with an apricot stuffing. Sometimes she baked meat in a dough blanket, and when she roasted prime ribs Grandpa would have to flee the kitchen. She used a salt blanket that he was sure would ruin the ribs for everyone. She would take cube steaks, roll them out as far as they would go without tearing, stuff them with fresh sautéed mushrooms, and serve them with a fresh mushroom sauce.

Grandma could also do great things with sweetbreads. We always had sweetbreads on Grandpa's birthday because that was his favorite dish. They were always lightly precooked, rolled in flour and white corn-meal, sautéed in butter, and served with broiled pineapple slices. We don't include that recipe here, but if you like sweetbreads, you'll love our Creamed Sweetbreads and Mushrooms.

There are also some excellent pork recipes in here, and we hope you will try them all. At one time, when we lived up on Hilltop Farm, we raised some of our own pigs. That gave us a great chance to try many new ways of preparing pork.

Grandma said you couldn't run a business unless you could make great-tasting food from inexpensive cuts of meat. She did this often, but the meat had to be of the best grade. Of course, with butter at 15 cents a pound, it was lavishly used, and everything tasted wonderful! Today's crafty cook devises other ways of using inexpensive cuts; we have a number of such recipes in this section. Whether your choice for a meat dish is Skewered Lamb with Cranberry Burrs or Grandma's Pot Roast, you'll be sure to please all diners in your home.

ROASTED CANADIAN BACON

4 pounds Canadian bacon
Whole cloves
1⅓ cups brown sugar
¾ cup water
¾ cup white wine

8 ounces currant jelly
1 tablespoon vinegar
1 teaspoon dry mustard
½ teaspoon ground cloves

Dot bacon with cloves. Cover with brown sugar. Put in roaster. Add water and wine. Bake in a 350-degree oven 1½ hours. Baste occasionally. Combine jelly, vinegar, dry mustard, and cloves in a small saucepan. Heat until jelly melts. Slice bacon and serve with sauce. Serves eight.

STUFFED BEEF ROLL

1½ pounds round steak
   (about ¼ inch thick),
   trimmed
¼ pound ground veal
1 egg, slightly beaten
¼ cup small bread cubes
2 tablespoons grated
   Parmesan cheese
2 slices (2 ounces) salami,
   cut in strips
2 slices (2 ounces)
   Provolone cheese, cut
   in strips

2 hard-cooked eggs, sliced
2 tablespoons shortening
1 10¾-ounce can
   condensed tomato soup
½ cup water
½ cup chopped onion
¼ cup Burgundy or other
   dry red wine
1 medium clove garlic,
   minced
1 small bay leaf

Pound steak with meat hammer or edge of heavy saucer. Combine veal, egg, bread, and Parmesan cheese. Spread mixture evenly on steak to within 1 inch of edges. Press salami, Provolone cheese, and sliced eggs into meat mixture. Starting at narrow end, roll up; tuck in ends. Tie with string or fasten with skewers. In skillet, brown roll in shortening; pour off fat. Add remaining ingredients. Cover; cook over low heat 1 hour. Turn; cook 1 hour more. Stir now and then. Serves six.

GOLDEN CORNMEAL RING
WITH BEEF SAUCE

1 cup enriched cornmeal
3½ cups cold water
Salt
1 cup sharp cheddar
  cheese, grated

½ teaspoon
  Worcestershire sauce
Beef Sauce (below)

Mix cornmeal with 1 cup cold water. Bring 2½ cups water to a boil, then add salt. Add cornmeal mixture to boiling water, stirring constantly. Cook over low heat 10 minutes, or in double boiler 20 minutes. Add cheese and Worcestershire sauce, stirring until cheese is melted. Pour into a greased 8-inch ring mold. Keep warm until ready to serve. Serves six.

BEEF SAUCE

2 tablespoons vegetable oil
1 small clove garlic, minced
½ cup coarsely chopped
  onion
½ cup coarsely chopped
  green pepper

1 cup diced celery
¾ pound ground beef
2½ cups tomatoes
2 ounces pimiento
1 teaspoon salt
1 bay leaf

Heat vegetable oil in large skillet over moderate heat. Add garlic, onion, green pepper, and celery. Brown slightly, cooking over low to medium heat for about 15 minutes, then add ground beef and cook only enough to brown. Add tomatoes, pimiento, salt, and bay leaf. Cook slowly until mixture is sauce-like in consistency, about 20 minutes. Serve ring on platter and fill center with sauce.

ANN POLISCHTAK'S
LAS VEGAS CABBAGE ROLLS

When we managed the 500-room Hacienda International Hotel in Sepulveda, California, next door to the Los Angeles International Airport, John and Ann Polischtak managed our food department. When the airlines called to tell us fog had grounded them, and they were sending 250 people over for dinner at 2:00 A.M., we scurried like mad for the kitchen to get ready. No time to call in any employees, so we did it ourselves. Ann always made her famous Cabbage Rolls.

The Polischtaks have worked for us in Los Angeles; Venice, Florida; Biloxi, Mississippi; Big Springs, Texas; Jacksonville, Florida; and Rochester and Wabasha, Minnesota. They are always ready to come running if the bell tolls! Now they summer at home and winter in Las Vegas; the Cabbage Rolls are well known there as well.

1 medium head cabbage
  (about 1½ pounds)
Salt and pepper to taste
1 pound ground beef
3 cups cooked rice
2 cups grated sharp
  cheddar cheese
½ cup minced onion

1 large clove garlic, minced
½ teaspoon salt
¼ teaspoon pepper
2 tablespoons dried parsley
2 8-ounce cans tomato
  sauce
¼ cup Parmesan cheese

Remove 12 large outer leaves from cabbage. Place in boiling salted water and cook until leaves begin to soften. Drain. Shred remaining cabbage; season with salt and pepper. Place in buttered 9 x 13 inch baking pan. Combine ground beef, rice, cheddar cheese, onion, garlic, ½ teaspoon salt, ¼ teaspoon pepper, and parsley. Spoon equal amounts of mixture (about ⅓ cup) in center of each cabbage leaf. Fold two sides over stuffing and roll up from the end. Secure with a toothpick. Arrange rolls, seam side down, on shredded cabbage. Pour tomato sauce over rolls. Cover and bake at 375 degrees for 40 minutes. Sprinkle each roll with Parmesan cheese. Serves six.

CASSOULET

3 cups navy beans (cover
with water and soak
overnight)
2 tablespoons salt
¼ teaspoon thyme
1 bay leaf
1 pound Polish sausage
½ pound lean salt pork,
diced
4 tablespoons shortening
(not oil)

2 pounds shoulder of lamb,
cut into stewing pieces
(bite-sized)
2 large onions, chopped
4 tablespoons tomato paste
2 cloves garlic, finely
chopped
¼ teaspoon pepper
3 tablespoons bread
crumbs
Butter

Drain the beans and put in large kettle. Cover with water. Add ½ tea-spoon salt, thyme, bay leaf, and sausage. Bring to a boil and simmer for about 30 minutes. Remove sausage and set aside. Continue simmering for 1 hour. In a saucepan cook the salt pork in boiling water for 5 minutes. Drain and set aside. In a large skillet heat shortening, then add lamb and the remaining salt; sauté until lightly browned on all sides. Pour off excess fat. Add onions and cook until soft. Cover with water, add tomato paste, garlic, pepper, and salt pork. Bring to a boil and simmer gently for 30 minutes uncovered. Drain the beans, removing bay leaf, and add the lamb mixture to the beans; add sausage. Cover and simmer 1 hour or until the meat and beans are tender. Rub the inside of a large casserole with garlic. Remove some of the lamb and sausage. Pour bean mixture into the casserole. Cut sausage into slices about ½ inch thick. Arrange lamb and sausage on top of the beans. Sprinkle with bread crumbs and dot with butter. Broil until browned. Serves six.

CIRCUS STEW

When my boarding school roommate and I were in our junior year at Holy Angels Academy in Minneapolis, we had a burning desire to join the circus. After an elaborate plan in which her family thought she was with me, and my family thought I was with her in Cincinnati, we made our way to Florida with vivid dreams of sailing through the air from swing to swing in rhinestones and feathers, walking the tightrope, or riding an elephant. We looked four or five years older than we were, and boarding school had made us sophisticated enough to sound older than we were, so we were hired on the spot. We had to find a temporary place to live, then we went back to the man who hired us. We were immediately dispatched to the tent they called K.P. where we were set to work making hamburgers and opening sodas. We must have made a million hamburgers a day, and when night came we fell into bed too tired to talk. It soon became obvious we were not going to ride any elephants or walk any tightropes, so after three weeks we called it a day and headed for home. The snake charmer's wife invited us into her trailer for Circus Stew our last night. After all those hamburgers, we thought it was food for the gods.

½ cup butter
2 pounds ground beef
½ cup chopped celery
2 cans dark-red kidney beans
2 cups chopped onion
2 #2½ cans tomatoes (not whole), drained (reserve juice)

2 green peppers, chopped
1 pound fresh mushrooms
½ cup dried parsley flakes
2 tablespoons chili powder
Salt (if needed)

Melt butter in a large frying pan. Add the ground beef and brown on medium heat, turning occasionally. Add celery and cook another 15 minutes. Remove from heat. Preheat oven to 350 degrees. Put remaining ingredients in large bowl and mix carefully (drain kidney beans and tomatoes before adding). Place mixture in 2-quart casserole. Bake about

1½ hours, covered. Stir occasionally so that the top portion is moved to the bottom. If it seems dry, add the reserved tomato juice from the canned tomatoes. Serve at once with a big tossed salad. Serves eight.

BARNBURNER CHILI

½ cup butter
¼ cup vegetable oil
10 onions, chopped
5 pounds ground chuck
20 cloves garlic, minced
6 tablespoons chili powder
1 teaspoon oregano
1 tablespoon cumin

1 teaspoon celery salt
Salt and pepper to taste
6½ cups canned whole
  tomatoes (include juice)
6 tablespoons tomato paste
½ cup finely chopped
  green peppers
¾ cup cooked pinto beans

Heat butter and oil in heavy cast-iron skillet. Sauté onions for about five minutes or until translucent. Add meat and stir, being careful to break up any clumps of meat. Brown. Add garlic, chili powder, oregano, cumin, celery salt, salt, and pepper. Stir until well blended. Add tomatoes, tomato paste, and green peppers. Cook, stirring often, at least 1 hour, probably more. Add previously cooked pinto beans. Thin with tomato juice or beef broth. Serves eight to ten.

Note: Jim Klobuchar, a Minneapolis Tribune columnist, calls this "John's Incendiary Chili." We serve it to his skiing troops when they come down from the bluffs after an afternoon of skiing. John is co-owner of the inn, and spends a lot of time in the kitchen—the fourth generation of the family to find the serving of good food great fun, and a real challenge.

DILLED LASAGNE ROLLUPS

12 lasagne noodles
  (about 8 ounces)
1 tablespoon salt
3 quarts boiling water
¾ pound ground beef
2 tablespoons minced onion
Thick White Sauce
  (see index)

¾ cup chopped dill pickles
½ cup grated mozzarella
  cheese
1 8-ounce can tomatoes
⅓ cup grated carrots

Gradually add lasagne noodles and salt to rapidly boiling water so that water continues to boil. Cook uncovered, stirring occasionally, until barely tender. Drain in colander. Reserve. Meanwhile, in medium skillet brown beef and onion. Stir ⅔ cup white sauce and pickles into beef. Mix in cheese; reserve. Add tomatoes and carrots to remaining white sauce; simmer 10 minutes. To assemble, spread about ¼ cup beef-pickle mixture on each lasagne noodle; roll up. Place rolls, seam side down, in shallow baking dish. Pour sauce over rolls. Bake in 375-degree oven 25 minutes. Garnish with additional pickle slices. Serves six.

HERMAN KLINE'S
HUNGARIAN GOULASH

1 pound lean chuck roast,
  cut in ½-inch cubes
1 pound onion, thinly sliced
¼ cup water
2 tablespoons vegetable oil
1½ teaspoons to 1 table-
  spoon Hungarian paprika
  (according to taste)
½ teaspoon salt
1 teaspoon marjoram

2 pinches caraway seeds
  (optional)
2 garlic cloves, finely
  chopped
2 tablespoons tomato paste
1 10½-ounce can beef
  broth (more, if needed)
¼ cup sour cream
Noodles or Hungarian
  Spaetzles (below)

Cook onion and meat in oil until onion is limp and beef is browned. Add the remaining ingredients except sour cream and noodles. Simmer 2 to 3 hours until meat is tender. If the mixture becomes too dry, add more broth. Just before serving, add sour cream. Serve over noodles or Hungarian Spaetzles. Serves four to six.

Note: The goulash may be poured over noodles or spaetzles and frozen. Defrost and bake until hot.

HUNGARIAN SPAETZLES

1 cup flour
1 egg
1 egg yolk
5½ tablespoons milk
¾ teaspoon salt

Dash nutmeg
1 tablespoon minced
  parsley
2 tablespoons butter
¼ cup soft bread crumbs

Mix the first seven ingredients and place in a coarse colander over a large kettle of rapidly boiling, salted water. Press through the colander with a wooden spoon or a glass. Cook for about 5 minutes after all the mixture has been pressed through the colander. Rinse under cold water. Drain and set aside. Melt butter. Add soft bread crumbs and brown lightly. Stir into the spaetzles and brown lightly over low heat for about 10 minutes.

BELLEWEATHER PLANTATION HAM AND CHICKEN SHORTCAKE

4 chicken breasts
4 medium-thick slices
   baked ham
½ cup melted butter
4 tablespoons flour

2 cups rich chicken stock
Salt to taste
Dash white pepper
12 ounces fresh mushrooms
Cornbread

Lightly flour and brown chicken in butter in a skillet. Grease baking pan. Place ham slices in the pan. On top of each slice place one breast of chicken. Bake in a 350-degree oven until chicken is done. While chicken is baking, prepare mushroom sauce: cream ¼ cup butter and flour. Add chicken stock, stirring constantly over medium heat until it thickens. Add salt and pepper. Saute fresh mushrooms in ¼ cup butter and add slowly to white sauce. Pour over chicken and ham and garnish with parsley flakes on top of mushroom sauce. Serve on square of cornbread split to make two thin slices. Serves four.

HAM LOAF

1 pound ground ham
1 pound ground fresh pork
2 eggs, beaten
½ cup milk
2 tablespoons catsup
2 tablespoons
   Worcestershire sauce
10 drops Tabasco sauce
3 tablespoons chopped
   onion

¼ teaspoon salt
1/8 teaspoon pepper
1 slice soft bread, torn
   into small pieces
1 cup brown sugar
¼ cup water
¼ cup vinegar
1 teaspoon dry mustard
1 #2½ can pineapple
   chunks

Mix together first eleven ingredients (through bread). Place in a greased 5 x 9 inch loaf pan. Combine brown sugar, water, vinegar, and mustard. Pour half the brown sugar sauce over the uncooked meat and bake 1 hour at 350 degrees, basting every 10 to 15 minutes. Use rest of sauce to brown pineapple tidbits; serve with ham loaf. Serves six.

CORNED BEEF
AND DUMPLINGS

An English boiled beef dinner includes root vegetables and almost always dumplings. Buy short ribs or brisket and a marrow bone for richness. Buy extra meat so that you will have leftovers.

5 to 6 pounds short ribs or brisket
13 to 17 carrots, peeled
1 marrow bone
1 teaspoon dried thyme leaves

1 sprig parsley
1 onion, peeled
1 teaspoon salt
Egg Dumplings (below)

Put beef, 1 carrot, and remaining ingredients, except dumplings, in kettle and add water to cover. Bring to boil, reduce heat, and simmer, allowing 25 minutes per pound. One hour before meat is done, add carrots. Ten minutes before end of cooking time, drop dumpling batter on top of liquid. Cover and steam without uncovering 10 minutes. Serve beef with fresh horseradish, mustard, and good pickles. Have potatoes if you like, but they are not necessary with the dumplings. Serves six with beef left over.

EGG DUMPLINGS

2 eggs, separated
1 tablespoon milk
½ teaspoon salt

3 tablespoons all-purpose flour, unsifted

Mix egg yolks, milk, and salt. Beat in flour. Continue beating until light. Beat egg whites until stiff but not dry. Fold in yolk mixture.

PENNSYLVANIA DUTCH
HAM POT PIE

Once I asked Grandma Anderson if she had been poor when she lived in Pennsylvania. She thought it over quite a while before she answered. "Well, there were times when we had a whole lot of pot pie. But, then, Mother was so clever that you didn't realize how often you had it. Some days it would be ham pot pie, some days it would be chicken pot pie." She looked thoughtfully out the window and said, "We had a great big garden with potatoes, tomatoes, squash, onions, pie plant, every kind of vegetable you could think of. We had apple trees and berry bushes, 12 cows, and chickens, and Mother spun her own wool from our sheep. We had a springhouse to keep things cool, and Grandpa had a smokehouse, so I guess we had aplenty. We had two buggies and two horses. We didn't go into town except when we took in vegetables for the market. Mother was always canning everything from chickens to fruit to meat. We had a big barrel full of brine with pickles in it. We had pie for breakfast...sometimes two or three kinds. I thought it was a great life. The Dutch are fine farmers and very frugal, and my Mother taught me that. I guess I loved every minute of it. She taught me to make a pot pie when I was seven years old and I've been making it ever since." Here's the recipe, and it goes a long way if you have lots of people and not much money!

1 ham hock, or a 1½ pound piece of ham	**¼ teaspoon pepper**
2 quarts cubed potatoes	**Chopped parsley**
1 quart chopped onions	**Dough Squares (below)**

Cook the ham in 2 quarts water to cover until tender, about 1 hour. Add more water to make 2 quarts liquid, if necessary. Add vegetables and then drop in, piece by piece, the Dough Squares, made according to the following recipe. Keep the broth boiling during the additions. Sprinkle with pepper and parsley. Cover tightly and simmer until the begetables and dough are cooked, about 10 minutes. Serves eight.

Note: For a ham soup, cut the dough in ½ inch squares, cut the ham in small cubes, and omit the potatoes and onions. Substitute 1 3-pound chicken for Chicken Pot Pie.

DOUGH SQUARES

1 tablespoon butter,
  softened
1 egg or 2 egg yolks,
  beaten
¾ cup lukewarm water

1½ cups sifted flour
1¼ teaspoons baking
  powder
½ teaspoon salt

Prepare a dough by adding the butter and egg to the lukewarm water. (Or substitute ham stock for the water, and then omit the shortening.) Sift together 1 cup of the flour, baking powder, and salt, and combine smoothly with the first mixture. Add more flour to make a rather stiff dough. Knead lightly on a floured board for 1 to 2 minutes. Roll out 1/8 inch thick. Cut into 3-inch squares.

HAM TIMBALES

1¾ cups milk
4 tablespoons butter
1⅓ cups stale bread
  crumbs
2 cups chopped cooked
  ham

1 tablespoon parsley,
  chopped
1 teaspoon minced onion
4 eggs, slightly beaten
Salt to taste
1/8 teaspoon pepper

Make a white sauce with milk, butter, and bread crumbs. Cook 5 minutes, stirring constantly. Add ham, parsley, onion, and eggs. Salt to taste and add pepper. Turn into buttered molds, two-thirds full, and bake surrounded by hot water. Serve with creamed mushrooms. Serves four.

HANK THE WRANGLER'S
TIN-PLATE SPECIAL

If we talk a lot about Hank, the wrangler at the C Lazy U Dude Ranch, it's because he could have been a great chef had circumstances been different. When he cooked his simple food it was always perfectly flavored and perfectly prepared. I gave him one of my cookbooks, and he gave me every recipe I asked for.

1 huge ham hock, the
   biggest you can find
   (½ pound or so)
1 large onion, chopped

2 pounds fresh green beans
Salt and pepper to taste
6 small potatoes, chopped

Cover the ham hock with water in a dutch oven. Add onion. Cook over medium heat for about 2 hours. String the beans. Remove ham hock from its broth and remove the meat from the bone. Discard bone, place meat in broth, add beans, salt, and pepper. Cook for 1½ hours. Add potatoes and cook until beans and potatoes are tender, about ½ hour. When done, dish with a slotted spoon. Serves four.

GLAZED HAM ROLL-UPS
WITH APPLES

1 cup shredded Winesap
   apples
½ cup fine dry bread
   crumbs
¼ teaspoon salt
1/8 teaspoon pepper
1 teaspoon dry mustard

1 teaspoon sugar
2 tablespoons melted
   butter or margarine
6 ½-inch thick slices
   boiled ham
Syrup (below)

Combine apples, crumbs, salt, pepper, mustard, sugar, and butter or margarine in a bowl and blend well. Spread each slice of ham with a spoonful of the mixture and roll up like a jelly roll. Fasten with toothpicks. Arrange the ham rolls in a shallow baking pan and pour syrup over them. Bake in a 400-degree oven for 30 minutes, basting several times during baking. Remove toothpicks before serving. Serves six.

SYRUP

¾ cup light corn syrup
3 tablespoons water
¼ cup cider vinegar
2 teaspoons grated
    orange rind

6 whole cloves
1 2-inch stick cinnamon

Combine all ingredients in saucepan. Bring to a boil and simmer for 5 minutes.

HAM-AND-SAUERKRAUT BALLS

1 cup diced ham
1 cup diced cheese
    (mozzarella, Swiss, or
    cheddar)
¼ cup diced onion
¼ cup diced green pepper
2 cups sauerkraut, drained
    and squeezed as dry as
    possible
1 egg, beaten

2 teaspoons prepared
    mustard
1 teaspoon celery seed
¼ cup grated Parmesan
    cheese
2 cups flour
2 eggs, beaten
2 cups bread crumbs
1 quart oil

Mix together ham, cheese, onion, green pepper, sauerkraut, egg, mustard, celery seed, and Parmesan cheese. Firmly shape into balls the size of golf balls; dredge balls in flour, dip in egg wash, and roll in bread crumbs. Cook in deep fryer at 350 to 375 degrees for 3 to 5 minutes, or until a dark golden brown. Makes about 10 ham and sauerkraut balls. Serves four.

LOREN'S LAMB AND BEANS

2 tablespoons vegetable oil
2 pounds boneless lamb
   shoulder, cut in 1-inch
   pieces
1 cup coarsely chopped
   onions
1 large clove garlic, minced
½ cup water
1 pound fresh green beans,
   cut in 1-inch pieces

2 medium potatoes, pared
   and cut into 1-inch
   squares
1 tablespoon finely
   chopped fresh hot
   chili peppers
¼ teaspoon thyme
1 teaspoon salt
Pepper to taste
Rice (below)

In a 12-inch heavy frying pan, heat the oil over moderate heat. Add the lamb and brown a little at a time. Turn the pieces often, being careful to keep heat low enough so they won't burn. When brown, transfer to a small dish and hold. Pour off all but 2 tablespoons of fat from frying pan and place the onions and garlic in the pan. Stir frequently, scraping any particles at bottom of pan. Cook over moderate heat for about 10 minutes until onions are a light brown. Return the lamb with any liquid that has accumulated around it to the frying pan. Reduce heat to low, cover, and simmer for 45 minutes. Stir in the water, green beans, potatoes, chili peppers, thyme, salt, and pepper. Bring to a boil. Cover pan and again reduce heat to low; stir occasionally and simmer for about 1½ hours until lamb is tender. Serve with hot rice (below). Serves eight.

RICE

2 cups rice
1 tablespoon butter

4 cups beef consommé

Place all ingredients in a saucepan. Bring to a rolling boil. Cover and turn heat to low. Cook until consommé is absorbed and rice is dry, about 10 minutes.

SKEWERED LAMB WITH CRANBERRY BURRS

½ cup catsup
¼ cup cranberry juice
2 tablespoons
    Worcestershire sauce
3 tablespoons sugar

2 tablespoons steak sauce
3 tablespoons vinegar
1 teaspoon salt
1½ pounds lamb shoulder,
    cut in 1½-inch cubes

Combine all ingredients except the lamb. Heat to the boiling point. String lamb on skewers, allowing 3 or 4 cubes to each skewer. Place on the broiler rack. Spoon part of sauce over the cubes. Broil 3 inches from the heat 25 to 35 minutes. Turn and baste every 5 minutes. Place skewers of lamb as spokes on a wheel with the center of the wheel filled with Cranberry Burrs. Between the spokes, place wild rice and mushrooms. Serves four.

CRANBERRY BURRS

1 16-ounce can jellied
    cranberry sauce
Flour (for rolling
    cranberry balls)
1 cup all-purpose flour

½ teaspoon salt
⅔ cup milk
2 eggs, well beaten
Cornflakes, crushed
Fat for frying

Chill cranberry sauce thoroughly; remove from the can and shape sauce into balls with ball cutter. Roll balls in flour, then in batter made by combining the 1 cup flour, salt, milk, and eggs. Roll in cornflakes and fry in deep fat heated to 390 degrees, or hot enough to brown a cube of bread in 40 seconds. Drain and serve. Makes 50 small balls, or 20 to 25 using larger ball cutter.

Note: This recipe won first prize for us in a joint contest hosted by the Lamb Producers Council and the National Cranberry Association several years ago.

LAMB HASH

2 tablespoons finely
  chopped onion
¼ cup butter (more if
  needed)
2 cups finely chopped
  cooked lamb
2 cups finely chopped
  cooked potatoes

½ teaspoon salt
1/8 teaspoon powdered
  sage
Dash pepper
½ cup milk

In large skillet, sauté onion in 1 tablespoon of the butter until tender-crisp. In bowl, mix together onion, lamb, potatoes, seasonings, and milk. In same skillet brown mixture in remaining butter, turning and flattening mixture with a pancake turner. When turning, scrape up bits in skillet; additional butter may be added, if necessary. Serves four.

LEG OF LAMB WITH
BRAISED RED CABBAGE

1 5- to 6-pound boned
  rolled leg of lamb
Olive oil
3 cloves garlic, slivered
3 cups dark beer
3 onions, thinly sliced
Herb bouquet (tie with
  string: 3 sprigs parsley,
  1 bay leaf, ½ teaspoon
  dried rosemary leaves,
  ¼ teaspoon dried
  thyme leaves)

¾ cup plus 2 tablespoons
  olive oil
1½ cups beef broth
¼ cup butter or margarine
¼ cup all-purpose flour
Salt
Steamed rice
Braised Red Cabbage
  (below)

Rub leg of lamb with olive oil. Slash meat in several places; insert slivers of garlic. Place meat in large glass bowl or baking dish; add beer, onions, and herb bouquet; cover. Refrigerate at least 12 hours, turning occasionally. Remove lamb from marinade; reserve marinade. Brown lamb in hot olive oil in Dutch oven. When brown on all sides, add onions, herbs, marinade, and beef broth. Heat oven to 300 degrees. Cover lamb tightly. Bake until done, about 2 hours and 45 minutes. Remove lamb from Dutch oven; keep warm while preparing gravy. Strain drippings and return 4 cups of liquid to Dutch oven. Melt butter in skillet; blend in flour. Cook, stirring constantly, until smooth and light brown. Add to drippings in Dutch oven; cook and stir until thick. Salt to taste. Serve lamb on platter with steamed rice. Serve Braised Red Cabbage and gravy separately. Serves six to eight.

BRAISED RED CABBAGE

2 heads red cabbage
  (about 2 pounds each),
  shredded
1 teaspoon salt
½ cup butter or margarine
½ teaspoon salt

½ teaspoon pepper
1 cup dry red wine
2 tablespoons caraway
  seeds
2 tablespoons brown sugar
1 tablespoon wine vinegar

Place cabbage in two large bowls or Dutch oven. Cover with cold water. Stir in 1 teaspoon salt. Soak 30 minutes; drain thoroughly. Melt butter in Dutch oven. Add cabbage; cook and stir 5 minutes. Stir in salt, pepper, wine, and caraway seeds. Heat to boiling; reduce heat. Simmer 5 minutes over medium heat; stir in brown sugar and vinegar. Cover and simmer until tender, about 30 minutes. Serves six to eight.

SPANISH LAMB WITH SPAGHETTI

1 medium onion, finely
  chopped
1 clove garlic, minced
3 tablespoons vegetable
  oil
1 3-ounce can whole
  mushrooms
1 20-ounce can tomatoes
1 8-ounce can tomato sauce

1 bay leaf
7 cups cubed cooked lamb
¼ cup sliced pimiento-
  stuffed olives
12 ounces spaghetti,
  cooked
½ cup grated Parmesan
  cheese

Cook onion and garlic in hot oil until golden. Mix in undrained mushrooms, tomatoes, tomato sauce, and bay leaf. Cover and simmer 1½ hours or until slightly thickened; stir occasionally. Mix in lamb and olives; simmer 10 minutes longer. Meanwhile, cook spaghetti according to package directions; drain. Pour lamb sauce over spaghetti; sprinkle with cheese. Serves six to eight.

LAMB-STUFFED EGGPLANT

1 large eggplant, cut in
  half lengthwise
3 tablespoons vegetable
  oil
1 small onion, chopped
1 medium green pepper,
  diced

1½ cups cooked rice
1 16-ounce can tomatoes
½ teaspoon basil
½ teaspoon garlic salt
2 cups diced cooked lamb
Salt and pepper to taste

Cut center from eggplant leaving ½ inch shell; reserve shell. Dice eggplant. Combine oil, onion, green pepper, and eggplant; sauté until vegetables are tender. Add rice, tomatoes, basil, and garlic salt. Heat to boiling point, stirring occasionally. Cook over low heat 15 minutes. Add lamb, salt, and pepper; mix well. Fill eggplant shells with lamb mixture. Place in shallow baking pan. Bake in 350-degree oven for 45 minutes. Serves four.

JOHN HALL'S
STRANGE LAMB SHANKS

John Hall, who is now co-owner of the Anderson House, was thrown into the hotel field at an early age. When he was 13, I was a traveling supervisor for a large hotel chain with headquarters in Biloxi, Mississippi. I could keep a watchful eye on him when he was at St. Stanislaus, a school at Bay St. Louis, Mississippi, but summers were another thing. John and Ann Polischtak were managing a hotel in Port Arthur, Texas, so I put them in charge of John. He filled in for vacationing employees and finally ended up doing the night transcript for a 200-room hotel. That's where he received his start in the kitchen, and ever since, he's been master of that terrain.

The story of the creation of this dish shows John's talent in the business. One Sunday, John was looking at the leftovers from Saturday night and found a good-sized pot of gazpacho. Lamb shanks were on the Sunday menu, so John browned them, poured the leftover gazpacho over them, put them in to bake, and went about his business. Two hours later he proclaimed them the best he'd ever done! His finest hour was when they asked for the recipe! So, whenever we have leftover gazpacho, and lamb shanks are on the menu, that's where it goes.

6 1-pound lamb shanks   **1 quart leftover gazpacho**
5 cloves garlic   **(see index)**

Brown lamb, then place on rack in roaster. Make slits in lamb and insert garlic. Do not season otherwise. Pour gazpacho over meat. Put in 350-degree oven and roast for 3 hours. Serves six.

SAUERBRATEN MEATBALLS ON FLUFFY WHITE RICE

3 slices fresh bread
½ cup milk
1 pound ground beef
2 teaspoons grated onion
Dash garlic powder
1 teaspoon salt
½ teaspoon black pepper
¼ cup all-purpose flour
3 tablespoons cooking fat
¼ cup cider vinegar
1½ cups water
1½ teaspoons beet or cane sugar

1 cup sliced onions
3 peppercorns (or add black pepper to taste to gravy)
1 bay leaf
4 whole cloves
1 cup uncooked white rice
1 teaspoon salt
2 cups water
4 gingersnaps, crumbled

Tear the bread into small pieces and place in a large bowl. Pour milk over bread. Add ground beef, grated onion, garlic powder, salt, and pepper. Mix well. Form into 12 meatballs about 1½ inches in diameter. Roll meatballs in flour. Melt fat in large skillet. Brown meatballs on all sides. Add vinegar, water, sugar, and onions. Tie peppercorns, bay leaf, and cloves in a piece of cheesecloth. Add to meat. Cover with a lid and simmer 30 minutes. About 10 minutes before the cooking time is up, put the rice, salt, and water in a 2-quart saucepan. Bring to a vigorous boil. Turn the heat as low as possible. Cover with a lid and simmer for 14 minutes. Remove saucepan from heat but leave the lid on until ready to serve, or at least 10 minutes. After meatballs have simmered 30 minutes, remove the bag of spices. Add gingersnaps and continue cooking, stirring occasionally, for 10 to 15 minutes or until the gravy thickens. To serve, spread the hot cooked rice on hot platter. Top with the meatballs and gravy. Serves four to six.

Note: We can thank Annie Mertins, a one-time cook who came directly from Germany, for this one. She said she had come husband-hunting and successfully found one after he fell under the spell of her wonderful cooking.

FLORENTINE MEATBALLS

2 pounds ground chuck
2 teaspoons salt
Freshly ground black
  pepper
½ cup plus 1 tablespoon
  finely minced parsley
¼ cup grated Parmesan
  cheese
1 clove garlic, pressed
1 teaspoon oregano
1 teaspoon basil
1 teaspoon thyme
2 slices white bread,
  soaked in milk

2 eggs, beaten
Flour
2 tablespoons olive oil
2 tablespoons butter
1 cup finely diced carrot
1 cup finely diced onion
1 cup finely diced celery
2 tablespoons flour
1 10½-ounce can
  condensed beef broth
1 to 2 tablespoons lemon
  juice

In advance, combine chuck, salt, a little black pepper, ½ cup parsley, Parmesan cheese, garlic, oregano, basil, and thyme. Soak bread in milk to saturate and beat into meat mixture. Beat eggs until frothy; add to meat. Shape mixture into 1-inch balls and roll in flour. Set aside until flour no longer appears white. Heat oil and butter in skillet and brown meatballs. Remove meatballs to an oven-proof serving dish. Pour off all but 2 tablespoons grease from skillet. Sauté carrots, onion, and celery until limp. Stir in the 2 tablespoons flour and beef broth. Stir until smooth and of sauce consistency. Pour over meatballs. Cover and refrigerate. To serve, place meatballs in a 375-degree oven. Bake, uncovered, 1 hour. Remove from oven and sprinkle with 1 to 2 tablespoons lemon juice and 1 tablespoon parsley. Serves six to eight.

Note: This first appeared in the Minneapolis Tribune. *We tried it at once and found it to be a great change from other types of meatballs. It has become a regular on our noon menus, and we are sure you will like it as much as we do. Reprinted with permission from the* Minneapolis Tribune.

FROSTED MEAT LOAF

1 10½-ounce can
condensed cream of
mushroom soup
2 pounds ground beef
½ cup fine dry bread
crumbs
⅓ cup finely chopped
onion

1 egg, slightly beaten
1 teaspoon salt
⅓ cup water
2 to 3 tablespoons
drippings

Mix thoroughly ½ cup soup, beef, bread crumbs, onion, egg, and salt. Shape firmly into loaf (8 x 4 inches); place in shallow baking pan. Bake at 375 degrees for 1 hour and 15 minutes. Blend remaining soup, water, and drippings. Heat; stir now and then. Serve with loaf. Serves six.

FROSTED MEAT LOAF

4 cups mashed potatoes

Shredded cheddar cheese

Prepare loaf as above; bake for 1 hour. Frost loaf with mashed potatoes; sprinkle with cheese. Bake 15 minutes more.

ANN POLISCHTAK'S UKRAINIAN MEAT LOAF

1 small head cabbage
1½ pounds ground chuck
1½ teaspoons salt
½ teaspoon pepper
1 cup soft bread crumbs
½ cup undiluted beef broth
1 tablespoon parsley flakes

1 medium onion, minced
5 strips bacon
1 8-ounce can tomato
sauce
1 tablespoon sugar
1 teaspoon Worcestershire
sauce

Cut cabbage in quarters and remove the core. Cover with boiling water and cook 10 to 15 minutes. Drain. In a mixing bowl, mix all ingredients except cabbage, bacon, tomato sauce, sugar, and Worcestershire sauce. Put two strips of raw bacon on the bottom of a loaf pan. Cover with layer of cabbage, then a layer of the meat mix. Alternate cabbage and meat layers until all ingredients are used, ending with meat. Cover with the remaining three strips of uncooked bacon. Mix tomato sauce, sugar, and Worcestershire sauce, and pour over top of meat loaf. Bake at 375 degrees in preheated oven about 1 hour. Remove from oven and place on cake rack. Allow to set for about 15 minutes. Turn out of pan on foil. Serves six.

BRAISED OXTAILS

6 pounds disjointed oxtails
Flour
1 teaspoon salt
Pepper to taste
3 tablespoons shortening
1 cup carrots, diced
1 clove garlic, minced
12 small whole white onions, peeled

12 ounces beer
1 bay leaf
Dash thyme
1 10½-ounce can beef consommé
1 cup mushroom caps and stems, sliced
2 tablespoons parsley, chopped (garnish)

Roll pieces of oxtail in flour seasoned with salt and pepper. Melt shortening in heavy skillet; brown meat. Transfer to casserole or small roaster. Add carrots, garlic, and onions to shortening in skillet and brown. Add to oxtail. Add beer, bay leaf, thyme, and beef consommé. Cover and bake in 350-degree oven for 2½ to 3 hours, or until meat is tender. Sauté mushrooms in shortening and add to casserole during last 30 minutes of cooking. Serve sprinkled with chopped parsley. Serves six.

JOHN HALL'S
OCTOBER MOOSEBURGERS

When John collects all the hunters who want to make a foray into the Canadian wilderness in October in search of moose, they look mighty ridiculous starting out. First goes the 45-passenger bus in the lead. Behind it goes the Anderson House jitney to bring back the moose, and behind the jitney is the big trailer used as a command post and telephone contact. They're left behind on the mainland while the eager hunters fly to their lodge. Sometimes only ten or twelve moose make it back, but there are always boxes and boxes of huge fish. Getting the moose back on home ground means skinning, cleaning, cutting, wrapping, and storing. I won't tell you what part of the moose John finds most succulent, but he loves to make mooseburgers. Here is his recipe.

2 pounds ground moose meat	1 clove garlic, pressed
2 onions, finely chopped	Salt and pepper to taste
4 slices white bread, lightly soaked in milk	8 strips bacon
	⅓ cup butter
	⅓ cup vegetable oil

Select a heavy, large cast-iron skillet. Fry 4 strips bacon until crisp. Be sure grease does not burn. Reserve bacon drippings. Mix moose meat, crumbled bacon, onions, soaked bread, garlic, and salt and pepper to taste. Make four good-sized mooseburgers. Each will be ½ pound. Put butter, ⅓ cup bacon drippings, and oil in skillet. Take the remaining four strips of bacon, wind around the mooseburgers, and fasten with toothpick. When oil, butter, and fat are hot, place burgers in skillet, cover at once, and cook very slowly until the steam partially cooks them. Remove cover and brown on both sides if not already brown. Remove patties to a warm serving dish. Make a gravy from the pan drippings, using browned flour and beef consommé. Serve with a slice of red onion on top. Serves four.

PLAYBOY GUESTHOUSE
MEAT LOAF

2 eggs
½ cup milk
Salt to taste
1 envelope Lipton Onion
  Soup Mix
1½ cups dry bread crumbs
2 pounds ground pork
2 pounds ground chuck

¼ cup chopped parsley
½ cup finely chopped
  onion
1 10¾-ounce can tomato
  soup
2 large onions, sliced
½ cup butter

Preheat oven to 350 degrees. Beat eggs, milk, salt, and onion soup mix. Stir in the bread crumbs and let mixture stand about 10 minutes. Add ground meats, parsley, and onion. Mix lightly until well combined. Grease a 9 x 5 inch loaf pan and bake 1 hour. Remove the meat from the pan and place on oven-proof platter. Turn off heat and place meat loaf in oven. When ready to serve, cover with 1 can undiluted tomato soup, warmed and mixed well. Cover with onion slices sautéed in butter. Include the butter the onions were sautéed in. Serves eight.

ALTERNATE SAUCE

2 pounds potatoes,
  quartered
2 teaspoons salt
½ cup half-and-half

¼ cup butter
¼ teaspoon white pepper
2 egg yolks, beaten
Parsley flakes (garnish)

Cook potatoes, covered, over high heat until tender. Drain. Return to saucepan. Pour half-and-half and butter into the pan until butter melts. Do not boil; remove from heat, put in mixer and beat until light and fluffy. Add pepper and egg yolks. Beat well. Spread mashed potatoes over meat loaf, return to oven until topping is golden. Sprinkle with chopped parsley flakes over top.

RAY BROADWATER'S
PORK BALLS
AND SAUERKRAUT

It's not only the Dutch and Germans who can do great things with sauerkraut. John Hall's wife, Gayla Broadwater Hall, is Norwegian, and occasionally she treats us to some great family dishes that are always unusual and appealing. Her father, Ray, raises pigs now and then, and we are treated to fine pork dishes. Here is a favorite dish made from Ray's ground pork.

2 pounds ground pork
1 medium onion, grated
4 slices white bread,
**   crusts removed,**
**   soaked, and drained**
1 6-ounce can tomato
**   paste, diluted with**
**   1 can water**
1 8-ounce can tomato
**   sauce, diluted with**
**   1 can water**

¾ cup brown sugar
Salt and pepper to taste
2 onions, diced
1 green pepper, diced
2 16-ounce packages
**   sauerkraut, drained**

Mix together the pork, grated onion, bread, tomato paste, and water. Form into balls. Mix the remaining ingredients together. Place meatballs and sauce in a 9 x 13 inch pan. (You may use only 1 package of sauerkraut if you wish, but we find 2 packages disappear in a hurry.) Cover with foil and cook in a 350-degree oven for 1½ to 2 hours. Serves eight.

Note: When we lived up at Hilltop Farm this dish was served to the threshing crews, and they thought it was great!

SAUERKRAUT AND POLISH SAUSAGE CASSEROLE

1 #2½ can sauerkraut
  (about 3 cups)
1 cup grated raw potato
1½ cups sour cream
1 2-ounce jar pimiento

1 teaspoon caraway seeds
1 pound Polish sausage,
  sliced lengthwise and
  cut in 3-inch pieces

Heat sauerkraut and add grated potato. Cook over medium heat in skillet, stirring frequently with fork until potato is tender. Add sour cream, pimiento, and caraway seeds. Place in a round casserole and cook for 30 minutes at 300 degrees. Boil sausage, discard the water, and finish cooking in the skillet until brown. Remove casserole from oven, place mixture on a platter, and surround with Polish sausage, cut side down. Serves four.

MAYOR LATIMER'S CHRISTMAS PORK PIE

1¼ pounds fresh lean
  ground pork
1 cup water
1 medium onion, chopped
½ teaspoon cinnamon

¼ teaspoon sage
Salt and pepper
2 pie crusts (top and
  bottom), unbaked
Flour

Put meat, water, onion, and seasonings in a heavy pot and cook until thoroughly done. Cool meat slightly, and in the meantime make pie crust. Pour meat mixture and juice into bottom crust, and sprinkle with flour. Put top crust on. Bake 30 minutes at 400 degrees. Serve warm with cheese or apple pie. Keep leftovers in refrigerator. Serves six.

Note: Mayor Latimer is St. Paul's competent and progressive mayor.

APPLE AND ONION
PORK CHOPS

1 apple, cored
2 tablespoons vegetable
  oil
4 pork chops, cut ¾ inch
  thick
⅔ cup chopped celery
1½ cups soft bread crumbs

3 envelopes Lipton's
  Onion Cup-a-Soup
½ cup jellied cranberry
  sauce
1 teaspoon flour
¾ cup boiling water

Preheat oven to 350 degrees. Cut four rings ½ inch thick from apple and finely chop remainder. In medium skillet, heat oil and brown chops; remove. Add celery and chopped apple and cook until celery is tender. Stir in bread crumbs, 1 envelope Lipton soup, and ¼ cup cranberry sauce. Place chops in a baking dish; top each chop with one-fourth of the celery-apple mixture and an apple ring. In a small bowl combine remaining envelopes of soup mix and cranberry sauce, flour, and water. Pour over chops. Bake 1 hour or longer if necessary until chops are done. Serves four.

PORK CHOPS ITALIANO

4 thick loin pork chops
  (about 8 ounces each),
  closely trimmed
2 ounces liverwurst
1 teaspoon chervil
Salt
Pepper
1½ pounds (5 medium)
  potatoes, sliced ½ inch
  thick

1 large onion, sliced
2 zucchini, sliced ½ inch
  thick
4 medium tomatoes,
  thickly sliced
1 green pepper, cut into
  ¼-inch rings
2 tablespoons grated
  Parmesan cheese

Prepare a pocket in each pork chop by cutting a slit in center of meat from fat side through to bone. Stuff each pocket with one-quarter of the liverwurst. Using a small amount of trimmed pork chop fat, lightly grease a large heavy skillet or Dutch oven. Add pork chops and brown well on both sides; remove and set aside. Meanwhile, preheat oven to 375 degrees. To assemble casserole, in same skillet, layer meat and vegetables in the following order, sprinkling each layer with chervil, salt, and pepper; potatoes, onion, pork chops, zucchini, tomatoes, and finally, green pepper rings. Cover tightly and bake 1 hour, or until chops and vegetables are fork-tender. Remove cover, sprinkle with grated cheese and bake 5 minutes more. Serves four.

SCHWEINKOTELETTEN MIT BIRNE
(Pork Chops with Pears)

6 pork chops, cut 1 inch
  thick
1½ teaspoons salt
¼ teaspoon pepper
2 onions, cut in wedges
¼ cup seedless raisins

½ cup sweet sherry
½ cup water
3 tablespoons brown sugar
1/8 teaspoon thyme
¼ teaspoon nutmeg
4 fresh Bartlett pears

Fry pork chops in skillet for 5 minutes on each side; drain. Arrange chops in baking dish; sprinkle with salt and pepper. Top with the onions, raisins, sherry, water, brown sugar, thyme, and nutmeg. Cover and bake at 375 degrees for 1¼ to 1½ hours, or until chops are tender when pierced with a fork. Pare, halve, and core pears. Cut each half lengthwise into 4 slices. Place pears over the chops about 5 minutes before dish is ready, just long enough to heat through. Serves six.

HANK'S HEAVENLY
PORK CHOPS

Another goodie from Hank the Wrangler's private recipe file, which he said he kept in his head. Sometimes he "grubbed" for the other wranglers, and whatever came from his makeshift stove was a real gem. While the guests at the elegant C Lazy U Dude Ranch in Granby, Colorado, were being served gourmet dinners inside, Hank was doing his thing outside.

1 head cabbage	**1 tablespoon cream**
½ cup melted butter	**8 pork chops, cut ¾ inch**
⅓ cup butter	**thick**
⅓ cup vegetable oil	**Bread crumbs**
1 clove garlic, pressed	**Salt and pepper to taste**
2 eggs	

Using a sharp knife, cut cabbage in half. Then cut down on each half grating the cabbage by hand in long strips. Melt the ½ cup butter in a 9 x 13 inch pan. Place cabbage in pan and put in 350-degree oven. Stir constantly so cabbage on the bottom gets to the top occasionally. Meanwhile, heat the ⅓ cup butter and the vegetable oil, adding garlic. Beat eggs and cream together. Dip pork chops in egg wash and bread crumbs and fry until browned. When browned on both sides, lift out, and cover cabbage. Salt and pepper to taste. Put foil over the top of pan and bake 1½ hours at 350 degrees or until done. Be careful to check cabbage occasionally so it doesn't get too well done. Hank said the pork chop fat drippings on the cabbage was the secret of this dish's success. Serves eight.

Note: I had a birthday while I was at C Lazy U, and in a blaze of high spirits took a T-bone steak and some birthday cake down to Cream Puff, my horse for the duration. I went to the wrong side of the horse, which caused some commotion, offered the steak and cake, which were rejected, and carefully retreated in a chastened mood. But Hank's horse Papoose saved the day by reaching over for the cake. Fabulous quarter horses on that ranch, but too sly for me!

WRANGLER'S PORK CHOP TIN-PLATE SPECIAL
(From the world's most delightful and exciting dude ranch, the C Lazy U at Granby, Colorado)

The C Lazy U Ranch is probably the most beautiful and the most elegant in the world. We spent a summer there some years ago and were delighted to find the food was superb. One day I found one of the older wranglers working some magic of his own outdoors, and when we asked him what it was, he said it was the Wrangler's Blue Plate Special. Invited to sample, we did just that and rolled our eyes with appreciation. Here is how he did it.

8 pork chops, cut about ¾ inch thick
Flour
½ cup butter or margarine
6 long potatoes, peeled and quartered or cut in eighths

4 large tomatoes, peeled and sliced
3 large onions, sliced
3 cloves garlic, pressed
2 tablespoons flour
2½ cups milk
Salt and pepper to taste

Dip pork chops in flour and fry in butter or margarine. Your pan probably won't hold 8 chops, so do 4 at a time, adding additional margarine or butter, being careful not to let the margarine or butter get too dark since you will be using it later. Remove chops from pan. Reserve drippings. Place potatoes in the bottom of a 9 x 13 inch pan. Cover with chops. Cover the chops with tomato and onion slices and sprinkle garlic over top. Cover with aluminum foil and bake 1½ to 2 hours, depending on the chops. When complete, add 2 tablespoons flour to the drippings in the frying pan, stir until you have gotten all the scrapings from the bottom of the pan and margarine or butter and flour are well mixed. Add milk and stir constantly until thickened. Salt and pepper to taste. Serve over chops and potatoes. That's Hank's Tin Plate Special—tasting all the better under a Colorado summer sky. Serves eight.

POLISH-STYLE
PORK TENDERLOIN

1½ pounds pork tenderloin,
  cut in 1-inch cubes, or
  2 x 1 inch strips
1½ tablespoons all-
  purpose flour
Salt
Pepper
2 tablespoons bacon
  drippings or vegetable
  oil

1 medium onion, coarsely
  chopped
1 rib celery, coarsely
  chopped
2 cups chicken broth
2 teaspoons dillweed
1 teaspoon vinegar
1 cup sour cream (room
  temperature)
Buttered noodles or rice

Sprinkle pork with flour, salt, and pepper. In large skillet, brown meat in bacon drippings or oil over medium heat. Add onion and celery. Reduce heat and cook about 10 minutes more. Add chicken broth, dillweed, and vinegar. Cover and simmer for 45 minutes. Add sour cream and simmer over very low heat about 15 minutes more, but do not boil. Serve with buttered noodles or rice. Serves five.

GRANDMA'S POT ROAST

½ cup butter
4 to 5 pounds rump or
  round beef
Salt and pepper
8 potatoes, cut in wedges
6 large carrots, julienne cut

3 medium onions, peeled
  and quartered
2 large cloves garlic,
  pressed
¼ cup dried parsley

Melt butter in heavy skillet. Brown roast on all sides. Remove from skillet and place in small roaster or Dutch oven with cover. Salt and pepper all sides of roast. Cover with pan drippings. Cover with lid to pan and roast 1 hour at 375 degrees. Turn oven down to 350 degrees and roast another 1½ hours. One hour before removing from oven, put potatoes in bottom of pan. Add carrots, onions, and garlic. Return to oven, basting occasionally so all vegetables are covered with the gravy of the roast. Remove from oven, slice and serve meat with vegetables on each plate and sprinkle with parsley and gravy from pan. Serves six.

HOEDOWN RIBS AND CHICKEN
(For the grill)

5 pounds pork spareribs, trimmed of excess fat
2 3-pound broiler chickens, quartered
Salt and pepper
2 cups catsup
2 cups pineapple juice
2 cups dry red wine
1 tablespoon salt
¼ to ½ cup Worcestershire sauce
½ teaspoon Tabasco
1 onion, grated
2 large cloves garlic, mashed

Sprinkle ribs and chicken on all sides with salt and pepper. Place ribs and chicken in a large pan. Combine all remaining ingredients and pour over ribs and chicken. Let marinate, covered, for at least 2 hours or overnight in the refrigerator. Turn at least once. Drain ribs and chicken well and place 8 inches above moderately hot coals; grill until done (about 1 hour). Turn ribs and chickens every 15 minutes, brushing frequently with marinade. Pour marinade into a saucepan, and heat on grill. Cut ribs into individual pieces; serve chicken and ribs with marinade as dipping sauce. Serves eight to ten.

NORA'S PENNSYLVANIA
DUTCH SCRAPPLE

Back in Grandma's growing-up days, scrapple was an ingenious use of leftover food. It's a wonderful blend of pork and cornmeal. Everything is simmered together, set in bread tins, and allowed to thicken in the refrigerator. When ready to use, remove from tins, slice, and fry. Used for breakfast and other meals as well.

1 cup cornmeal
¼ cup flour
1 quart meat stock
1 cup shredded pork
1 teaspoon salt

¼ teaspoon pepper
1 sage leaf
1 tablespoon grated onion
Butter

Mix cornmeal and flour together and add enough water to make a paste. Add meat stock, pork, salt, pepper, sage leaf, and grated onion. Cook in a double boiler over hot, not boiling, water for several hours and put in three or four bread tins until cool. After several hours in the refrigerator, it will be ready to slice and serve. Fry over low heat in butter in cast-iron skillet until crisp, 10 to 15 minutes. Serves eight.

DUTCH-OVEN STEAK

4 pounds round steak
  (8 ounces per serving)
1 cup flour
1 teaspoon salt
½ teaspoon paprika
½ teaspoon pepper
½ cup butter
2 cloves garlic, minced

2 large onions, coarsely
  chopped
1 green pepper, coarsely
  chopped
1 cup tomato sauce
2½ cups beef broth
6 carrots, cut in
  julienne strips

Cut the steak in the portions you wish. Pound each piece on both sides until it is 1 inch thick. Mix the flour, salt, paprika, and pepper. Rub well into steak. Heat the butter and brown meat on both sides. Be careful not to burn butter. Add garlic, onions, and green pepper, and cook about 5 minutes. Combine the tomato sauce and beef broth. Pour over meat and bring to a boil. Transfer to a casserole or baking dish of your choice, preferably a Dutch oven. Cover. Bake at 350 degrees for 2 to 2½ hours. Add carrots ½ hour before removing from oven. Make sure there is enough liquid as it cooks. Serves eight.

CREAMED SWEETBREADS
AND MUSHROOMS

3 pair sweetbreads
3 tablespoons butter
1 cup sliced fresh
    mushrooms
1 tablespoon minced
    parsley
Dash curry powder
2 tablespoons flour

1 cup chicken broth
½ cup half-and-half
¼ cup Madeira
Salt and pepper to taste
1 tablespoon butter
½ cup slivered almonds
7 or 8 pastry shells

Cook sweetbreads over medium heat for about 15 minutes. Plunge into cold water, then remove the fine, delicate skin. Dry, cut in slices, and brown in the 3 tablespoons of butter over medium heat with mushrooms, parsley, and curry powder. Stir in flour and cook for a few minutes, but do not brown. Add chicken broth, half-and-half, and Madeira. Salt and pepper to taste. Blend well and stir until it is the right consistency, resembling a light cream sauce. Let stand, covered, over hot water for ½ hour until flavors are well blended. Just before serving lightly brown the slivered almonds in the 1 tablespoon of butter. Add to the sweetbread mixture. Serve in heated pastry shells. This dish can be prepared ahead of time and kept in the refrigerator. Serves six.

BUSY GIRL'S
GREAT SHORT RIBS

The gal who brought this recipe over to us says she cooks everything with a pressure cooker, crock pot, electric frying pan, or toaster oven. She's a traveling executive who lives most of her life in hotel rooms. John Hall would have a fit, because she confesses to traveling with all or part of her cooking equipment and preparing food in hotel rooms, which is a no-no in most places unless there is a kitchenette. She says her biggest problem is triggering the fire alarm. How about keeping the cooking smell out of the hallways? She says going into the bar and dining room alone in most hotels makes most everyone think she is out for fun and frolic. So, it's room service for her or cook your own. We sympathize. For fifteen years as traveling supervisors for a hotel chain, we spent most of our time in the air or in hotels, and that was long before there were very many of us.

1 cup catsup	2 tablespoons bacon
1 teaspoon salt	drippings
2 teaspoons brown sugar	2 tablespoons finely
½ teaspoon celery seed	chopped onion
2 teaspoons lemon juice	2 tablespoons chopped
¼ teaspoon cumin	green pepper
2 tablespoons mustard	2 tablespoons flour
1 teaspoon Worcestershire	2 tablespoons cold water
sauce	
6 pounds short ribs	
of beef	

Make a marinade from catsup, salt, brown sugar, celery seed, lemon juice, cumin, mustard, and Worcestershire sauce. Trim short ribs and put in deep bowl; cover with marinade. Cover and let stand in refrigerator for 6 hours, turning occasionally. Remove the ribs and pour the marinade into a two-cup measuring cup, adding whatever water is necessary to make two cups. Heat the bacon drippings in a pressure cooker. Brown ribs until brown. Pour off excess fat. Add the marinade, onion, and green pepper. Cover and set control at 10. Cook 30 to 35 minutes after the control begins to jiggle. Reduce pressure normally for at least 5 minutes. Then place cooker under cold running water. Remove cover. Mix flour and water and use to thicken the pan juices. Boil 2 minutes, stirring constantly, and serve with ribs. We serve with whole carrots, oven-browned potatoes, and boiled cabbage. Serves six.

COUNTRY-FRIED STEAK

Back in Grandma Anderson's day, a peddler (as they were then called) moaned that all his teeth ached; he hadn't eaten for days because he couldn't chew. He then said he would like a bowl of bread and milk. "Would you like a steak if you could chew it?" asked Grandma. He moaned with anticipation, "You bet!" And this is how she made the peddler's steak.

1 8-ounce top sirloin steak   **½ cup water**
½ cup butter   **Salt and pepper to taste**
Flour

Melt the butter in a frying pan. Pound steak flat with a heavy mallet on both sides until it looks three times larger. Dip in flour on both sides. Cook briefly in frying pan on both sides. Remove, add ½ cup water to pan drippings, stir until thickened, and pour over steak. Salt and pepper to taste. Serves one.

TAMALE RUMAKI

1 16-ounce can tamales   **24 slices bacon**

Cut each tamale into four or five pieces crosswise. Cut each bacon slice in half and wind one piece around each piece of tamale. Secure with toothpick. Place in pan and bake at 375 degrees until bacon is done, about 5 to 10 minutes.

RIBS AND KRAUT

5 pounds pork spareribs,
  trimmed of excess fat
  and cut in serving pieces
Barbecue Sauce (below)
3½ cups undrained
  sauerkraut
2 medium tart red apples,
  unpared

¼ cup butter
½ cup finely chopped onion
½ cup diced green pepper
2 tablespoons sugar
Black pepper to taste

Place ribs in shallow roasting pan; cover with foil and bake at 325 degrees for 1 hour. Increase oven temperature to 400 degrees. Pour off fat from pan and wipe ribs with paper towels to remove excess fat. Brush ribs on all sides with Barbecue Sauce. Roast ribs uncovered for 45 minutes or until fork tender and dark brown. About 25 minutes before ribs are done, drain kraut juice into bowl and set kraut aside. Slice apples into ½-inch-thick wedges; toss into kraut juice immediately to prevent browning. Melt butter in saucepan over medium heat. Add onion and sauté until golden; stir in green pepper. Cook, stirring occasionally, until green pepper is tender-crisp. Drain apples and add with kraut, sugar, and black pepper to onion mixture. Heat thoroughly and serve with spareribs. Serves six.

BARBECUE SAUCE

½ cup honey
½ cup light molasses
1 cup catsup
½ teaspoon grated
  orange peel
⅔ cup orange juice
1 clove garlic, minced

1 tablespoon A-1 Sauce
2 teaspoons prepared
  mustard
1/8 teaspoon ginger
½ teaspoon salt
¼ teaspoon pepper

Simmer 5 minutes, stirring constantly. Set aside until needed.

NEW YEAR'S EVE KIDNEY AND LOIN VEAL CHOPS

½ cup melted butter
2 large cloves garlic, minced
8 veal chops, cut 1 inch thick (this must be loin chop with a part of the kidney still on)

Flour
2 cups whipping cream
12 ounces fresh mushrooms, sliced
¼ cup butter
4 tablespoons finely chopped fresh parsley

Melt ½ cup butter in a 12-inch skillet. Add minced garlic. Dip both sides of the veal chops in flour and lower into skillet carefully. Brown on both sides. Do not burn butter. Remove to a small roaster. Scrape pan, loosening remaining bits, and add cream. Stir until it thickens slightly. Sauté mushrooms in ¼ cup butter and add to cream mixture. Stir to blend. Add parsley and pour over veal chops. Roast until tender (about 1½ hours) in a 350-degree oven. Serves eight.

LITTLE JOHN HALL'S FAVORITE WIENERS

1 medium onion, finely chopped
2 tablespoons butter
3 tablespoons Worcestershire sauce
½ tablespoon prepared mustard
2 tablespoons vinegar

½ cup water
2 tablespoons brown sugar
4 tablespoons lemon juice
1 cup tomato catsup
½ cup chopped celery
Salt and pepper
1½ pounds cooked wieners

Sauté onion in butter. Combine onion with all ingredients except wieners. Simmer slowly for 30 minutes. Place wieners in 9 x 9 x 2 inch pan. Pour the sauce over them. Bake 45 minutes in a 350-degree oven. Serves four.

BEEF TONGUE, ANDERSON STYLE

1 beef tongue
2 cups diced carrots
2 cups finely diced celery
2 cups diced white onion

1 cup diced parsnips
 (optional)
¼ cup butter
½ cup flour

Allow beef tongue to soak two hours in cold water. Drain. Refill pot with cold water and bring to boiling point. Cook for 3 hours over medium heat. Remove tongue from water. Reserve water. Cool. Skin tongue and remove gristle you will find at the end. Put tongue in roasting pan and cover with the cut vegetables. Pour 4 cups of the reserved water over the tongue and the vegetables. Cover and roast for 2 hours at 325 degrees. Remove to a serving dish. In a separate pan, melt butter, add flour, and blend. Add this to the stock in the baking pan, making a not-too-thick gravy. Serve separately in a gravy boat or pitcher. Serves six.

Note: There are those who turn a cold shoulder on tongue and miss one of the greatest delights the food world has to offer. When Peter Klas worked for us in Chicago, we knew there was another dedicated tongue addict, allowing little chance for leftovers. Peter also liked it sliced cold with whipped horseradish sauce.

Poultry

We like to think we have some of the most inventive cooks in the country, but even *they* weren't quite sure what they would do with the six-hundred-bird flock we purchased from a chicken farmer who, due to health problems, needed to winter in a warmer climate.

Fortunately, we found someone to clean and wrap the chickens for the freezer, but they were ever-present in our minds as we planned each day's special dishes. We served them broiled, baked, fried, in salads, in soups, in casseroles, and, of course, in Grandma Anderson's Chicken and Dumplings (a five-star dish as far as our customers are concerned).

As we learned from that experience, there must be a million ways to serve chicken. We've served it with sweetbread stuffing (see Baked Stuffed Broilers) and in casseroles with wild rice (see Muriel Humphrey's Special Occasion Dish). We've made Chicken Spaghetti, a real winner with those who do not eat red meat. Other notable Anderson House chicken dishes are Baked Chicken Pie (a Pennsylvania Dutch tradition), Plum-Glazed Chicken, and Chicken à la King. One of Grandma Anderson's specialties was Chicken Piquant in a Pancake Shell, which remains popular today. Chicken Liver Sauté is another favorite at our inn.

Try these and others in this section—you're sure to build hearty and delicious meals around them.

BAKED STUFFED BROILERS

3 broilers, halved
Salt
Pepper
Sweetbread Stuffing
  (below)
3 onions, sliced
6 tablespoons chicken fat
  or butter

4 tablespoons flour
2½ cups hot chicken stock
  or boiling water
Salt and pepper to taste
2 tablespoons sour cream
Orange shells filled with
  orange ice (garnish)

Season chickens with salt and pepper. Fill cavities with stuffing and tie halves together. Place in a roasting pan with a sliced onion and 2 tablespoons chicken fat or butter over each chicken. Bake 1 hour in a hot oven (375 degrees) until tender, basting frequently.

To 4 tablespoons of the fat in which the chickens were cooked, add flour and brown. Gradually pour into hot chicken stock or boiling water. Cook until smooth and thick. Season to taste and add sour cream. When ready to serve, split chickens in half, garnish platter with orange shells filled with orange ice. Serve with gravy. Serves six.

SWEETBREAD STUFFING

4 slices dry bread
Water
3 tablespoons chicken fat
1 onion, sliced
2 egg yolks, lightly beaten
1 egg white, lightly beaten
¼ pound chicken livers,
  pureed

½ pound boiled
  sweetbreads, broken
  into small pieces
1 tablespoon minced
  parsley
Salt
Pepper
Paprika

Soak the bread in water. Squeeze dry. Brown onion in fat. Add bread and cook until the fat is absorbed. Cool. Add egg yolks and white, livers, sweetbreads, and seasonings. Set aside until ready for stuffing.

Note: You may omit livers and increase amount of sweetbreads to ¾ pound.

CHICKEN À LA KING

We probably serve more chicken à la king to ladies' luncheons, bus tours, wedding parties, and other large groups than any other dish on our menu. We serve it on rice, patty shells, and homemade tart shells. We think we have perfected it—even men love it. The secret, of course, is lots of good, fresh chicken (white meat preferred).

2 tablespoons finely
  chopped onion
¼ cup chopped green
  pepper
½ pound mushrooms,
  chopped
⅓ cup boiling water
⅔ cup flour
1 cup cold milk
2 cups chicken broth

2 teaspoons salt
Pepper to taste
½ teaspoon poultry
  seasoning
4 cups diced cooked
  chicken
2 tablespoons chopped
  pimiento
Cooked rice

Cook onion, green pepper, and mushrooms in boiling water in a covered saucepan for 5 minutes. Drain; reserve the liquid. Blend flour with milk. In a saucepan combine reserved liquid, broth, and seasonings; slowly stir in flour mixture. Bring to a boil, stirring constantly; cook 1 minute. Add chicken, cooked vegetables, and pimiento. Heat thoroughly and serve on rice. Serves six.

CHICKEN CASSEROLE

1 3½-pound chicken,
  cooked
3 eggs, beaten
3 to 5 slices bread,
  torn into pieces

1 cup cooked rice
¾ cup milk
1 cup soup stock
1 10¾-ounce can
  mushroom soup

Cut up chicken after cooking. To eggs add bread, rice, milk, and soup stock. Pour into casserole. Bake at 325 degrees for 1 hour. Dilute soup with ½ can water. Mix in blender. Heat until warm. Serve with chicken as gravy. Serves four.

GRANDMA ANDERSON'S CHICKEN AND DUMPLINGS

1 3-pound stewing chicken
Flour
2 tablespoons fat
1½ teaspoons salt
1/8 teaspoon pepper

2 tablespoons chopped parsley
¼ teaspoon celery seed
Southern Dumplings (below)

Cut the chicken into pieces for serving, wash, and dry. Dredge lightly with flour and brown on all sides in hot fat. In a large saucepan, cover the chicken double its depth with water. Add the salt, pepper, parsley, and celery seed. Simmer until the meat separates easily from the bone, about 45 minutes to 1 hour. Lift carefully from the broth, using a large slotted spoon. Keep warm until serving time. Reserve the broth for cooking the dumplings. Pour the dumplings and gravy over the warm chicken just before serving. Serves six.

SOUTHERN DUMPLINGS

2 cups sifted flour
1 teaspoon salt
1 teaspoon baking powder

1 tablespoon shortening
Chicken broth (see above)

Sift the flour, salt, and baking powder together. Cut in the shortening and gradually add about two-thirds cup of chicken broth, until a stiff dough results. Roll out on a floured board and cut into strips 1 inch wide and 2 to 2½ inches long. Bring remaining chicken broth to a boil. Drop a few strips at a time into broth. Cover and cook for 10 to 15 minutes. Serves four.

CHICKEN LIVER SAUTÉ

½ cup finely chopped
bacon
2 tablespoons finely
chopped onion
2 tablespoons finely
chopped green pepper
1 pound chicken livers,
dredged in flour

Sprig of fresh thyme
½ cup red wine
½ cup pitted ripe olives
¼ cup chopped parsley
Cooked rice

Sauté bacon, onion, and green pepper in skillet over medium heat.
Add chicken livers and cook them for 3 to 5 minutes, browning them
carefully on all sides. Add thyme and wine and cook a few minutes longer.
Add olives and parsley and cook, stirring constantly, until olives are
heated through. Serve over buttered rice. Serves four.

CHICKEN LOAF
(From Grandma Anderson's
Primer for Brides)

2 cups chopped cooked
chicken
1 cup bread crumbs
Chicken stock (enough to
moisten chicken and
crumbs)
2 eggs, well beaten

1 2-ounce jar pimiento,
finely chopped
Salt and pepper
1 10¾-ounce can cream
of mushroom soup
Minced parsley (garnish)

Put chicken and bread crumbs in a mixing bowl. Moisten with stock.
Add eggs and pimiento. Season. Grease a bread pan, and form mixture
into loaf. Bake 1 hour at 375 degrees. To make a sauce, heat cream
of mushroom soup according to directions, but reduce liquid added to
½ can. Ladle sauce over loaf. Sprinkle with parsley. Serves four.

QUICK AND EASY
OVEN-FRIED CHICKEN
(From Grandma Anderson's
Primer for Brides)

1 ounce whole or
   evaporated milk
1 egg
1 frying chicken, cut up

1½ cups crushed
   cornflakes
Salt and pepper to taste
Melted butter

Combine milk and egg. Beat lightly. Dip chicken into egg wash and then coat with cornflakes. Butter a 9 x 13 inch pan and lay chicken in, skin side up. Season with salt and pepper. Drizzle with melted butter and bake in a 350-degree oven, uncovered, for about 1 hour. Serves four.

PICKLED CHICKEN GIZZARDS

3 cups vinegar
2 cups water
1 teaspoon salt
2 tablespoons sugar
1 tablespoon allspice
1 clove garlic, minced
1 large onion, peeled
   and sliced

2 quarts cooked chicken
   gizzards (can be
   pressure cooked at 15-
   pound pressure for
   15 minutes)

In a large saucepan, combine vinegar, water, salt, sugar, and allspice; boil for 5 minutes. Remove from heat and cool. Stir in garlic. In crockery container, alternately layer gizzards and onion slices. Pour vinegar mixture over and allow to sit one hour at room temperature. Refrigerate until used. Serves twelve as a snack. Serve with pickled eggs.

CHICKEN MOLD

4 cups cooked and
  chopped chicken
2 cups soft bread crumbs
2 cups cooked rice
¼ cup pimiento

4 eggs, beaten
3 cups chicken stock or
  milk
¼ cup butter or chicken fat
Filling (below)

Mix all ingredients except filling and place in a well-buttered 2-quart ring mold. Cook slowly for 1¼ hours at 320 degrees. Place filling in center of mold.

FILLING

2 tablespoons plus
  5 tablespoons butter
½ pound mushrooms,
  sliced
2 egg yolks, beaten

½ cup heavy cream
4 tablespoons flour
2 cups chicken stock
1 teaspoon minced parsley
1 teaspoon lemon juice

In a skillet melt the 2 tablespoons butter, and sauté mushrooms over moderately high heat; set aside. Mix together egg yolks and cream; set aside. In a saucepan melt the 5 tablespoons butter and stir in flour. Stir in the stock; when thickened, add yolk-cream mixture. Add mushrooms, and cook until thickened, about 10 minutes. Mix in parsley and lemon juice. Serves ten to twelve.

BAKED CHICKEN PIE

1 4-pound chicken
Pot-Pie Dough (below)
5 medium potatoes,
  quartered

1 onion, minced
2 tablespoons minced
  parsley
Salt and pepper to taste

Boil the chicken in salted water for 45 minutes. Reserve broth. Remove meat from bones and cut in 1-inch pieces. Make pastry as directed below and line bottom and sides of a baking dish. Fill with layers of chicken, potatoes, onion, parsley, salt, and pepper. Pour enough chicken broth over mixture to almost cover. Cover with pastry, fastening edges securely. Cut holes in the top to allow steam to escape. Bake at 350 degrees for 1 hour.

POT-PIE DOUGH

2 cups flour   **⅓ cup shortening**
1 teaspoon baking powder   **½ cup milk**
½ teaspoon salt

Cut shortening into the combined flour, baking powder, and salt. Moisten with the milk as in regular pie dough. Roll out on lightly floured board until 1/8 inch thick.

Note: Pot-pie is one of the most renowned Pennsylvania Dutch meat dishes. When mother announced pot-pie for dinner, we always wondered whether it would be boiled or baked. Some of us hoped for a baked pot-pie while others begged for the boiled. For baked pot-pie, I use regular pastry to line the baking dish that is to be filled with meat and potatoes and then covered with a top crust. Baked to a golden brown with the rich juice bubbling through the crust, this pot-pie will tempt even the poorest of appetites.

COUNTRY-CRUST CHICKEN PIE

1½ cups flour
2 teaspoons baking powder
½ teaspoon salt
2 teaspoons butter
3 egg yolks, beaten until
 fluffy
¾ cup milk
3 egg whites, stiffly
 beaten
2 cups diced cooked
 chicken

½ cup finely cubed
 carrot
1 cup frozen peas
¼ cup finely chopped
 onions, sautéed in butter
3 cups rich chicken stock,
 thickened with ½ cup
 flour

Combine flour, baking powder, and salt; add butter. Mix. To egg yolks, add flour mixture and milk. Beat vigorously. Fold in egg whites; set aside. Combine chicken, carrot, peas, onions, and chicken stock. Place in baking dish; spread flour mixture over top. Bake at 375 degrees for 25 minutes or until done. Serves six.

CHICKEN PIQUANT IN A PANCAKE SHELL

2 tablespoons chicken fat
 or margarine
¼ cup flour
2 cups chicken broth or
 milk
1½ teaspoons salt

½ cup diced, cooked celery
½ cup diced, cooked carrots
1½ cups diced, cooked
 chicken
Pancake Shell (below)

Melt fat or margarine in saucepan; stir in flour. Add broth or milk and salt. Cook over medium heat, stirring constantly, until thickened, 10 to 15 minutes. Add remaining ingredients, except shell, and simmer gently about 15 minutes, stirring constantly. Keep chicken piquant warm while preparing Pancake Shell. When shell is done, pour in mixture. Serve hot. Serves four.

PANCAKE SHELL

½ cup pancake mix   2 tablespoons melted butter
¼ cup milk   1 egg

Combine pancake mix, milk, butter, and egg, beating with a rotary beater until smooth. Lightly grease sides and bottom of a 9- or 10-inch frying pan and heat until very hot. Pour in the batter, immediately rolling the pan until sides and bottom are evenly coated. Cook pancake over moderate heat until dry on top. Prick bottom of pancake in several places. Bake in a 400-degree oven for 5 minutes or until brown. To remove pancake from pan, run knife around edge, tilt pan and very gently slide pancake onto serving dish.

PLUM-GLAZED CHICKEN

¾ cup plum jam
2 tablespoons
   Worcestershire sauce
2 tablespoons soy sauce
1 tablespoon catsup
2 teaspoons finely chopped
   fresh ginger, or 1
   teaspoon powdered
   ginger

½ teaspoon cinnamon
¼ teaspoon dry mustard
1/8 teaspoon ground cloves
1/8 teaspoon hot pepper
   sauce
1 3- to 3½-pound chicken,
   cut into serving pieces

Make the plum sauce by placing all the ingredients except chicken in a small saucepan and heating gently until the jam melts. Place chicken pieces in a 9 x 13 inch pan. Brush chicken with plum sauce and bake for 30 minutes in a preheated 375-degree oven. Turn chicken pieces over, and brush with the sauce; bake an additional 20 to 25 minutes. Serve any remaining sauce with the chicken. Serves four.

Note: This recipe works well with ducklings, also.

CHICKEN 'N' POTATO CASSEROLE

4 chicken breast halves,
  skinned and deboned
2 slices bacon, cut in half
1 teaspoon chopped parsley
½ teaspoon sage
Salt and pepper
¼ cup butter or margarine
1 pound potatoes
  (3 medium), boiled
2 egg yolks

½ cup milk
1 pound Swiss chard,
  coarsely chopped
  (separate white stems
  from green leaves)
2 medium carrots,
  coarsely grated
1 green onion, chopped
2 tablespoons grated
  Parmesan cheese

With mallet or rolling pin, pound chicken pieces to flatten. Top each piece with a half bacon slice; sprinkle with some of parsley, sage, salt, and pepper. Roll up each piece jelly-roll fashion; secure with string or toothpicks. In a heavy skillet, melt 2 tablespoons butter or margarine. Brown chicken rolls slowly on all sides, about 15 minutes. Preheat oven to 375 degrees. Meanwhile, in large bowl combine potatoes, egg yolks, milk, remaining 2 tablespoons butter or margarine, salt, and pepper. Using electric mixer, beat until well blended; set aside. In large heavy saucepan with tight-fitting lid, in 1 inch of salted water, cook white chard, carrots, and green onion, covered, 2 minutes; add green chard and cook 4 minutes more or until vegetables are tender. Drain; season vegetables with salt and pepper to taste and set aside. In bottom of shallow, 2-quart casserole, arrange chard mixture; spread potato mixture evenly on top. Place chicken rolls on potato layer; sprinkle with Parmesan cheese. Bake, uncovered, 30 minutes or until chicken is tender. Serves four.

CHICKEN AND RICE

We know practically everyone has this recipe, but because it is requested nearly every day at the Anderson House, we offer it here. We hope you will like it as well at home as you do at the Anderson House.

2 3½-pound chickens
1 cup long-grain rice
1 package onion soup mix
2 cups chicken broth
1 10¾-ounce can cream
of mushroom soup
1 8-ounce can chopped
mushrooms or 8 ounces
fresh mushrooms sautéed
in butter

Seasoning salt
Salt and white pepper
to taste
Paprika
¼ cup dried parsley flakes

Quarter chickens and remove wings. Place in pot and cook over medium heat for 45 minutes. Reduce broth to 2 cups. Set aside. Pour dry rice into a large casserole or baking pan. Pour onion soup mix (dry) over the rice. Mix broth and mushroom soup and pour over the rice. Add mushrooms. Rub insides of chicken with seasoning salt, salt, and pepper. Place chicken on top of mixture and sprinkle with paprika. Bake, covered, at 350 degrees for 1½ hours. Remove cover and bake an additional 15 minutes. Sprinkle with dried parsley and serve at once. Serves eight.

Note: We suggest Sweet Potato Buns, Pennsylvania Dutch Green Beans, and Pennsylvania Dutch Go-to-Meeting Hot Slaw as accompaniments (see index).

CHICKEN ROLLS

6 chicken breasts,
  boned and split (allow
  1½ per person)
12 thin slices prosciutto
  ham
12 thin slices Muenster
  cheese

6 teaspoons butter
  (½ teaspoon per breast)
1 egg, lightly beaten
Seasoned bread crumbs
Mushroom Sauce (below)
Fresh minced parsley
  (garnish)

Remove skin from breast halves and pound thin between sheets of waxed paper. Place 1 slice ham and 1 slice cheese on each breast and dot with butter. Roll up, tucking in ends and tying with string. Dip in beaten egg and then roll in bread crumbs. Place on cookie sheet with seam side down and freeze until firm. Remove and put into heavy plastic bag and return to freezer.

To bake, place breasts (not touching) in greased shallow baking dish. Bake at 350 degrees for 1¼ hours. (If you don't have time to freeze the rolls, place for 4 to 6 hours in refrigerator and then bake, without bringing to room temperature, at 350 degrees for 45 minutes.) Put on heated platter or serve from baking dish. Ladle Mushroom Sauce over rolls; garnish with parsley. Serves eight.

MUSHROOM SAUCE

2 tablespoons butter
2 tablespoons flour
1 cup rich chicken stock
½ teaspoon tarragon
Salt and pepper to taste

1 4-ounce can mushroom
  pieces or ¼ pound fresh
  mushrooms, sliced and
  sautéed in butter for
  5 minutes
½ cup half-and-half
1 egg yolk, beaten

Melt butter in saucepan, add flour, and cook, without browning, stirring constantly for several minutes. Slowly add stock and spices. Simmer several minutes, add mushrooms, and simmer for 5 minutes. Remove from heat and stir in cream mixed with egg yolk. Cook, stirring, until heated through. Do not let boil. May be made a day ahead of time and reheated.

CHICKEN SPAGHETTI

1 5½-pound hen, or 2 cups
  cut up cooked chicken
Water
2 onions, sliced
1 bell pepper, quartered
5 ribs celery
Salt
Black pepper
Poultry seasoning
¼ cup margarine
2 onions, chopped
1 cup chopped celery
1 bell pepper, chopped
2 cloves garlic, crushed
4 tablespoons flour

1 2-ounce jar pimiento,
  drained and sliced
1 4-ounce can mushrooms,
  drained, or ½ pound
  fresh mushrooms
2 tablespoons chopped
  parsley
Worcestershire sauce
  to taste
Tabasco sauce to taste
2 ounces red wine (optional)
Cooked spaghetti
4 ounces Parmesan cheese,
  grated

Simmer chicken approximately 2 hours until tender in enough water to cover the hen or chicken parts, with onions, bell pepper, celery ribs, salt, black pepper, and poultry seasoning to taste. Remove chicken; skin, debone, and cut up if you are using a whole hen. Strain the broth and set aside. Saute onions, celery, bell pepper, and garlic in ¼ cup margarine for 5 minutes. Add the flour and sauté for 5 minutes more. Slowly add 2 cups of the reserved chicken broth. Simmer for 10 minutes. Add chicken, pimiento, mushrooms, parsley, salt, pepper, Worcestershire sauce, and Tabasco sauce. Add wine if desired, cover, and simmer for 2 minutes. Cook spaghetti in the chicken broth, according to the directions on the package, except do not add salt. Spoon chicken over spaghetti. Provide grated Parmesan cheese for sprinkling over dish according to individual taste. Serves eight.

MURIEL HUMPHREY'S
SPECIAL OCCASION DISH

1 3- to 3½-pound frying
   chicken, cut up
2 cups milk
1¼ teaspoons salt
½ cup butter
1½ teaspoons lemon juice
1 5- to 6½-ounce package
   prepared white and
   wild rice

2 cups sour cream
1/8 teaspoon pepper
1 bouillon cube, dissolved
¼ cup chopped chives
Pinch oregano or
   seasoned salt

Marinate chicken in milk and 1 teaspoon salt for about 2 hours. Remove chicken, saving marinade. Brown chicken lightly in butter and squeeze 1 teaspoon lemon juice lightly over the top. Salt and pepper to taste. Cook rice according to directions. Place rice mixture in bottom of casserole and put browned chicken over rice. In saucepan, put sour cream, ½ cup of the milk marinade, ¼ teaspoon salt, pepper, ½ teaspoon lemon juice, bouillon cube, chives, and oregano or seasoned salt. Heat just to blend. Pour over the chicken and rice mixture in casserole and bake at 375 degrees for 2 hours, covered except for the last 20 minutes. This could be baked for 1 hour at 400 degrees and then turned down to 325 degrees until ready to serve. Serves four.

Note: My mother, who came to know and appreciate the Humphreys when she was president of the Democratic Women of Minnesota, said Muriel Humphrey bought more copies of our first cookbook than any other individual. It made us feel good to think of copies of our book floating around in Washington. So we are doubly pleased to include one of Muriel Humphrey's recipes in this book.

ROSY GLAZED GOOSE
WITH APPLE STUFFING

¼ cup butter or margarine
2 medium onions, chopped
2 ribs celery, sliced
½ cup extra dry vermouth
12 tart apples (about
  2½ pounds), sliced into
  8 pieces
1½ cups apple juice

1 bag (8 ounces) herb-
  seasoned stuffing mix
1 teaspoon salt
¼ teaspoon pepper
1 10- to 12-pound goose
  or 2 4- to 5-pound ducks
Rosy Glaze (below)

In a large skillet melt butter. Add onions and celery and sauté until limp, about 3 minutes. Add vermouth and simmer 10 minutes. Add apples and sauté 5 minutes. Add apple juice, stuffing mix, salt, and pepper, stirring well to combine. Remove from heat and allow to cool for about 10 minutes. Preheat oven to 325 degrees. Stuff cavity of goose with cooled stuffing and skewer closed. Place goose on rack in roasting pan. Cook in oven for 2½ to 3 hours or until meat thermometer reads 185 degrees. Carefully drain accumulating fat at least twice during cooking, or as necessary. Discard fat. During the last ½ hour of cooking baste goose with Rosy Glaze. Carve goose and arrange on serving platter with stuffing. Serve goose with remaining glaze. Serves four to six.

ROSY GLAZE

1 cup orange juice
¼ cup lemon juice
½ cup cranberry juice
¾ cup sweet vermouth
1 teaspoon mustard

¼ teaspoon garlic powder
¼ teaspoon onion powder
2 tablespoons cornstarch
1 10-ounce jar currant jelly

In a small saucepan, combine all ingredients. Heat over medium heat for 12 minutes or until mixture boils, stirring occasionally. Lower heat and simmer for 15 minutes.

Vegetables

We close the Anderson House from January 4 until January 24 so we can catch up on maintenance and decoration. After the wallpaper is ordered, we can give our attention to the seed catalogs. We plant some of our own vegetables in the small space not taken by the flowers, but we know that when summer comes our vegetable lady, Claire Hall (she's not related to us), will come down from the hills with her marvelous, scientifically grown veggies.

Claire is one of those fine-boned natural beauties who looks a little like Greta Garbo and Marlene Dietrich combined. She is young and strong and works from dawn to dusk during the season. She comes every Tuesday to deliver her goodies. One of the nice things about Claire is that she too spends winters with seed catalogs and dares to plant exciting and unusual things. This year she planted a new, small striped squash that we couldn't get into the kitchens fast enough. Overall, our vegetable supply brings real joy to all of our creative cooks.

We start our summer season for home-grown goodies in May when the first rhubarb comes up bright and green and pink. Our peak season is late August or early September and from then until November first we have abundant supplies. Our fresh vegetable plate is a popular entrée, and our soups and salads are especially appealing. Our season is short but we don't waste a day of it. The day the first frost is announced we call Claire and ask for all the green tomatoes left in her fields. Then it's back to Grandma Anderson and the thrifty Dutch. We serve pan-fried green tomatoes with a cream gravy. That dish is so popular that people order in advance. Then my sister Ann, who is the greatest cook I know, takes over the green-tomato supply and makes an absolutely elegant green tomato relish that we serve as a garnish.

Among our favorite vegetables is the tomato; we serve it in many ways. We marinate tomatoes overnight, then serve them with an olive oil and chive sauce; stuff and then broil them; and use them in salads. Of course, we subject cucumbers to the same treatment. Many people don't know that cucumbers can be stuffed or gently sautéed and served with a light sprinkling of parsley. Cucumbers make an elegant sauce for fish as well. We pickle our own beets and use them for soup and for salad. Pea Pods go into many of our dishes as do green and red peppers. Zucchini is plentiful; we use it in bread, in soup, pickled, and broiled. Everybody's favorite, however, is fried zucchini slices. We use corn for corn chowder, corn pudding, Mexican corn, pickled relish, and many other dishes. When corn is in season, we like corn on the cob.

Of all vegetables, the potato is our specialty. We serve Creamed Browned Potatoes with Bacon, we make Baked Potato Pudding, and we still use Grandma Anderson's recipe for Sesame Potato Spears. Our most important advice in preparing this delightful vegetable is to never wrap it in foil for baking because you end up with a steamed, not baked, potato. At the Anderson House, we're blessed with a variety of vegetables—even a vegetarian need never have a boring meal!

BARLEY-AND-MUSHROOM CASEROLE

1 pound fresh mushrooms
½ cup butter
1 cup finely chopped onion
1 cup diced celery
4 cups cooked medium-sized barley
¾ teaspoon salt
½ teaspoon marjoram leaves, crushed
1/8 teaspoon sage
Dash black pepper
¾ cup chicken broth
2 eggs, lightly beaten

Preheat oven to 350 degrees. Rinse, pat dry, and slice fresh mushrooms. In a large skillet, melt ¼ cup of the butter. Add onion and celery; sauté until tender, about 5 minutes. Reserve. Melt remaining ¼ cup butter. Add mushrooms and sauté until golden, about 10 minutes. Add barley, salt, marjoram, sage, black pepper, chicken broth, eggs, and reserved onion and celery. Spoon into a buttered 2-quart casserole. Cover and bake 30 minutes; uncover and bake until firm, about 10 minutes longer. Let stand about 10 minutes before serving. This may be used as a vegetable or stuffing for a small turkey or large roasting chicken. Makes about 7 cups. Serves eight.

ELEGANT BAKED BEANS

1 pound dry navy beans
1 medium onion studded
  with 2 or 3 cloves
2 cloves garlic
½ teaspoon thyme
1 bay leaf
¼ cup butter or margarine
1 small onion, chopped
1 cup tomato paste

2 tablespoons dry parsley
¼ cup cognac
½ cup dry red wine
Salt and pepper to taste
1 teaspoon
  Worcestershire sauce
2 tomatoes (optional)
1 eggplant (optional)
Oil (optional)

Soak beans overnight in water to cover. Place in large kettle with onion, garlic, thyme, bay leaf, and water to cover. Simmer gently 1½ to 2 hours or until beans are tender. Drain; reserve 1 cup liquid. Discard onion, bay leaf, and garlic. Melt butter in skillet and sauté onion until tender. Add tomato paste, parsley, bean liquid, cognac, and wine. Simmer at least 15 minutes. Season with salt, pepper, and Worcestershire sauce. Add beans to sauce; mix well. Lightly grease a large casserole and pour in beans. If desired, peel and thickly slice tomatoes and eggplant. Brush with oil and place under broiler a few minutes until browned on both sides. Overlap tomato and eggplant slices in a circle on top of beans. Cover and bake at 325 degrees for 1 to 1½ hours. Serves six to eight.

DUKE ELLINGTON'S
RED BEANS AND RICE

When Duke Ellington came to our Athearn Hotel in Oshkosh, Wisconsin, we had great fun with him. He checked in with his band to play at the county fair. They had been booked into the new, modern hotel up the street, but when the advance men stumbled across our elegant Victorian hotel, and sampled our famous cuisine, they immediately changed reservations.

Ellington arrived late in the afternoon and almost immediately picked up the phone and asked for room service. "What I'll have," he said, "is fried chicken with cream gravy, hush puppies, fried catfish, red beans and rice, spoon bread, okra, and ten scoops of ice cream, all different. Don't bring the ice cream till I call down." The switchboard operator came out to the kitchen in awe. "Look at what that Duke Ellington wants for dinner tonight! Do we have this kind of stuff?" My sister Ann, who just has to be the world's best cook, took a look and laughed. "I'll bet he thinks he won't get a third of that food. I'll fix him!" We had Southern Plantation Candlelight Dinners at that hotel every Friday night, a kind of nostalgia trip for me (I once lived in New Orleans), so we were able to cope and then some!

Ann busied herself with the help of her two cooks and salad girl, and in exactly one hour the cart rolled up to the Athearn suite with the order complete. She had added southern biscuits and honey butter as a kind of final touch. Shortly afterward, Ellington called down and expressed a desire to talk with the chef. "Are you the chef?" he inquired of Ann. "I'm in charge of the kitchen, I do a lot of cooking, and I also own the hotel with my two sisters," she replied. "Well," said Ellington, "food on the road is a pain in the neck. These are the best vittles I've had since I left home. Your red beans and rice are just like Mama's. Forget the ice cream. I'm hooked on ice cream, and my boys tell me yours is homemade, but I'd never find the space." "Well, that's too bad," said Ann. "We have some great Sweet Potato Pie down here too." Ellington groaned, "Send the whole pie up."

It was great fun the three days they were there. Johnnie Hodges played in our Gay Nineties bar after the nightly appearance at the fair was over. Ellington played at our private parties after our bar closed. After it was all over, he went back to Chicago with carefully packed red beans and rice and two sweet potato pies.

1½ cups red kidney beans	Salt
1 clove garlic, chopped	Pepper
½ teaspoon thyme	Few drops Tabasco sauce
1 large onion, chopped	½ pound salt pork, diced

Wash beans and soak overnight. Boil in water they were soaked in. When beginning to get soft (after 15 minutes or so), add remaining ingredients. When tender (in 30 minutes), take out 1 cup beans, mash, and put through sieve. Add to the other beans and cook 20 minutes longer. Serve over boiled rice. Serves eight.

BARLEY CASSEROLE

Old-fashioned cooks used barley chiefly for soup. But more than a dozen years ago some modern cooks found it made an admirable accompaniment in casserole form for poultry, meat, and fish—and a welcome change from potatoes, rice, or pasta. Here's a recipe I'm certain adventurous cooks will enjoy.

¼ cup butter
1 medium onion (4 ounces),
   finely chopped
½ pound mushrooms,
   thinly sliced

2 chicken bouillon cubes
1 quart water
1 cup medium-sized
   pearled barley
1 teaspoon salt

Melt butter in a 10-inch skillet over moderately low heat. Add onion and mushrooms and cook, stirring often, until wilted. In a 1½- or 2-quart saucepan bring bouillon cubes and water to boil, stirring to dissolve cubes. Turn barley into a round ungreased 2-quart casserole; stir in onion-mushroom mixture, the very hot bouillon, and salt. Bake uncovered in preheated 350-degree oven, stirring several times, for 1 hour. Cover tightly; continue baking until liquid has been absorbed and barley is tender but chewy, about 30 minutes. Serve hot. Serves eight.

PICKLED RED CABBAGE

Red Cabbage
Salt
Peppercorns

Ginger or allspice
Sugar

Slice red cabbage (not too thinly). Lay in a deep dish; sprinkle with salt. Let stand 24 hours and drain. Fill jars. Prepare a spiced vinegar. This can be done in advance. To each quart vinegar add 1 ounce peppercorns, 1 tablespoon ginger or allspice, and 1 cup sugar. Simmer 20 minutes. Cool and pour over cabbage. Seal.

OUTDOOR
CAMP-TOWN BEANS

2 tablespoons oil
1 large green pepper,
  chopped
½ pound mushrooms,
  thickly sliced
1 16-ounce can stewed
  tomatoes, undrained

1 20-ounce can kidney
  beans, drained
1 20-ounce can chick
  peas, drained
½ cup apricot preserves
2 tablespoons lemon juice
Salt

In a skillet, 6 inches above moderately hot coals, heat oil. Sauté green pepper and mushrooms until tender but still crisp (about 5 minutes). Stir in remaining ingredients except salt. Bring mixture to a boil, stirring occasionally; cook about 5 minutes more until piping hot. Season to taste with salt. Serves eight to ten.

CITY-SLICKER BEANS

1 16-ounce can lima
  beans, drained
1 16-ounce can kidney
  beans, drained
1 16-ounce can navy
  beans, drained
3 onions, chopped
1 clove garlic, minced

3 tablespoons oil or
  bacon drippings
½ cup catsup
3 tablespoons brown sugar
3 tablespoons cider vinegar
1 teaspoon salt
1 teaspoon dry mustard
¼ teaspoon pepper

Combine all ingredients in 1½-quart baking dish and cover. Bake at 350 degrees about 1 hour. Remove cover and cook 15 minutes more. Serves six.

PENNSYLVANIA-DUTCH GREEN BEANS

By now, a variation of this recipe must be in every cookbook in the whole world. But since enchanted customers keep asking for it, we are including it in this collection. When Grandma Anderson cooked green beans, they simmered for an hour and a half; this is a streamlined version. At the Anderson House we try not to serve canned vegetables. Once in a while a customer overload catches us unawares and only then do we reach for this version of great green beans.

8 strips bacon
1 large onion, sliced
2 tablespoons cornstarch
½ teaspoon salt
½ teaspoon dry mustard
2 20-ounce cans cut
　green beans

2 tablespoons brown sugar
2 tablespoons cider vinegar
2 hard-cooked eggs, sliced
　(garnish)
1 2-ounce jar pimiento

Fry bacon in skillet until crisp. Remove from pan, drain on paper toweling, and then crumble. Drain off all but 4 tablespoons of bacon drippings, add onion, and brown lightly. Stir in cornstarch, salt, and dry mustard. Drain beans, reserving 1 cup of liquid. Pour liquid into skillet, and stir until the mixture starts to boil. Blend in sugar and vinegar. Add the well-drained green beans and heat thoroughly. Turn into a serving dish and garnish with egg slices, crumbled bacon, and pimiento. Serves eight.

JOSEPHINE SENDERHAUF'S WONDERFUL BAKED BEANS

1 16-ounce package large
　dried lima beans
3 large Bermuda onions,
　sliced ¼ inch thick

1 pound thick bacon,
　cut into four sections
　crosswise
¾ cup light brown sugar

Soak the beans overnight. Bring them to a boiling point the next morning in the same water in which they have been soaked. Lower heat to medium and cook about 20 minutes. Drain and reserve one pint of the liquid. Grease a 2-quart casserole. Take one-third of the beans and place in casserole. Cover with onion rings until entire top is covered. Salt lightly. Add strips of bacon until entire area is covered. Dust lightly with ¼ cup brown sugar. Repeat for another layer. Use the remaining one-third of the beans. Cover with onion slices and bacon. If there is bacon left over, use it all on the top. Sprinkle with the last ¼ cup of brown sugar. Place cover on casserole. Place in oven heated to 350 degrees. After an hour, check to be sure there is liquid in the casserole. If it seems dry, add some of the bean water you have held in reserve. Sometimes this dish will bake in 2 hours depending on the beans, your oven, and other factors. Normally it will be done in 3 hours. Serves six.

SWEET-AND-SOUR
RED CABBAGE

8 cups finely shredded
 cabbage (about 2 pounds)
1 large apple
1 tablespoon salt
1 large onion, finely
 chopped

1 tablespoon bacon
 drippings, or other fat
⅓ cup sugar
1 cup water
⅓ cup cider vinegar

Combine cabbage, apple, and salt. Cook onion in bacon drippings in cast-iron skillet until onion is soft. Add cabbage and apple and simmer slowly, turning occasionally for about 15 minutes. Add sugar and one-third of the combined vinegar and water. Steam, covered, for about 1 hour. Then add the remaining vinegar and water. Serves six.

Note: We serve this with our barbecued ribs and special garlic rolls.

JOHN HALL'S
MOOSE HUNTER'S
BEANS AND RIBS

Enough ribs for 4 people
(we suggest 4 racks of
4 ribs each)
3 16-ounce cans pork
and beans
1 cup barbecue sauce
1 teaspoon dry mustard
1 cup brown sugar
1 cup maple syrup
¼ cup chopped parsley

2 teaspoons seasoning salt
6 large cloves garlic,
sliced
2 16-ounce cans pineapple
rings
6 large onions, sliced
6 green peppers,
sliced in rings
8 strips bacon

Parboil ribs over medium heat for about 1½ hours. Remove from water and drain. Mix the beans, barbecue sauce, mustard, brown sugar, maple syrup, parsley, seasoning salt, and garlic. Place ribs in a 9 x 13 inch or slightly larger baking pan and cover with bean mixture. Cover with pineapple rings, onion rings, and then green pepper rings. Lay bacon strips over the top. Cover with foil, tightly fastening around sides. Bake for 1 hour at 375 degrees. Check after 30 minutes to be sure ribs are covered. Remove foil and take pan out to the grill and keep on the edge of the grill until the rest of your meal is ready. Serves four. (There are enough beans and liquid to serve more people. You may wish to use this sauce with ribs you have done on the grill as well.)

Note: Every fall when the Anderson House Moose Hunt takes off for the Canadian wilds, the fixings for this great dish are always on board.

CARROTS ANDERSON

½ cup catsup
½ cup melted butter
½ cup honey

1 16-ounce bag frozen carrots
(whole miniature preferred),
or 4 fresh carrots

Blend catsup, butter, and honey in blender. Cook carrots as directed. Near the end of the cooking process, add the sauce. (It sounds terrible, but everybody loves it.) We suggest you use carrot sticks in fresh vegetable season. Split each carrot down the middle, then in fourths. Make 4 to 6 sticks from each carrot depending on size. It makes an elegant dish. Serves four.

Note: If you use twice the amount of carrots specified above, you will still have enough sauce. Carrots can then be frozen with sauce for future meals.

FRENCH-FRIED CARROT CHIPS

Carrots (as many as you
    wish to do)

Scrape carrots and cut crosswise into the thinnest possible slices. Heat fat to 375 degrees. Put a layer of carrots in frying basket. Lower carefully into fat and cook until tender, being careful that they do not get too brown. Drain on paper toweling and continue until all are fried. Just before serving, heat fat to 395 degrees. Put chips in basket and lower carefully into fat and cook until crisp. Keep basket in constant motion. Drain on paper toweling and sprinkle with salt.

CHEESE SOUFFLÉ WITH FRESH MUSHROOM SAUCE

7 eggs, separated (room temperature)
⅓ cup butter
6 tablespoons flour
¾ teaspoon salt
1¼ cups whole milk
¾ cup grated Parmesan cheese

¼ teaspoon cream of tartar
½ cup grated sharp cheddar cheese
Spinach Filling (below)
8 slices mild cheddar cheese
Mushroom Sauce (see index)

Grease a 15 x 10 x 1 inch jelly-roll pan. Line pan with waxed paper and grease the top of the waxed paper as well. Melt butter over low heat. Remove from heat and stir in flour and ½ teaspoon salt. Gradually stir in milk. Bring to a boil, stirring constantly. Reduce heat and simmer until thick, about 10 to 15 minutes. Beat in ½ cup Parmesan cheese and cheddar cheese. Beat yolks, add to cheese mixture. Beat whites with remaining ¼ teaspoon salt and cream of tartar until stiff peaks form. Carefully fold ⅓ of whites into cheese mixture. Carefully fold in remaining whites to combine. Turn into greased pan. Bake at 350 degrees for 15 minutes or until surface is puffed and firm. With metal spatula loosen edges of soufflé. Invert on waxed paper sprinkled with ¼ cup Parmesan cheese. Peel off waxed paper. Spread surface with spinach filling. Roll up the long side. Place seam side down on greased cookie sheet. Cut cheese slices in half diagonally. Place triangles of cheese over the top of the roll. Broil about 4 inches from the heat until cheese melts. Cut in slices and cover with Mushroom Sauce. Serves eight.

SPINACH FILLING

2 10-ounce packages frozen spinach, chopped
2 tablespoons butter
¼ cup finely chopped onions

¼ teaspoon salt
¼ cup grated cheddar cheese
½ cup sour cream

Cook spinach according to package directions. Drain very well. In skillet sauté onion in butter until onion is soft. Remove from heat. Add spinach, salt, cheddar cheese, and sour cream. Mix well. Set aside until ready to use.

PERRY COUNTY
FRESH CORN CASSEROLE

4 to 5 strips bacon
2 cups chopped onions
9 ears corn
2 cups grated cheddar
** cheese**
1 cup half-and-half

1 2-ounce jar chopped
** pimiento**
Salt and pepper
¾ teaspoon powdered
** ginger**

Cook bacon until crisp. Remove and set aside. In drippings, sauté onions until soft but not brown. Cut corn off the cob and scrape cob to get milk. (Cut only about halfway through kernels, then scrape the rest off.) Add corn and cheese to onions. Cook at a rapid boil, stirring, about 10 minutes. Add half-and-half, pimiento, seasonings, and crumbled bacon. Pour into 2-quart casserole. Bake in 350-degree oven until bubbly, about 45 minutes. Serves eight to ten.

CARROT CIRCLES
AND PINEAPPLE

2 cups sliced carrots
½ cup pineapple chunks,
    drained (reserve juice)
½ cup pineapple juice
    (from can)
½ cup carrot stock (reserved
    from cooking carrots)

1 tablespoon cornstarch
½ teaspoon salt
1/8 teaspoon pepper
1 tablespoon butter

Cook carrots in water over medium heat until soft. Drain, reserving ½ cup stock. Thicken juice and carrot stock with cornstarch in saucepan; bring just to boil. Add salt, pepper, butter, carrots, and pineapple chunks. Heat over medium heat until thickened and serve. Serves four.

CARROT-POTATO SCALLOP

3 heaping tablespoons
    flour
2 teaspoons salt
1/8 teaspoon pepper
2 cups potatoes, pared
    and thinly sliced
2 cups carrots, scraped
    and thinly sliced

½ cup diced celery
2 tablespoons chopped
    onion
2 cups milk, scalded
3 tablespoons butter or
    margarine

Combine flour, salt, and pepper. Arrange a layer of half the potatoes, then a layer of half the carrots in greased 1½-quart casserole. Sprinkle each layer with celery, onions, and flour mixture. Repeat. Pour in milk, and dot with butter or margarine. Bake in 375-degree oven about 45 minutes. Serves four.

GRANDMA'S CORN FRITTERS

In the mid-1920s, the boarders paid $7.50 a week for a room and three meals a day, the ever-present full cookie jar in the lobby, and as much coffee as they could consume. The days Grandma served fried chicken and cream gravy, real mashed potatoes, corn fritters, and hot apple cobbler were the days the roomers smiled in bliss. Once, a boarder married and moved out but left a standing order to call him when these gustatory delights were being served.

4 eggs, separated
2 cups cream-style
**   canned corn**
½ teaspoon salt
2 tablespoons plus ½ cup
**   melted butter**

1 cup cracker crumbs
1 teaspoon baking powder
½ cup vegetable oil

Beat the egg whites until stiff. Beat the yolks until foamy and add the corn, salt, and the 2 tablespoons butter. Mix the cracker crumbs and baking powder and combine with the corn mixture. Gently fold in egg whites. Mix vegetable oil and the ½ cup melted butter and heat in skillet. When hot, drop spoonfuls of batter and fry until brown on both sides. Serves six.

Note: This recipe is somewhat different in that many recipes for fritters indicate deep-frying. These fritters more closely resemble thickened pancakes.

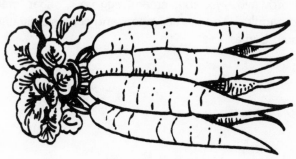

BRAISED CUCUMBERS

4 slices bacon
4 cups peeled ¼-inch-
  thick cucumber slices

2 tablespoons cider vinegar
½ teaspoon salt
Pepper to taste

In a large skillet, cook bacon until crisp. Drain bacon on paper towels, crumble, and set aside. Drain off all but about 2 tablespoons of fat in skillet and add cucumbers. Stir-fry for 5 minutes over medium-high heat. Reduce heat and add bacon, vinegar, salt, and pepper. Cover and simmer until the cucumbers are tender-crisp, about 5 minutes. Don't overcook. Serves four.

FRIED CUCUMBERS

2 tablespoons butter
2 tablespoons chopped
  onion
4 large cucumbers,
  sliced ¼ inch thick
¼ cup water
½ cup sour cream

1 egg yolk, beaten
2 tablespoons sugar
3 tablespoons vinegar
1½ teaspoons salt
1/8 teaspoon pepper
1/8 teaspoon paprika

Melt butter in a skillet; add onion and sauté over low heat until a delicate brown. Add cucumbers and water. Cook until water is absorbed and cucumbers browned. Mix sour cream, egg yolk, sugar, vinegar, salt, pepper, and paprika. Add to cucumbers and cook slowly until mixture begins to boil. Serves four.

FROZEN CUCUMBERS

12 cucumbers, peeled
  and sliced
1 medium onion, peeled
  and very thinly sliced
1 tablespoon salt

2 cups sugar
2 cups white vinegar
¼ cup pickling salt
1 tablespoon minced
  fresh or dried parsley

Sprinkle salt over cucumbers and onion and let set for 1 hour. Drain and rinse with cold water, and drain again. Boil together the sugar, vinegar, and pickling salt for 10 minutes, then pour over drained vegetables. Add parsley. Let stand 6 hours. Freeze in containers. Thaw in refrigerator when ready to use.

Note: The idea that cucumbers and tomatoes can't be frozen is a myth slowly being dispelled. Try these and you'll become addicted! Makes about 1 quart, depending on size of cucumbers.

ESCALLOPED CUCUMBERS

6 medium-sized cucumbers
Salt and white pepper
  to taste
2 ounces minced pimiento

1½ cups buttered white-
  bread crumbs
Fresh chopped or dried
  parsley (garnish)

Peel and slice cucumbers about ¼ inch thick. Sprinkle with salt and white pepper to taste. Preheat oven to 350 degrees. Select small shallow pan for cucumbers and butter sides and bottom of casserole. Place a layer of cucumbers and minced pimiento and cover with crumbs. Alternate layers, ending up with crumbs on top. Bake until tender but do not overbake, about 15 to 20 minutes. Sprinkle with parsley before serving. Serves four.

JOYCE'S EGGPLANT CREOLE

½ pound ground chuck
1 small eggplant, peeled
  and cut into small pieces
1 cup mushrooms, fresh
  or canned
1 medium onion, chopped
1 teaspoon wine vinegar

½ teaspoon salt
½ teaspoon sugar
1/8 teaspoon pepper
Pinch oregano
1 16-ounce can tomatoes
½ cup chopped celery

Brown meat, add rest of ingredients and cook over medium heat until consistency you desire, about 40 minutes. We double this recipe and freeze it. Serves four.

CREAMED ONIONS WITH PEANUTS

2 tablespoons butter
  or margarine
2 tablespoons flour
Pinch pepper
1 teaspoon salt
Dash paprika
2 cups milk

4 cups drained cooked
  or canned small onions
½ cup coarsely chopped
  salted peanuts
¼ cup dried bread crumbs
2 tablespoons melted
  butter or margarine

Melt butter or margarine over low heat in saucepan and stir in the flour, pepper, salt, and paprika until smooth. Then slowly add the milk, stirring constantly, until sauce is creamy and thickened. Pour over onions in mixing bowl; add peanuts, then lightly toss together. Turn into a 1½-quart greased casserole. Preheat oven to 375 degrees. In small bowl toss bread crumbs with melted butter or margarine, then sprinkle over onion mixture. Bake the casserole about 20 minutes or until the top is brown and crusty. Serves six.

KEESLER FIELD'S
MUSHROOM AND WILD RICE

12 ounces wild rice
3 ribs celery, finely chopped
1 green pepper, chopped
1 large onion, chopped
12 ounces fresh
  mushrooms, sliced

4 tablespoons butter
1 teaspoon salt
¼ teaspoon pepper
½ cup finely chopped
  pecans
1 cup heavy cream

Prepare rice as directed on package. Over low heat, brown celery, pepper, onion, and mushrooms in butter until onions are transparent, about 10 minutes. Combine with rice, salt, pepper, and pecans in 3-quart casserole. Cover with cream. Bake at 325 degrees about 1 hour or until rice has absorbed cream. Serves eight.

ANDERSON HOUSE
ONION AND CORN SCALLOP

2 tablespoons margarine
1 large onion, sliced
1 cup sour cream
¼ teaspoon salt
¼ teaspoon dill weed
1¼ cups shredded
  cheddar cheese

1½ cups corn muffin mix
1 egg, beaten
⅓ cup milk
1 16-ounce can cream corn
2 drops hot sauce

Preheat oven to 425 degrees. Melt margarine in skillet and sauté onions until tender. Combine sour cream, salt, dill, and ½ cup cheese; add to onions. Set aside. Combine remaining ingredients, except cheese. Mix well and spread in 9-inch square pan. Cover with sour cream mixture. Top with the remaining cheese. Bake 25 to 30 minutes at 350 degrees. Serves six.

PEAS À LA ANDERSON
(From Grandma Anderson's
Primer for Brides)

2 tablespoons butter
2 tablespoons water
1 clove garlic, mashed
½ cup small white onions
3 large lettuce leaves,
    cut in julienne strips

1 teaspoon sugar
¼ teaspoon salt
Dash pepper
2 10-ounce packages
    frozen peas

In a skillet melt butter, add water, garlic, onions, lettuce, sugar, salt, and pepper. Cover and simmer 30 minutes. Stir in peas. Cover and simmer about 30 minutes at low heat. Correct seasoning, stir well, and serve. Serves six.

BAKED POTATO PUDDING
(From Grandma Anderson's
Primer for Brides)

6 to 8 large Idaho
    potatoes, grated
½ cup grated onion
3 eggs, beaten well

1 cup hot milk
6 tablespoons melted
    butter
½ teaspoon salt

Combine all ingredients, beat well, and pour into well-buttered 8 x 12 inch shallow baking pan. Bake at 350 degrees for one hour and 15 minutes. This is an Anderson House special. Serves four.

SESAME POTATO SPEARS
(From Grandma Anderson's
Primer for Brides)

6 to 8 medium potatoes
½ cup melted butter
2 teaspoons salt

2 teaspoons paprika
¼ cup sesame seeds

Pare and cut potatoes in strips. Grease a cookie sheet and place potatoes on the sheet, arranging them so they do not touch. Brush with melted butter. Sprinkle salt, paprika, and sesame seeds over the top. Bake for 1 hour at 350 degrees. Turn if you wish. Serves six.

COUNTRY CLUB POTATOES

1 cup sour cream
1 10¾-ounce can cream
of celery soup
1 soup can milk or light
cream
1 2-pound package frozen
hash browns
6 green onions, finely
chopped

1 small green pepper,
finely chopped
1 2-ounce jar pimiento,
drained and chopped
1½ teaspoons salt
½ teaspoon black pepper
Paprika

Mix together all ingredients except paprika. Do not thaw potatoes before baking. Turn into prepared casserole. Sprinkle with paprika to taste. Bake in a 350-degree oven 1½ to 2 hours until a light crust forms. Serves eight to ten.

MAHALA'S PENNSYLVANIA DUTCH POTATOES AND SAUERKRAUT

The Irish have their colcannon (potatoes mashed with cabbage), and a very tasty dish it is. The Dutch have their potatoes and sauerkraut; we offer this recipe for your consideration. We serve this with our stuffed ham.

6 medium potatoes,
  peeled and quartered
1 teaspoon salt
½ cup butter
½ cup whipping cream
2 tablespoons butter
1 large onion, minced

1 16-ounce can or bag of
  sauerkraut, well drained
1 cup water
2 ounces pimiento,
  drained and chopped
2 tablespoons butter

Boil potatoes in salted water until tender but not mushy, about 10 minutes. Drain well, place on cookie sheet, and put in 350-degree oven for 5 minutes to dry. Remove, press through potato ricer, place in a bowl, stir in ½ cup butter and cream, and beat well. In a skillet, melt the 2 tablespoons butter and sauté onion until soft and transparent. Stir in sauerkraut and water, and simmer for ½ hour. Stir occasionally so sauerkraut doesn't burn. You may need to add more water. When sauerkraut is tender, let water evaporate, then blend sauerkraut well with potatoes, using an electric mixer. Add pimiento, mixing on low speed. Serve very hot in heated bowl with 2 tablespoons butter in the middle. Serves six.

LOREN'S RAMP-AND-EGG SCRAMBLE

Ramps are a kind of wild onion, found in forests during the spring, and they are powerful! Garlic addicts die with delight over these things. Prepare to wash your hands a thousand times after cleaning them. We didn't know we had them in Wabasha until Mr. Clem Heins found some in the Zumbro bottoms and brought them to us to replant.

3 tablespoons bacon grease
1 tablespoon chicken broth
2 cups cleaned and sliced
**   ramps**

6 eggs
Salt to taste

In a skillet heat bacon grease with chicken broth. Add ramps and sauté until they are tender. Season the eggs as desired and beat until well blended. Pour this mixture over the ramps and stir constantly. This is a gourmet delight for woodsmen and those raised on ramps. Serves four.

Note: Ramps can also be fried like onions. Remember, you've got a tiger by the tail with ramps—they let people know you've been partaking of them!

RUTABAGA EN CASSEROLE

1 large rutabaga (2 to
**   2½ pounds)**
Salt and pepper to taste
1 10¾-ounce can
**   condensed cheese soup**
½ cup half-and-half
¼ cup melted butter

2 ounces pimiento
1½ cups soft bread
**   crumbs**
½ cup shredded mild
**   cheddar cheese**
2 tablespoons grated
**   Parmesan cheese**

Peel rutabaga, dice, and place in 2-quart saucepan. Cook over medium heat until tender. Place cooked rutabaga in 1½-quart casserole. Sprinkle lightly with salt and pepper. Combine cheese soup and cream and beat well. Pour over diced rutabaga. Mix melted butter, pimiento, crumbs, and cheese. Sprinkle over rutabaga. Bake at 375 degrees for 20 to 25 minutes, or until cheese is melted and crumbs are light brown. Sprinkle Parmesan cheese on top before serving. Serves four.

SCALLOPED RICE
(From Biloxi, Mississippi)

1 cup chopped celery
½ cup chopped onion
½ cup chopped green
  pepper
1 4-ounce can sliced
  mushrooms, drained,
  or ½ pound sliced
  fresh mushrooms
¼ cup butter
1 10¾-ounce can cream
  of celery soup
1 cup milk

2 cups cooked rice
1 2-ounce jar pimiento,
  drained and chopped
1 teaspoon salt
¼ teaspoon pepper
1 cup crushed potato chips
3 slices or 6 ounces
  grated sharp cheddar
  cheese
2 tablespoons minced
  parsley

In a skillet sauté celery, onion, green pepper, and mushrooms in butter. In a mixing bowl, blend soup with milk, then add rice, pimiento, seasonings, and vegetables. Spread potato chips on bottom of buttered 1½-quart casserole. Add rice mixture. Cover and bake at 350 degrees for 30 minutes. Cut cheese in half and arrange on top of the rice. Bake 10 minutes longer. Sprinkle parsley over the cheese and serve immediately. Serves six to eight.

Note: When we lived in Mississippi and New Orleans we entered a whole new culinary area. We fell in love with the cities, the Gulf Coast, the food, and the customs, and we go back every chance we get. You'll find recipes from that locale as you look through our book.

CREAMED BROWNED POTATOES WITH BACON

4 medium-sized potatoes
½ cup cream

1 clove garlic, minced
4 strips lean bacon

Boil potatoes in their skins until tender. Remove skins, put potatoes in bowl, mash lightly with a fork and stir in cream. Add garlic. Fry bacon until crisp, being careful not to let it get too dark. Remove from skillet, and drain on paper toweling. Drain all but three tablespoons of bacon grease from pan. While still hot, put potato mixture in skillet and brown well on one side over medium heat, about 10 to 15 minutes. Check carefully to see if underside is brown, and using a broad spatula, turn and brown the other side. Serves four.

Note: In a household full of Dutch, it is nice to know there are some Irish and Norwegians for balance. This goodie comes from the Irish part of the family.

POTATOES WHY?

6 medium potatoes, put
through a meat grinder
4 medium onions, ground

¼ pint cream
¼ cup melted butter
Salt and pepper to taste

Mix all ingredients. Place in a buttered 2-quart casserole. Bake in a slow oven, 175 to 200 degrees, for about 4 hours. Serves six.

Note: This recipe came from a patient at the Mayo Clinic who discovered our little country inn was a fine place to spend his weekends between appointments. One day he gave us this recipe, and while it isn't practical for the dining rooms, we use it in our homes. When he gave us the recipe and informed us of the cooking time, we all asked, "Why?" His answer was, "Just because!"

DUTCH
SAUERKRAUT CASSEROLE

When Grandma Anderson made this, she mixed it, put it in a 9 x 13 inch pan, and placed breaded pork chops on top to bake, claiming the pork chop fat oozing down into the sauerkraut made it a perfect dish. (She breaded her pork chops by dipping them in beaten egg and soft, fresh bread crumbs and browning them in butter.)

1 20-ounce bag sauerkraut	2 medium onions, chopped
5 large carrots, scraped and grated	2 tablespoons plus 3 tablespoons butter
6 large potatoes, peeled and grated	Salt and pepper to taste

Remove sauerkraut from bag, place in colander, and run cold water through it for several minutes. Remove to large bowl. Add carrots and potatoes. Sauté onions in 2 tablespoons butter until transparent but not brown. Add to sauerkraut mixture, and salt and pepper to taste. If you are cooking as a casserole, butter a 2-quart casserole, spoon in mixture, dot with butter, and bake about 1 hour at 300 degrees. If you are cooking with chops, spread mixture out in 9 x 13 inch pan, place breaded chops on top, cover with a cookie sheet, and bake 1½ hours until pork chops feel tender to the touch. Serves eight.

SPINACH BALLS

2 10-ounce packages frozen spinach, thawed, or 2 16-ounce cans spinach, squeezed dry and chopped	¾ cup melted butter or margarine
	½ cup Parmesan cheese
	1 tablespoon garlic salt
	½ teaspoon thyme
2 cups herb stuffing mix	½ tablespoon black pepper
2 onions, finely chopped	1 tablespoon monosodium
6 eggs, beaten	glutamate

Mix all ingredients together, blending thoroughly. Form into small balls (marble-sized). Bake on cookie sheet in 350-degree oven for 20 minutes.

SAUERKRAUT BALLS

8 ounces Italian sausage,
crumbled
¼ cup well-chopped onion
1 14-ounce can sauerkraut,
well drained and chopped
2 tablespoons plus 1 cup
soft bread crumbs
1 3-ounce package cream
cheese, softened
2 tablespoons pimiento,
chopped

2 tablespoons minced
fresh or dried parsley
1 teaspoon prepared
mustard
1 small clove garlic,
minced, or dash garlic
salt
¼ teaspoon pepper
¼ cup all-purpose flour
2 eggs, well beaten
⅓ cup milk

Cook sausage and onion until meat is brown and onions are transparent. Drain. Add sauerkraut and 2 tablespoons bread crumbs. In a bowl, combine cream cheese, pimiento, parsley, mustard, garlic or garlic salt, and pepper. Stir into sauerkraut mixture. Chill for 1 hour in refrigerator. Remove. Shape into small balls, and coat with flour. Add milk to eggs. Dip balls into egg-and-milk mixture and roll in bread crumbs. Fry in deep fat until brown. Do not overcook. Then place in 375-degree oven and bake for about 15 to 20 minutes. Serve with ribs, ham, or as cocktail tidbits. Serves six.

SPINACH-AND-CHEESE SQUARES

2 15-ounce cans spinach
⅔ cup whole milk
½ cup melted butter
½ cup finely chopped
  onion
2 tablespoons minced
  fresh or dried parsley
1 teaspoon Worcestershire
  sauce

1 teaspoon salt
½ teaspoon thyme
4 eggs, beaten
2 cups cooked rice
2 cups shredded mild
  cheddar cheese
1 2-ounce jar pimiento,
  drained and chopped

Open spinach and drain for 15 minutes in colander. Add milk, butter, and seasonings to eggs. After the spinach is drained, squeeze it a few times to be sure most of the liquid is gone. Then add spinach, rice, cheese, and pimiento. Pour into a 12 x 9 inch pan. Bake at 350 degrees for about 45 minutes in the middle rack of your oven. Cut into squares. You may sieve hard-boiled eggs and sprinkle on top before serving if you wish. Serves eight.

GLAZED HUBBARD SQUASH

3 cups pared and cubed
  squash
¼ cup melted butter
½ teaspoon salt
1 tablespoon brown sugar

1 tablespoon honey
2 tablespoons lemon juice
¼ cup chopped almonds
¼ cup shredded coconut

Combine all ingredients except almonds and coconut; mix well. Arrange in shallow buttered 9 x 9 inch baking dish. Cover and bake at 400 degrees for about 30 minutes. Remove cover; sprinkle with almonds and coconut. Continue baking for 15 minutes. Serves six.

JOHANNA HALL'S
PINEAPPLE SQUASH

1 10-ounce package
  frozen squash
1 cup crushed pineapple,
  drained

¼ cup orange marmalade
6 tablespoons brown sugar
½ teaspoon salt
1 tablespoon butter

Thaw squash. Combine with pineapple and marmalade, brown sugar, and salt. Place in a 2-quart casserole. Dot top with butter. Bake in 350-degree oven about 30 minutes. Serves four.

Note: To serve this dish, we cut oranges in half, scoop out centers, and slice off bottom so orange will stand straight. Fill with the squash casserole and reheat until ready to serve.

PARTY SWEET-POTATO BALLS

6 sweet potatoes
Butter, salt, and pepper
  to taste
Pineapple juice

Pineapple tidbits
2 cups cornflake crumbs
¼ cup melted butter

Boil sweet potatoes until soft. Peel and mash potatoes. Season well with butter, salt, and pepper to taste. Add small amount of pineapple juice to soften. Roll 1 tablespoon of sweet potato at a time around a pineapple tidbit so that it is the center of the ball. Roll in finely crushed cornflakes, dip in melted butter, and place on baking sheet. Brown in 400-degree oven. These can be made ahead and warmed just before serving. Serves four.

THOSE THINGS

Vegetables never seem to send children into ecstasies of delight, but we do serve one vegetable for special parties that always does the trick. "Bring us more of those things," they say. We have heard it so often that we call this dish precisely that.

BATTER

1 egg yolk
2 cups ice-cold water

¼ teaspoon baking powder
1⅔ cups flour

VEGETABLES

Onions, sliced
Green beans, cut into
  1½-inch lengths
Mushrooms, halved

Zucchinis, cut very thin
Carrots, cut very thin
Green pepper, sliced

Mix ingredients for batter. Heat oil (we like peanut oil for this) to 375 degrees. Dip vegetables individually into batter and carefully drop into hot oil one at a time. Don't overload; cook about 10 pieces at a time. Fry just until crisp—it won't take long. Remove with slotted spoon and drain on paper towel.

BAKED TOMATOES
FLORENTINE

6 medium-sized tomatoes
Salt
½ cup light cream
1 egg yolk
12 ounces fresh spinach,
  cooked, drained, and
  chopped

¼ teaspoon horseradish
3 tablespoons melted
  butter
2 hard-cooked eggs, sieved

Cut top off each tomato. Scoop out the juice and seeds. Sprinkle insides with salt. Combine the cream and egg yolk; add chopped spinach, horseradish, and 1 tablespoon of butter. Salt to taste. Heat and stir just until it simmers. Fill tomatoes with the creamed spinach. Place in a 10 x 6 inch baking dish. Top each with 1 teaspoon melted butter. Bake at 375 degrees for 25 minutes. Serve hot with eggs sprinkled on top of each tomato. Serves six.

LOREN'S
FRIED GREEN TOMATOES
(From Rainelle, West Virginia)

Salt and pepper
2 cups cornmeal
4 large green tomatoes
(nearly ripe)

12 slices bacon
¾ cup grated cheddar
cheese

Salt and pepper cornmeal to taste. Slice each tomato into ½-inch slices. Dip slices in cornmeal, coating both sides. Fry bacon until crisp (but not burned), and drain on paper toweling. Add tomato slices to bacon grease and fry on each side until coating is crisp. Remove. Place cheese on top and sprinkle with crumbled bacon. Serves six.

Note: Loren's mom used to add some flour and milk to pan drippings to make a cream gravy to pour over tomatoes.

ZUCCHINI PARADISIO

4 strips bacon
½ cup chopped Bermuda
  onion
1 large zucchini, thinly
  sliced

2 boiled Idaho potatoes
(cold), thinly sliced

Fry bacon until crisp, being careful not to burn or allow bacon grease to get too dark. Remove bacon from pan and drain on paper toweling; crumble. Add onion to bacon grease and sauté for about 5 minutes. Add zucchini slices, potatoes, and bacon. Cover frying pan. Stir potatoes occasionally so they do not stick. Cook about 20 minutes, depending on how well done you want the zucchini. When done, remove from pan along with pan scrapings. Serves two.

Note: A man going to the Mayo Clinic came to dinner one night and spied our vegetable garden out back with zucchini running wild (as they are prone to do). He offered to go into the kitchen and show us a fine dish. We loved the result and use it often. When he goes back to the clinic for yearly check-ups, he always has a new recipe, and it's always one we like as well.

BELLE'S STUFFED ZUCCHINI

3 zucchini
Salt
½ cup finely chopped
  onion
¼ cup chopped green
  pepper
⅓ cup finely chopped
  celery

1 cup ground beef
1 slice bread, cubed
1 8-ounce can tomato sauce
½ cup grated mild
  cheddar cheese
¼ cup grated Parmesan
  cheese

Cook whole zucchini in boiling salted water for 3 minutes. Drain off water. Cut lengthwise and scoop out pulp. Reserve. Cook onion, green pepper, celery, and meat until lightly browned; add bread cubes, tomato sauce, and pulp. Mix well and stuff into zucchini shells. Sprinkle cheddar and Parmesan cheeses over tops. Place in shallow baking pan and bake in 375-degree oven. Serves six.

Note: This recipe comes to us from the Golden Nugget, *a supplement to several southeastern Minnesota newspapers, and a constant source of unusual recipes. "Just Plain Belle," Manie Hoelz of Belle Plaine, writes a spirited and creative column, and we always look for that first when our* Northfield News *arrives. We serve this for our "Thank God It's Friday" Luncheon occasionally, and everybody likes it!*

ZUCCHINI WITH BACON AND EGG SAUCE

4 slices bacon
2 green onions, finely
  chopped
¼ cup tarragon vinegar
2 pounds zucchini, cut
  in very thin diagonal
  slices

Boiling salted water
3 hard-cooked eggs,
  chopped

Fry bacon until crisp and remove bacon from fat. Drain and crumble bacon. Add onions to bacon fat and sauté until wilted; stir in vinegar. Cook zucchini in a small amount of boiling salted water for 3 minutes— no longer. Drain and put in a heated serving dish. Sprinkle eggs on top, and then crumbled bacon. Finally pour hot vinegar mixture over all. Serves six.

PLAYBOY GUESTHOUSE
WILD RICE CASSEROLE

12 ounces wild rice
6 stalks celery, chopped
1 green pepper, chopped
1 large onion, chopped
12 ounces fresh mushrooms

¼ cup butter
Salt to taste
¼ teaspoon pepper
2 ounces pimiento
1 cup heavy cream

Prepare rice as package directs. Brown celery, green pepper, onion, and mushrooms in butter. Combine with rice, salt, pepper, and pimiento in 2-quart baking dish. Cover with the cream. Bake at 325 degrees for about 1 hour or until rice has absorbed the cream. Serves six.

Breads

Grandma's bread! How could I ever forget it! When I came home from school each day her kitchen was flooded with sunshine and the counter was filled with fresh bread just out of the oven. The wonderful aroma permeated the entire house.

She was surely way ahead of her time, for she made bread out of everything! Grandpa Anderson had an enormous garden in back of the Anderson House and an even larger garden in back of his house directly across the street and fronting the Mississippi. He swore there was a night mist that arose off the river and sunk into his garden that made every vegetable larger and more delectable. The gardens supplied the inn with a bounty of marvelous fruits and vegetables and flowers, and when there was an oversupply Grandma found something to do with it. She made tomato bread, lettuce bread, apple bread, pear bread, squash rolls, sweet potato bread, rhubarb bread, plum bread, and grape bread long before I ever saw them in other cookbooks. Nothing was wasted. If something didn't turn out right, at least the birds enjoyed it.

It took me a long time to figure out Grandma's deep involvement with bread. She was twenty-five years younger than my grandfather and a second wife as well. She was bright, beautiful, merry, and jolly with an angelic disposition. She woke up singing, and I know because I lived with her for twenty-two years. My grandfather was a business genius, somewhat taciturn, slightly dour, and not much of a smiler but a good provider, which seemed to be most important in those days. Wives just didn't argue with their husbands at that time, so when Grandma disagreed with her husband she made a huge batch of bread and kneaded it with force and fury!

He ate the same breakfast every day of his life (and he lived to be ninety-six): steak, hot biscuits, fresh doughnuts, and apple pie. The biscuits had to be hot out of the oven, the steak fried in a red-hot iron skillet for two minutes on each side, the doughnuts had to be hot and varied, and the pie absolutely had to be still warm. Sometimes there was fresh, homemade grape-nut ice cream on top. It depended on his moods but you can see that Grandma Ida Anderson had to be up mighty early to meet those demands.

For those fortunates who lived there, room and board was $7.50 a week at the Anderson House, and the vittles were superb! Ida Anderson started our famous bread tray the year they bought the inn, and when the boarders spied the great array of cinnamon rolls, squash biscuits, batter bread, tomato bread, and honey biscuits, they went into gastronomic shock. The breakfast rolls were huge, like small loaves of bread. The favorites were wild cherry, walnut-caramel, and cinnamon. We haven't changed the recipes or the size in all these years.

The family is still involved in the cooking. My sister Ann, whom I devoutly believe to be the world's greatest cook, still makes fragile, buttery, flaky pie crust and some of her special breads although she is officially retired. When we expect great crowds for special holidays, I'm busy with breads and desserts. (I especially like making them for the Christmas house party, New Year's Eve, and New Year's Day.)

Some of the recipes in this chapter have been sent by our wonderful customers. We try every one that is sent to us. Some are Grandma's recipes, and some have been created in our own test kitchen.

When Grandma sold the hotel to my mother she moved into her new house across the street and tried to retire. No way! She bought a large pair of binoculars, sat in her front window, and watched the dining room carefully during each meal to be sure the bread tray was loaded with a variety of delectables. That wasn't enough. So she converted a huge basement room in her new house to a fine kitchen and went back to baking bread, rolls, biscuits, and other goodies.

Grandma was a genius too!

CARROT MUFFINS

1 cup vegetable shortening
½ cup brown sugar
1 egg, beaten
¼ teaspoon nutmeg
¼ teaspoon cinnamon
1 tablespoon hot water
1½ cups flour
½ teaspoon salt
1 teaspoon baking powder
1½ cups grated carrots

Cream shortening and sugar thoroughly, then add egg. Dissolve spices in 1 tablespoon of hot water, and add to mixture. Add dry ingredients and carrots; mix until moistened. Bake at 350 degrees for about 1 hour; check after 45 minutes. Makes 12 muffins.

APPLE-MOLASSES BREAD

½ cup butter
1 cup sugar
3 eggs
2 cups flour
1 teaspoon baking powder
½ teaspoon salt
½ teaspoon ground
  cinnamon

¼ teaspoon ground nutmeg
1 cup applesauce
¼ cup dark molasses
1 cup raisins
½ cup chopped nuts

In a large mixing bowl, combine butter and sugar. Cream until light and fluffy. Add eggs one at a time, beating well after each addition. Combine flour, baking powder, salt, cinnamon, and nutmeg. Set aside. Combine applesauce and molasses. Add dry ingredients alternately with applesauce mixture to egg mixture. Fold in raisins and nuts. Pour into a greased loaf pan. Bake in a preheated oven at 350 degrees for an hour, or until a toothpick inserted into the center comes out clean. Cool ten minutes, remove from pan, and continue cooling on rack. Makes 1 loaf.

SANTA BARBARA
AVOCADO BREAD

2 cups sifted flour
½ teaspoon baking soda
½ teaspoon baking powder
¼ teaspoon salt
¾ cup sugar

1 egg, slightly beaten
½ cup mashed, ripe
  avocado
½ cup buttermilk
1 cup chopped nuts

In a mixing bowl sift flour, baking soda, baking powder, salt, and sugar. Add the remaining ingredients in the order given and mix until barely moistened. Pour into a greased loaf pan and bake at 350 degrees for about 1 hour. Remove to cake rack until cool. Makes 1 loaf.

BANANA COFFEE CAKE

½ cup butter or
  margarine, softened
1 cup sugar
2 eggs
1½ cups mashed ripe
  bananas (about 4 medium)
1 tablespoon lemon or
  lime juice

2 cups flour
1 teaspoon baking soda
½ teaspoon salt
½ teaspoon cinnamon
½ teaspoon grated lemon
  rind
½ cup chopped nuts
Topping (below)

In a large mixing bowl, cream together butter or margarine and sugar until light and fluffy. Add eggs one at a time, beating well after each addition. Stir in bananas and lemon or lime juice. Mix together flour, soda, salt, cinnamon, and lemon rind, and blend into creamed mixture. Stir in nuts. Turn into greased 9-inch baking pan and bake in a 350-degree oven for 40 minutes, or until a toothpick inserted in the center comes out clean. Add topping according to directions. Serves nine to twelve.

TOPPING

2 bananas
½ cup brown sugar
2 tablespoons melted
  butter or margarine

¼ cup flaked coconut

Slice 2 bananas over top and sprinkle with mixture of brown sugar, melted butter or margarine, and coconut. Broil 2 minutes or until topping is bubbly and lightly browned.

BANANA CALICO BREAD

½ cup shortening
1 cup sugar
2 eggs, beaten
2 cups flour
1 teaspoon baking powder
3 medium bananas,
  mashed

¼ cup chopped nuts
¼ cup maraschino cherries,
  halved
Grated rind of 1 orange
¼ cup chocolate chips

Cream shortening and sugar together. Add eggs and mix well. Sift flour and baking powder together. Add to egg mixture. Stir in mashed bananas. Add nuts, cherries, grated orange rind, and chocolate chips. Bake in a greased loaf pan at 350 degrees for 45 minutes. (These are especially nice if baked in 4 well-greased soup cans. Fill these only two-thirds full.) Remove from oven, and allow to stand for 5 minutes. Gently remove to a metal rack for further cooling. Makes 1 loaf or 3 or 4 small round loaves.

BLOCKBUSTERS

(A roll so great one of our customers calls them "Blockbusters.")

2 compressed yeast cakes,
  soaked in 1 cup
  warm water

1 tablespoon sugar
1 cup warm water
2 cups flour

Combine all ingredients. Let rise to a light sponge, 2 to 3 hours, in a warm place. Then add:

¼ cup sugar
⅔ cup melted butter
1 teaspoon salt

3 eggs, well beaten
5 cups flour

Let rise to double size, about 3 hours. Pinch off pieces large enough for a roll. Roll in melted butter. Let rise until very light, then bake about 30 minutes in a 350-degree oven. Makes 3 dozen rolls.

BLUEBERRY STREUSEL

1½ cups flour
½ cup sugar
2 teaspoons baking powder
½ teaspoon salt
1 egg

½ cup milk
2 tablespoons melted
    butter, cooled
¾ cup blueberries
Topping (below)

Sift dry ingredients. Beat egg, add milk and cooled butter, and barely mix. Fold in berries. Pour into an 8-inch square pan. Spread topping on top. Bake at 400 degrees for 25 minutes. Serves nine.

TOPPING

2 tablespoons butter
2 tablespoons sugar
¼ cup flour
¼ cup dry crushed bread
    crumbs or cereal

½ teaspoon cinnamon
¼ cup of nuts

Mix.

Note: This is the most popular bread served at the Anderson House. We can never keep enough on hand. We include it in every cookbook.

BROWN BREAD

There's a lot to be said for steamed brown bread but we think it's fussy and time consuming. We offer this as a satisfactory substitute that will freeze well.

2 cups raisins
2 cups hot water
2 teaspoons baking soda
1 tablespoon margarine
1½ tablespoons molasses

1 cup sugar
1 egg
2¾ cups flour
1 teaspoon baking powder
1 teaspoon salt

In a saucepan, boil the raisins and hot water together until the raisins are soft. Cool and add baking soda. Cream margarine, molasses, and sugar. Add egg. Combine flour, baking powder, and salt and add. Pour in raisin mixture. Blend well. Put in 3 greased and floured vegetable cans. Bake at 350 degrees for 1 hour. (We use soup cans and it makes 4 round loaves of bread. Be sure the mixture is poured in so cans are only two-thirds full.)

PENNSYLVANIA DUTCH OVERNIGHT RAISED BUCKWHEAT PANCAKES

Every day of his life after buying the Anderson House in 1896, Grandpa Anderson had buckwheat pancakes for breakfast along with steak and apple pie. He lived to be ninety-six!

½ cake yeast
1 quart lukewarm water
2 cups old-fashioned
   buckwheat flour

1 cup white flour
½ cup sugar
3 teaspoons salt
1 pinch baking soda

Dissolve yeast in water. Stir the flour, sugar, and salt into the yeast mixture until a smooth batter is formed. Let sit overnight in the refrigerator. Before using, remove from refrigerator, bring to room temperature (about 30 minutes), and add a pinch of soda. Pour ¼ cup of batter onto lightly buttered warm skillet. Turn when brown and cook other side. Serve with sausage patties and melted butter. Serves six.

Note: The recipe came from Mahala Hoffman in Pennsylvania. Mahala was Grandma Anderson's sister.

EMERGENCY CARAMEL-NUT ROLLS

2 16-ounce loaves frozen bread dough
½ cup butter
1 cup light brown sugar
1 teaspoon cinnamon

1 3¾-ounce box vanilla pudding (not instant)
1 tablespoon milk
½ cup chopped pecans

Remove frozen bread dough from your freezer, cover it loosely, and put it in the refrigerator overnight. Cut dough into 16 sections and arrange in a well-buttered 9 x 13 inch pan in rows of five down and three across. (One extra in a separate pan for you to sample!) Melt butter, add brown sugar, cinnamon, pudding, and milk. Stir until well blended. Pour this mixture over the cold dough pieces. Cover with nuts. Let rise on top of the stove for about 1½ hours, or until dough rises to top of pan. Bake at 350 degrees for about 35 minutes. Turn pan over onto a cookie sheet, let stand a minute so caramel all comes out of the pan. Makes 16 rolls.

CHEDDAR BRAN BREAD

1½ cups sifted flour
1½ teaspoons baking
  powder
¼ teaspoon baking soda
½ teaspoon salt
3 tablespoons butter
⅓ cup sugar

1 egg, well beaten
1 cup buttermilk
1 cup shredded cheddar
  cheese
1 cup finely crushed
  all-bran cereal

Mix together sifted flour, baking powder, baking soda, and salt. Cream butter and sugar; blend in egg. Add flour mixture alternating with buttermilk, beginning and ending with flour mixture. Fold in cheese and cereal. Spoon into well-greased loaf pan. Bake at 350 degrees for about 1 hour. Remove to rack and cool. Makes 1 loaf.

CHEESE-BACON STRIPS

1 package active dry yeast
1½ cups flour
1 tablespoon sugar
1 tablespoon shortening
1¼ teaspoons salt
¼ teaspoon garlic powder
½ teaspoon chili powder
1/8 teaspoon liquid smoke
  (optional)

½ cup crisp crumbled
  bacon (or bacon-like bits)
1 egg
¾ cup hot milk
2 cups shredded cheddar
  cheese
½ cup chopped ripe olives
1 teaspoon celery or
  poppy seed

Place first eleven ingredients in order in bowl. Beat at medium speed for 2 minutes. (Batter will climb beaters. Just push it down with rubber spatula.) Spread in a thin layer over bottom of greased 15 x 10 inch pan. Sprinkle with cheese, olives, and celery or poppy seed. Cover; let rise in warm place for 30 minutes. Bake at 450 degrees for 15 to 20 minutes, or until edges are golden brown. Cut into 4-inch long strips as wide as you wish. (Ours are about 1¼" wide.) Makes 3 dozen or more, depending on how it is cut.

CHEESE-OLIVE MUFFINS

2 cups flour
1 tablespoon baking powder
1 teaspoon seasoned salt
1 teaspoon dried dillweed
4 tablespoons melted
  butter

1 5-ounce jar sharp
  cheese spread
1 egg, beaten
1 cup milk
½ cup chopped pitted
  ripe olives

In mixing bowl combine flour, sugar, baking powder, seasoned salt, and dillweed. Blend together butter and cheese spread; stir in egg and milk. Add milk mixture all at once to dry ingredients, stirring just until moistened. Stir in olives. Fill greased muffin tins half full. Bake at 400 degrees for 20 to 22 minutes. Makes 12 muffins.

LONGFELLOW
CORN MUFFINS SUPREME

This recipe was given to us in 1947 by a waitress at Longfellow House in Pascagoula, Mississippi. If you are traveling along the Mississippi Gulf Coast it would be sheer heresy to miss dining at this wholly delightful spot. Now there are overnight accommodations as well and the entire experience is the kind that tourists hope for and hardly ever find.

2 cups cornmeal
1 teaspoon salt
2 cups boiling water
1 cup whole milk

2 eggs
4 teaspoons baking powder
1 tablespoon melted
  butter

Sift cornmeal and salt together, and mix with boiling water. Add cold milk at once and mix instantly. Add the eggs and beat well. Preheat the oven to 475 degrees. Add baking powder and melted butter. Pour into greased muffin tins dusted lightly with flour. Bake until golden brown, between 15 and 20 minutes. Remove from oven, turn upside down on cake rack, and serve while piping hot. Makes 12 muffins.

CHOCOLATE
SOUR CREAM BUNS

1 cup sour cream
3 tablespoons sugar
1 teaspoon salt
1/8 teaspoon baking soda
1 package active dry yeast
2 tablespoons warm water
1 egg, slightly beaten

2 tablespoons shortening
3 cups all-purpose flour
Chocolate Filling (below)
½ cup confectioners' sugar
  (optional)
2 teaspoons milk (optional)

In medium saucepan, heat sour cream just to lukewarm, stirring constantly. Remove from heat; add sugar, salt, and baking soda. Dissolve yeast in warm water; blend into sour cream mixture. Add egg, shortening, and 1 cup flour; beat until smooth. Stir in 1½ cups flour; turn out onto floured board, kneading in remaining ½ cup flour until smooth. Roll dough into an 18 x 12 inch rectangle. Cut crosswise into eighteen 1-inch strips. Gently roll each piece to a rope 15 inches long. Coil each strand loosely on greased baking sheet; group coils with sides just touching. Cover and let rise in a warm place 1 to 1½ hours or until doubled in bulk. Pat down center of each bun, leaving outside coil to form edge. Spoon in about 1 tablespoon Chocolate Filling. Bake in a 375-degree oven 12 to 15 minutes or until lightly browned. If desired, glaze with confectioners' glaze made by combining confectioners' sugar and milk. Serve warm. Makes 18 buns.

Note: Chocolate Sour Cream Buns can be baked a day ahead and warmed before serving. Cover buns loosely with aluminum foil and reheat 10 to 15 minutes in an oven preheated to 350 degrees. Chocolate Sour Cream Buns also can be frozen, thawed at room temperature, and warmed as directed above.

CHOCOLATE FILLING

¼ cup light corn syrup
2 tablespoons light brown
    sugar
2 tablespoons melted
    butter

1 tablespoon cornstarch
½ teaspoon vanilla
⅔ cup semi-sweet
    chocolate baking pieces
⅓ cup chopped pecans

Combine ingredients in a small bowl; mix well.

WHOLE WHEAT
FIG-HONEY BREAD

1½ cups whole wheat flour
¼ cup brown sugar
¼ cup chopped pecans
1 cup chopped dried figs
1½ cups flour
¾ teaspoon baking soda
2 teaspoons baking powder
1 teaspoon salt

1 egg, well beaten
1½ cups cold milk
½ cup honey
¼ cup melted butter
1 tablespoon sugar
½ teaspoon cinnamon
Melted butter

In a large mixing bowl, combine whole wheat flour, brown sugar, pecans, and figs. In a separate bowl, mix flour, baking soda, baking powder, and salt. Sift over whole wheat mixture; mix thoroughly. Combine egg, milk, honey, and butter. Mix well. Stir gently into the first mixture. Pour into a buttered loaf pan and let stand for fifteen minutes. Mix sugar and cinnamon and sprinkle over loaf. Brush with melted butter and bake at 325 degrees for about 1½ hours. Cool on cake rack before slicing. Makes 1 loaf.

CRANBERRY-ORANGE BREAD

2 cups flour
1 cup sugar
1½ teaspoons baking
  powder
½ teaspoon baking soda
½ teaspoon salt

2 tablespoons shortening
Grated rind of 1 orange
¾ cup orange juice
1 egg
1 cup raw cranberries,
  halved

Combine dry ingredients in a bowl. Mix in the shortening, rind, juice, and egg. Fold in cranberries. Pour into a greased loaf pan. Bake in a 350-degree oven 1 hour, or until a toothpick inserted in the center comes out clean. Cool well before slicing. Slice with a sharp knife. Makes 1 loaf.

CREOLE BREAKFAST CAKES

2 cups cooked rice
3 eggs, beaten
½ teaspoon vanilla
½ teaspoon cinnamon or
  nutmeg
6 tablespoons flour
3 teaspoons baking powder

¾ cup brown sugar,
  firmly packed
¼ teaspoon salt
1 quart vegetable oil
Powdered sugar
Nutmeg

Mix together the rice, eggs, vanilla, and cinnamon or nutmeg. Sift together the flour, baking powder, sugar, and salt and combine with the rice mixture. When well mixed, drop from a spoon into a deep kettle of hot oil. Fry until light brown, one or two minutes, at about 375 degrees and drain on paper towels. Sprinkle lightly with powdered sugar and dust lightly with nutmeg. Makes 12 cakes.

Note: This recipe was given to us by Bea, who was a cook in the Russ home in Biloxi, Mississippi. She served them to us in the middle of a hurricane. We've never forgotten them and make them often.

LOREN'S GARLIC BREAD

Although any kind of bread may be selected for this special garlic bread, we find French bread works especially well.

1 cup butter, softened
1 cup grated Parmesan
cheese
½ cup mayonnaise
6 cloves fresh garlic,
pressed

3 tablespoons fresh
parsley
1 long loaf French bread,
cut crosswise, but not
all the way through

Mix all ingredients well (except bread) and spread on each slice. Wrap the entire loaf in foil and bake at 350 degrees for 20 minutes. Unwrap and place under the broiler until slightly brown. Serve at once.

GINGER TEA BREAD

1 cup brown sugar
1 egg, well beaten
2 tablespoons melted butter
2 cups sifted flour
½ teaspoon baking powder
½ teaspoon nutmeg

¼ teaspoon salt
½ cup chopped walnuts
or pecans
⅓ cup finely chopped
crystallized ginger
1 cup buttermilk

Place sugar, egg, and butter in a medium-sized mixing bowl. Beat with an electric mixer until smooth and creamy. Sift together flour, baking powder, nutmeg, and salt; add the nuts and ginger. Stir the flour mixture alternately with the buttermilk into the egg mixture. Use folding motion—do not beat. Pour into a greased loaf pan and bake in a 350-degree oven about 40 to 45 minutes. Remove to cake rack and cool before slicing. Makes 1 loaf.

HONEY-FILLED BISCUITS

2 cups flour
3 teaspoons baking powder
¾ teaspoon salt

¼ cup butter
⅔ cup milk (or less)
Honey Spread (below)

Sift together flour, baking powder, and salt. Cut in the butter with two knives or pastry blender. Stir in milk lightly to make a soft dough. Turn dough onto a lightly floured board and knead it just enough to make the surface smooth. Roll into a rectangle about ½ inch in thickness. Spread the surface with Honey Spread and roll like a jelly roll. With a sharp knife, cut slices 1 inch thick; place in well-greased muffin tins or, if preferred, on a greased baking sheet. Bake at 400 degrees for fifteen to twenty minutes. Makes 12 biscuits.

HONEY SPREAD

¼ cup butter
¼ cup honey (or more)
¼ cup chopped dates

¼ cup chopped walnut meats

Cream together butter and honey. Add dates and walnut meats and blend thoroughly. Add additional honey if necessary to make mixture the proper consistency for spreading.

NEVER-FAIL HOLIDAY NUT ROLL

1 pound pecans
1 egg, beaten
1½ cups sugar

½ cup butter
Dough (below)

Grind nuts in blender or processor. Put nuts, egg, sugar, and butter in saucepan and cook over low heat until thick. Let cool while dough is made.

DOUGH

1 cup sour cream	2 eggs
3 tablespoons butter	1 package dry yeast
5 tablespoons sugar	3 cups flour
1/8 teaspoon baking soda	1 egg, beaten
½ teaspoon salt	

Boil sour cream in a large saucepan. Remove from heat and stir in the butter, sugar, baking soda, and salt. Cool until lukewarm. Stir in the 2 unbeaten eggs and yeast. Stir until yeast dissolves. Stir in flour gradually, using a wooden spoon. Turn dough onto lightly floured board. Gently knead for 5 minutes to form a small ball. Cover with clean towel and let stand 5 minutes. Divide into two balls. Roll out ¼ inch thick. Spread cooled pecan filling on and fold as you would a jelly roll. Brush the tops with beaten egg. Bake at 350 degrees for 30 minutes, or until brown. Check after 15 minutes because they bake fairly fast. Makes 2 rolls.

Note: These will freeze well. We serve them during our Christmas house party and other holidays.

MEXICAN SPOON BREAD

2 eggs	1 teaspoon salt
¾ cup milk	½ teaspoon baking soda
1 cup cornmeal	1 4-ounce can diced
½ cup cooking oil	green chilis
1 16-ounce can creamed	1½ cups grated cheddar
corn	cheese

Mix eggs and milk. Add cornmeal. Add remaining ingredients, except for chilis and cheese. Pour half the batter into a greased 9-inch square baking dish. Add chilis and cheese. Top with remaining batter. Sprinkle with more grated cheese. Bake at 400 degrees for 25 minutes. Cut into bite-sized squares. Good with cocktails. Serves four.

HOMEMADE BISCUIT MIX

8 cups enriched flour
¼ cup baking powder
4 teaspoons salt

1 cup lard for soft wheat,
or 1½ cups for hard
wheat flour

Sift together flour, baking powder, and salt. Cut in lard until the mixture has a fine even crumb. Cover closely and store in refrigerator until ready to use. The mixture will keep at least a month in the refrigerator. Makes 5 batches of biscuits.

TO MAKE BISCUITS:

2 cups Homemade
  Biscuit Mix

½ cup milk
Flour

Add milk to mix. Turn onto a lightly floured surface and knead gently for 30 seconds. Pat or roll ½ inch thick and cut with medium-sized biscuit cutter dipped in flour. Bake in 450-degree oven 12 to 15 minutes. Makes 10 to 12 biscuits.

JACKSONVILLE BISCUITS
AND GRAVY

1 pound sage seasoned
  sausage
1 heaping tablespoon
  flour

Milk
Biscuits (below)

Fry sausage. When done, remove from pan, leaving crumbs to make gravy. If there are not enough crumbs leave about ½ cup of sausage. Mix flour into the drippings and stir until the mixture is brown. Stir in enough milk to make gravy of consistency you desire. Serve over split baking-powder biscuits.

BISCUITS

2 cups self-rising flour
3 heaping tablespoons
  shortening

1 cup milk

Blend flour and shortening with pastry blender. Add milk. Stir with spoon. Press out lightly on waxed paper. Cut into biscuit shape and bake in 450-degree oven for 10 to 15 minutes.

Note: Two days is all it took, and I was hooked on biscuits and gravy, an everyday breakfast in northern Florida and southern Georgia. This is enough gravy to feed two people. Increase flour and milk for additional servings.

HIGH-CALCIUM BREAD

2½ cups flour
1 cup lukewarm water
1½ teaspoons salt
3 tablespoons high-fat
  soy flour

½ ounce yeast
3½ tablespoons nonfat
  dry milk solids
2 teaspoons shortening

Dissolve yeast in lukewarm water (about 85 degrees). Combine all dry ingredients in mixing bowl. Pour in the yeast solution and start mixing. Add shortening and mix until the dough is smooth. Place the dough in a well-greased bowl, cover, and allow to rise in a warm place (80 to 85 degrees) for 1½ hours.

After dough has risen, punch dough down by plunging your fist in the center of the dough. Fold over edges of dough and turn upside down. Cover and allow to rise for 15 to 20 minutes. Shape into a loaf and place in greased bread pan and cover. Allow to stand about an hour in a warm place until it fills the pan. Bake in a 400-degree oven for about 35 minutes.

Note: This recipe contains 8% nonfat dry milk solids and 6% full-fat soy flour.

MAHALA'S
LITTLE FRUIT DOUGHNUTS

½ cup sugar
2 egg yolks, beaten
½ cup sour milk
½ teaspoon baking soda
2 cups sifted flour
¼ teaspoon salt
½ cup finely chopped
  pecans

¼ cup finely chopped
  raisins
Grated rind of 1 orange
¼ cup finely chopped
  dates
2 tablespoons orange juice
32 ounces peanut oil
Sugar

Combine the ½ cup sugar and egg yolks. Mix the milk and baking soda together. Add to the egg mixture. Sift the flour and salt together and add. Stir in the pecans, raisins, orange rind, and dates. Add the orange juice. Drop from a teaspoon into hot fat. Turn while cooking. Fry until light brown. Remove from the fat and drain on absorbent paper. Sprinkle with sugar. Makes 2 dozen doughnuts.

Note: These should be quite small, only slightly larger than the hole in a regular doughnut. It helps to drop the amount spooned out of the dough briefly into flour, then each ball can be molded by hand. The flour coating keeps the grease from soaking in.

MOLASSES CORN BREAD

2 cups cornmeal
1½ cups flour
2 teaspoons baking powder
1 teaspoon salt

2 eggs, beaten
1½ cups whole milk
½ cup molasses
2 tablespoons melted butter

Sift dry ingredients together into a large bowl, and make a well in the center. Combine eggs, milk, molasses, and butter. Pour into the well, and mix just enough to combine ingredients. Bake at 425 degrees for about 20 minutes in 2 layer-cake pans.

MEXICAN BREAKFAST

6 eggs
¾ cup all-purpose flour
1½ teaspoons baking
  powder
½ teaspoon salt

½ teaspoon celery salt
1½ cups shredded
  cheddar cheese
Butter
Mexican Sauce (below)

Beat eggs at high speed of mixer until thick, about 10 minutes. Combine flour, baking powder, salt, and celery salt. Gradually add flour mixture to eggs, beating at low speed just until dry ingredients are moistened. Add cheese. Pour ½ cup of batter onto lightly buttered warm skillet. Turn when brown and bake other side. Serve three puffs for each person and cover with the warm sauce. Serves four.

MEXICAN SAUCE

¾ cup chopped green
  pepper
¾ cup chopped onion
¼ cup butter
1 tablespoon flour
1 15-ounce can tomato
  sauce

1 4-ounce can mushroom
  stems and pieces, or
12 ounces fresh
  mushrooms, chopped
  and sautéed in butter
½ teaspoon mild chili
  sauce

Sauté pepper and onion in butter until tender. Stir in the flour; add tomato sauce and mushrooms. Cook over low heat, stirring constantly until it thickens. Add chili sauce. Keep warm over hot water.

ONION SQUARES

2 cups sliced onions
2 tablespoons margarine
½ teaspoon salt
¼ teaspoon pepper
2 cups flour
4 teaspoons baking powder

1 teaspoon salt
5 tablespoons shortening
¾ cup milk
1 egg, well beaten
¾ cup sour cream

Cook onions in margarine until delicately browned. Season with salt and pepper. Sift flour, baking powder, and salt together. Cut in shortening until mixture resembles coarse crumbs. Add milk and mix to a soft dough. Spread dough in an 11 x 7 inch greased pan. Top dough with onions. Mix egg with sour cream and pour over onions. Bake at 450 degrees for 20 minutes. Serve in squares with roast or barbecued ribs. Serves twelve.

ORANGE-CREAM CHEESE
BREAD

⅔ cup honey
⅔ cup milk
2½ cups flour
⅓ cup sugar
1 teaspoon baking soda

1 teaspoon salt
½ cup shortening
1 egg
1 cup chopped nuts
Filling (below)

Combine honey and milk in large mixing bowl. Add flour, sugar, baking soda, salt, shortening, and egg; blend at low speed until smooth, about 1 minute. Stir in nuts. Spread half of batter in greased and floured 9 x 5 x 3 inch loaf pan. Pour filling over batter. Carefully spoon remaining batter over filling and spread gently. Bake at 325 degrees for 1 hour and 15 minutes to 1 hour and 25 minutes. Makes 1 loaf.

FILLING

1 3-ounce package cream
  cheese, softened
1 egg
2 tablespoons flour

1 tablespoon grated
  orange rind
¾ cup sugar

Combine all ingredients in small mixing bowl. Blend at low speed until well mixed. Set aside until needed.

FLAKY RASPBERRY ROLLS

1 cup butter
8 ounces cream cheese
1 teaspoon salt

2 cups sifted flour
10-ounce jar raspberry jam

In a bowl cream the butter with the cream cheese until smooth. Blend in the salt and flour. Mix thoroughly. Chill until firm enough to handle. Roll portions of the dough out on a floured board about 1/8 inch thick. Cut into 2½-inch squares. Spread each with about 1 teaspoonful of jam to within ¼ inch of edge. Roll up tightly and pinch edge to seal. Place on ungreased cookie sheet and bake at 375 degrees for about 15 minutes or until nicely browned. Remove to racks to cool thoroughly. Makes 1½ dozen.

Note: We serve these on special breakfasts such as Christmas, Easter, Thanksgiving, or other holidays.

PARK HOUSE
SOUFFLÉ PANCAKES

Pancakes date back to the Roman Empire, but the soufflé version is a more recent innovation. It is a super-light and fluffy variation of simple hot cakes.

6 eggs, separated
½ teaspoon cream of tartar
⅓ cup all-purpose flour
½ teaspoon baking powder
½ teaspoon salt

¼ teaspoon baking soda
⅓ cup sour cream
Butter
Maple syrup, honey, or
    preserves

In large mixing bowl, beat egg whites and cream of tartar at high speed until stiff but not dry, just until whites no longer slide when bowl is tilted. Set aside. In small mixing bowl, beat egg yolks at high speed until thick and lemon-colored, about 5 minutes. Beat in flour, baking powder, salt, and soda. Add sour cream. Gently but thoroughly fold yolk mixture into whites. For each pancake, pour ¼ cup batter onto hot, well-greased griddle (380 degrees for electric griddle), spreading to form cakes about 3 inches in diameter. Cook on both sides until golden brown. Serve hot with butter and topping. Makes about 16 pancakes.

Note: ⅓ cup pancake mix may be substituted. Omit flour, baking powder, and soda.

Note: We discovered the Park House in Augusta, Wisconsin, by accident and have been going there ever since. It's an eighteen-room Victorian house with a porch that extends across the entire front. Delightful, inventive meals are served, and for an incredible $275 a month you can live in comfort and ease under the eagle eye of Glenn Baumgardner, its proprietor. It's the last of the old-fashioned boardinghouses but has a club-like atmosphere. Meals are served at a long table in the large family kitchen, and Glenn does the cooking. Sunday is pancake day. These light charmers are flanked by all the sausage and bacon you can eat. I vacation there in preference to the Minnesota North Woods or more *exotic play areas. The Park House makes me feel warmly welcome and somewhat cherished. We hope it goes on forever.*

PEANUT BUTTER CINNAMON ROLLS

(The peanut butter is in the dough, the cinnamon is in the filling!)

¾ cup milk
2 tablespoons butter or margarine
⅓ cup mashed potato (add no seasoning or liquid)
½ teaspoon salt
3 tablespoons sugar
½ cup peanut butter

1 package active dry yeast
¼ cup warm water
1 egg, beaten
3 cups all-purpose flour, sifted
Filling (below)
Melted butter

Scald milk, pour over butter, potato, salt, sugar, and peanut butter, and mix well. Cool to lukewarm. Soften yeast in water. Add with egg to first mixture. Add 1 cup flour and beat 1 minute. Add enough additional flour (about 1¼ cups) to make a dough. Turn out on floured board and knead until smooth and satiny, using only enough flour to keep dough from sticking. Shape in a ball and put in greased bowl; brush with melted butter. Cover and let rise in warm place until doubled in bulk. Roll to a 16 x 9 inch rectangle. Spread with filling and roll up as for jelly roll, beginning at the widest side. Cut in 16 one-inch slices. Put close together in greased 9-inch square pan. Brush with melted butter, cover, and let rise until doubled. Bake in a 400-degree oven for 20 to 25 minutes. Makes 16 rolls.

FILLING

¼ cup butter
⅔ cup sugar

½ teaspoon cinnamon

Cream ingredients together. Set aside until needed.

PUFF BATTER

2 cups flour
2½ cups milk
2 tablespoons salad oil
1 teaspoon salt

1 teaspoon pepper
2 teaspoons monosodium
  glutamate
4 egg whites

Blend all the ingredients except egg whites together. Let stand one hour before adding egg whites. Beat and fold egg whites into blended mix just before use. Good for frying fish or vegetables.

SWEET POTATO BUNS

1 large sweet potato
1 compressed cake yeast,
  or 1 package active
  dry yeast
1 teaspoon salt

3 tablespoons sugar
1 tablespoon butter
1 cup milk
3½ to 5 cups sifted
  all-purpose flour

Peel the sweet potato and cut up into pieces. Cover with water and cook until tender. Drain after it is cooked and save ¼ cup of the water used for cooking. Let the sweet potato water cool until it's just barely warm and mix in the yeast. Mash the potato and mix in salt, sugar, and butter. Beat vigorously. Heat milk until a film forms on top. Skim the film off the top and stir into the sweet potato mixture. Cool again until just lukewarm. When the desired temperature has been reached, stir in the softened yeast. Adding one cup at a time, stir in the flour until the dough is stiff enough to knead. Place dough on the floured dough board and knead it until smooth and elastic. Put dough in a well-greased bowl, cover, and set in a warm place to rise until doubled in size. Push dough down with your fist, pinch off pieces the size of a golf ball, and put in greased muffin tins. Allow to rise again until doubled in size and bake at 425 degrees for about 15 minutes. Makes 20 buns.

SIXTY-MINUTE ROLLS

These are excellent as well as fast.

2 cakes yeast
¼ cup lukewarm water
3 tablespoons sugar
1¼ cups milk

1 teaspoon salt
¼ cup butter
4 cups flour

Soak yeast in water. Place sugar, milk, salt, and 2 tablespoons of butter in a pan. Heat until lukewarm. Add yeast and flour. Mix. Place in a warm place for 15 minutes. Turn onto a floured board and pat until ¾ inch thick. Cut with a biscuit cutter or glass. Fold the circle of dough in half and place a pat of butter inside of the fold. Place rolls on a baking sheet and let rise in a warm place for 15 minutes. Bake 10 minutes in a preheated oven at 400 degrees.

SOUR CREAM MUFFINS

1 egg, well beaten
1 cup thick sour cream
1 tablespoon melted butter
1⅓ cups flour
1½ teaspoons baking
  powder

½ teaspoon baking soda
½ teaspoon salt
2 tablespoons sugar

Combine egg, sour cream, melted butter, and sifted dry ingredients. Mix just until flour is moistened. (Batter will not be smooth.) Fill greased muffin tins two-thirds full. Bake in 400-degree oven for 25 minutes. Makes 12 muffins.

SWISS PEAR BREAD

FILLING

2 cups dried pears or
  apricots
½ cup dried pitted prunes
1 cup figs or fig preserves
½ cup raisins
½ cup chopped pecans,
  walnuts, or almonds

¼ cup citron
Juice of 2 lemons
1 teaspoon nutmeg
½ teaspoon cinnamon
½ cup sugar
½ cup red wine

DOUGH

1 cup milk, scalded
½ cup butter
½ cup sugar
1 teaspoon salt
2 packages dry yeast

1 egg, well beaten
5 to 6 cups all-purpose
  flour
Melted butter

GLAZE

1 cup confectioners' sugar
2 tablespoons hot water

1½ teaspoon almond
  extract

In just enough water to cover, cook pears or apricots and prunes until tender. Drain and seed prunes. Finely chop the pears, prunes, and figs and combine in a bowl with the rest of the filling ingredients. Allow the mixture to stand for several hours or overnight.

Scald milk. Stir in butter until melted. Add sugar and salt. Cool to lukewarm. Dissolve yeast in ½ cup of lukewarm water. Combine milk mixture, yeast, egg, and enough flour to make a soft dough. Knead on lightly floured board. Let dough rise until it doubles in bulk. Divide in half and roll each portion into a 12-inch square. Spread half the filling on each square, fold in ends, and roll like a jelly roll. Place on a lightly greased baking sheet. Prick top with a fork. Let loaves rise until doubled in bulk. Brush with melted butter. Bake at 350 degrees for 25 to 30 minutes or until golden brown. Combine confectioners' sugar, hot water, and almond extract. Mix and glaze loaves while hot. Makes 2 loaves.

Note: This recipe comes from Betty Cunningham of Baton Rouge who, some years ago, wrote her own delightful cookbook. It was beautifully illustrated by her daughter Lauren Tucker. We were so impressed that we contacted Lauren, who has been doing much of our artwork ever since. Lauren has done some of the illustrations for this book. Betty's book is a bedside companion for me—I read it often. The Swiss Pear Bread is well worth the effort.

ZUCCHINI BREAD

3 eggs
1 cup vegetable oil
2 cups sugar
1 teaspoon vanilla
2 cups chopped zucchini
3 tablespoons finely
  chopped and dried
  parsley

3 cups sifted flour
1 teaspoon salt
1 teaspoon cinnamon
1 teaspoon baking soda
1 teaspoon baking powder
Glaze (below)

Beat eggs until light. Add oil, sugar, and vanilla. Add zucchini, parsley, and dry ingredients. Mix well and pour into two greased loaf pans. Bake at 350 degrees for about 45 minutes.

GLAZE

¾ cup butter
⅔ cup brown sugar
1 cup coconut

1 cup chopped nuts
¼ cup milk

Mix together and cook about 3 minutes over medium heat. Pour over bread while it is still hot.

TOMATO-CHEESE MUFFINS

1¾ cups flour
2 teaspoons baking powder
½ teaspoon baking soda
¾ cup tomato juice
1 egg
⅓ cup vegetable oil

2 tablespoons sugar
½ teaspoon salt
3 ounces cream cheese,
  cut in small cubes
3 ounces American cheese,
  cut in small cubes

Mix flour, baking powder, and baking soda in mixing bowl. Put tomato juice, egg, oil, sugar, salt, and cream cheese in blender. Mix. Pour tomato mixture over dry ingredients. Stir until just moistened. Fill muffin tins half full. Add 1 American cheese cube to each cup. Fill with enough batter to cover. Bake at 400 degrees for about 25 minutes. Makes 12 muffins.

TROPICAL PEANUT BREAD

2 cups sifted flour
1 teaspoon baking powder
½ teaspoon baking soda
½ teaspoon salt
1 egg, slightly beaten
1 cup buttermilk
1 cup brown sugar

2 tablespoons peanut
  butter
1 cup mashed bananas
1 cup chopped peanuts
1 teaspoon sugar
½ teaspoon cinnamon

In a medium bowl sift flour, baking powder, baking soda, and salt. Mix together egg, buttermilk, brown sugar, peanut butter, bananas, and peanuts; add to dry ingredients, mixing just enough to moisten. Pour into a greased loaf pan, sprinkle with mixture of sugar and cinnamon. Brush with melted butter and bake at 350 degrees for 40 to 45 minutes. Remove to rack and cool. Makes 1 loaf.

Pies

Our Double Dutch Fudge Pie is famous all over the country. Every magazine article ever written about us mentions this pie, and every television program we are on dwells on it at some length. It's the only recipe we don't share because we sell it commercially. However, there are other great ones in this section. Our Lemon Meringue Pie is the dining-room favorite after the Fudge Pie. Lemon Elegance is a pie that makes its first appearance since, up until now, we have kept it a carefully guarded secret. Our Coffee Meringue Pie is great, and so is our Praline Eggnog Pie; if you like old-fashioned pies, it's hard to beat our Gooseberry Pie. Another pie in high demand is our Sour Cream-Raisin—its towering four-egg white meringue gets many appreciative looks.

We include the Rhubarb Pie from our first book because it just can't be improved upon. One of Grandma's secrets was to sugar the top crust of any fruit pies—it does something for them.

I hope I have included all the pies that have been requested. Some pies have lattice tops, some have whipped cream tops, and some have just a top crust. All of them are good, and it is tough-going living and eating at the Anderson House with all of these temptations.

ANN'S SPECIAL
DUTCH APPLE TART

When we had our choice of cakes on our birthdays, most of us chose Ann's Apple Tart instead. We ate it swimming with real whipped cream flavored with light rum.

1 cup butter
3 cups plus 1 tablespoon
  sugar
4 pounds tart green apples
  (Winesaps preferred)
½ teaspoon cinnamon

2 teaspoons lemon juice
Enough pie dough for
  1 crust
¼ cup light rum
1 cup whipping cream

Spread ½ cup of the butter in a 9-inch pie tin. Pour over this ½ cup sugar. Peel and slice the apples thin. Mix them with 1½ cups sugar. Place in pie tin. This will look very high. Sprinkle with the cinnamon and lemon juice and dot with butter. Roll out the pie dough and cover the apples pressing loosely on the sides of the tin. Bake in 450-degree oven for about 20 minutes. Turn the heat down to 350 degrees and bake until the apples are soft. Remove from oven, and cool slightly on a cake rack. Place a large cake plate on top of the pie and turn upside down. Cool. Caramelize 1 cup of the sugar, stirring constantly. Add rum and pour over apples. Serve with whipped cream topping (as follows). Place the 1 tablespoon sugar in bottom of bowl. Add whipping cream. Whip until stiff. Fold in rum to taste and serve on top of tart. Serves eight.

BLUE-RIBBON APRICOT PIE

1½ tablespoons quick-cooking tapioca
½ cup sugar
¼ teaspoon salt
1 tablespoon melted butter
2 cups cooked, dried apricots, drained

1 cup apricot juice
1 tablespoon lemon juice
½ cup canned crushed pineapple, drained
1 9-inch pie crust with lattice top

Mix together all ingredients except for pie crust and let stand 15 minutes while you prepare pie crust. Make a standing rim. Fill with apricot mixture, moisten edge with cold water and arrange a lattice of pie-crust strips across the top. Flute the rim with your fingers. Bake 10 minutes on bottom of 425-degree oven, then reduce heat to 350 degrees. Sprinkle with granulated sugar and bake an additional 10 minutes, or until a delicate brown. Serve with whipped cream or vanilla ice cream. Serves eight.

BLACK RUSSIAN PIE

1 cup cream-filled chocolate sandwich cookie crumbs (about 14 cookies)
2 tablespoons butter, melted
24 large marshmallows
½ cup cold milk

1/8 teaspoon salt
⅓ cup Kahlua (3 ounces)
1 cup whipping cream
Baker's solid semi-sweet chocolate for curls (optional)

Combine cookie crumbs and butter in an 8-inch pie pan. Mix well and press firmly in an even layer over bottom and sides of pan to form a crust. Place in freezer until firm. Meanwhile, melt marshmallows with milk and salt in a double boiler. Cool until mixture will mound on a spoon. Stir in Kahlua. Beat cream until stiff and fold into the marshmallow mixture. Chill about 30 minutes, until mixture holds ripples when stirred lightly. Turn into chilled cookie shell, and freeze firm. Before serving, arrange a circle of chocolate curls in the center (optional) and cut into wedges. Makes one 8-inch pie.

CHOCOLATE BOURBON PIE

1 8½-ounce box chocolate
  wafers
½ cup melted butter or
  margarine
21 large marshmallows
1 cup evaporated milk
2 cups heavy cream,
  whipped

4 tablespoons bourbon
Grated bitter chocolate
Fresh fruit for garnish
  (whole bing cherries with
  stems; whole straw-
  berries; orange slices,
  cut in half and twisted;
  fresh apricot halves)

Crush chocolate wafers with rolling pin or in blender. Mix wafer crumbs with melted butter. Pat this mixture evenly into 9-inch pie pan. Bake in preheated 350-degree oven, just to set. Cool. Make filling: melt marshmallows in hot evaporated milk, stirring over medium heat just until melted. Cool. Fold half of whipped cream into marshmallow mixture. Stir in bourbon. Pour into chocolate crust; chill 3 to 4 hours. Top with remaining whipped cream and a lavish sprinkling of grated chocolate. Ring pie with a wreath of seasonal fresh fruits. Serves eight.

CALICO SNOW

2 cups cream
2 cups marshmallow creme
2 teaspoons vanilla extract
1 cup plus ¼ cup coconut

2 baked pie shells
¼ cup shaved chocolate
Red candied cherries

Whip cream until stiff. Fold in marshmallow creme, vanilla, and 1 cup coconut. Sprinkle the chocolate and ¼ cup coconut over bottom of each pie shell. Spread creamed mixture on top, and sprinkle with cherries and more shaved chocolate. Makes 2 pies.

CHOCOLATE BAR PIE

Chocolate Petal Crust
   (below)
1 8-ounce milk chocolate
   bar or milk chocolate
   bar with almonds

⅓ cup milk
1½ cups miniature or
   15 regular marshmallows
1 cup whipping cream
Whipped cream for topping

Prepare Chocolate Petal Crust, and set aside. Break chocolate bar, chopping almonds, if used, into small pieces. Melt with milk in top of double boiler over hot water. Add marshmallows, stirring until melted. Cool completely. Whip cream until stiff, then fold into chocolate mixture. Pour into crust. Chill several hours until firm. Garnish with whipped cream topping. Serves eight.

CHOCOLATE PETAL CRUST

½ cup butter or margarine
1 cup sugar
1 egg
1 teaspoon vanilla

1¼ cups flour
½ cup cocoa
¾ teaspoon baking soda
¼ teaspoon salt

Cream butter, sugar, egg, and vanilla until light and fluffy. Combine flour, cocoa, soda, and salt. Add to creamed mixture. Shape soft dough into two 1½-inch rolls. Wrap in wax paper. Chill until firm. Cut one roll into 1/8-inch slices. Arrange, edges touching, on bottom and sides of greased 9-inch pie pan. (Small spaces in crust will not affect pie.) Bake at 375 degrees 8 to 10 minutes. Cool.

Note: Freeze any leftover dough and use for pie crust or cookies.

CHOCOLATE MOCHA CRUNCH PIE

Mocha Pie Shell (below)
1½ cups butter or margarine, softened
¾ cup firmly packed brown sugar
1 1-ounce square unsweetened chocolate, melted and cooled
2 teaspoons plus 1½ tablespoons instant coffee granules

2 eggs
2 cups whipping cream
½ cup powdered sugar
½ square semi-sweet chocolate, grated (optional)

Prepare pie shell. Set aside. Place butter in a small mixing bowl and beat until creamy. Gradually add brown sugar and beat at medium speed for 2 to 3 minutes, scraping sides of bowl occasionally. Stir in melted chocolate and 2 teaspoons instant coffee granules. Add eggs, one at a time, beating 5 minutes after each addition. Pour filling into cooled pie shell. Refrigerate at least 6 hours or overnight. About 1 or 2 hours before serving, combine cream, powdered sugar, and 1½ tablespoons instant coffee granules in a large, chilled mixing bowl. Whip cream until stiff (do not overbeat). Spoon over chilled filling. Sprinkle with grated semi-sweet chocolate, if desired. Chill. Serves eight.

MOCHA PIE SHELL

1 pie-crust stick, crumbled,
   or ½ 11-ounce-package
   pie-crust mix
1 1-ounce square
   unsweetened chocolate,
   grated

¾ cup finely chopped
   walnuts
¼ cup firmly packed
   brown sugar
1 tablespoon water
1 teaspoon vanilla extract

Use a fork to combine crumbled pie-crust stick or pie-crust mix and chocolate in a medium bowl. Stir in nuts and sugar. Combine water and vanilla; sprinkle over pastry mixture. Mix with fork until mixture forms a ball. Line a 9-inch pie pan with aluminum foil; place a circle of waxed paper over foil in the bottom of pie pan. Press pastry mixture evenly into pie pan. Bake at 375 degrees for 15 minutes; cool completely. Invert crust on an 8½-inch pie pan; remove foil and waxed paper. Return to pie pan. Makes 1 9-inch pie shell.

COFFEE MERINGUE PIE

In one of our earlier cookbooks, we had a recipe for Brazilian Coffee Pie that we thought was mighty nice. Along came a guest from a Western ranch who gave us this recipe, and now we are torn in two!

3 egg whites
½ cup sugar
¼ teaspoon salt

½ cup finely chopped
   pecans
Filling (below)

Beat egg whites until stiff, gradually adding sugar and salt. Gently fold in pecans. Spread the meringue into a buttered 10-inch pie tin. Bake at 350 degrees. Cool in oven.

FILLING

2 tablespoons instant
  coffee granules
½ cup milk
25 large marshmallows,
  cut in halves or fourths

3 egg yolks, beaten
2 cups whipping cream,
  whipped
1 tablespoon bourbon

In a double boiler over hot water mix coffee, milk, and marshmallows. Stir until marshmallows begin to dissolve. Add egg yolks. Cook about 5 minutes stirring constantly. Cool. Add bourbon. Gently fold in the whipped cream and pile mixture into the meringue shell. Store well covered in the refrigerator overnight. When you are ready to serve the next day, live dangerously and whip another cup of cream with sugar, spread over the top of the pie and cover with shaved chocolate and about ½ cup finely ground pecans. Makes a very high, rich pie. Serves eight.

MAPLE NUT PIE

2 cups chopped walnuts
1 10-inch unbaked pie crust
5 eggs
1 cup maple syrup
¼ teaspoon cinnamon

¼ teaspoon nutmeg
¼ cup melted butter
1 teaspoon maple flavoring
½ teaspoon salt

Sprinkle walnut pieces on pie crust. Combine eggs, syrup, cinnamon, nutmeg, butter, maple, and salt, and blend in mixer until smooth. Pour this mixture over the walnuts and bake 30 to 35 minutes at 325 degrees, or until the pie seems solid to the touch. Remove from oven and cool on cake rack. Serve with whipped cream flavored with maple flavoring and dust with finely chopped nuts. Serves eight.

MARY JOSLYN'S
LEMON MERINGUE PIE

When people in our dining rooms see our Lemon Meringue Pie go by on a tray there are plenty of incredulous stares. Our two-inch meringue is a towering, frothy topping for what I call the absolutely perfect lemon pie. We hope you'll like it as well as our guests do!

1½ tablespoons butter
2 cups hot water
2 cups sugar
3 tablespoons flour
5 egg yolks, beaten

Grated rind and juice of
  1½ lemons
1 9-inch pie crust
Meringue (below)

In the top of a double boiler melt butter in hot water. In a mixing bowl, mix sugar and flour well. Add beaten egg yolks and grated lemon rind and juice. Add this mixture to the butter and water. Cook until thick and cool thoroughly. Turn into baked pastry shell and top with meringue. Turn oven to 350 degrees and, when preheated, place meringue-covered pie in oven for 12 to 15 minutes to brown lightly. Serves eight.

MERINGUE

5 egg whites
Pinch salt

10 tablespoons sugar
¼ teaspoon cream of tartar

Beat the egg whites with salt until they hold a peak. Then add the sugar, one tablespoon at a time, beating thoroughly after each addition. Add cream of tartar, beating after that addition. Spread meringue smoothly. It will be stiff. Spread to the edge of crust. If your eggs are fresh your meringue will not weep. Overcooking the meringue will result in a tough meringue.

Note: Mary Joslyn came to the Anderson House just out of high school. That was thirty-five years ago, and she is still in the kitchen making her sensational Lemon Meringue, Sour Cream, Black Russian, Strawberry-Rhubarb, and Dutch Fudge pies. An inventive cook, she brings many new recipes to our test kitchen, and we are always glad to see them.

OLD-FASHIONED GOOSEBERRY PIE

It's amazing, but there are still people who have never seen gooseberries and have no idea what they taste like. Gooseberries are difficult to find, even in small country towns like ours. However, this spring I am going to plant four gooseberry bushes in back of the inn so we won't have that problem.

3½ cups gooseberries
2 tablespoons quick-cooking tapioca
1½ cups plus 2 to 3 tablespoons sugar
¼ teaspoon salt
1 teaspoon grated orange rind

1 9-inch pie shell, including top
1 egg white, slightly beaten
Flour
¼ cup melted butter

Remove stem and blossom ends from fresh gooseberries. Wash in cold water and cut large berries in half. Add tapioca, 1½ cups sugar, salt, and orange rind, and set aside for 20 minutes. Line 9-inch pie plate with pastry rolled 1/8 inch thick. Brush bottom and sides of pie crust with egg white. Sprinkle lightly with flour. Fill with gooseberry mixture, sprinkle with melted butter, and cover with the top crust. Make a few slits for escaping steam. Sprinkle top crust with 2 to 3 tablespoons sugar. Bake 10 minutes in 450-degree oven. Reduce heat to 350 degrees and bake 30 to 35 minutes longer. If served warm, serve with hard sauce if desired. Grandma poured thick cream on hers. Serves eight.

GRANDMA ANDERSON'S FAMOUS LEMON ELEGANCE PIE

1 tablespoon gelatin
¼ cup cold water
½ cup lemon juice
3 tablespoons water
10 large marshmallows
⅓ cup sugar

¼ teaspoon salt
3 egg whites
1 9-inch vanilla wafer,
  pecan, or cornflake crust
Topping (below)

Soften gelatin in cold water. In a saucepan combine lemon juice, 3 tablespoons of water, and marshmallows; cook over low heat until marshmallows melt. Stir constantly. Stir sugar and salt into mix, and add softened gelatin. Cool slightly. Place egg whites in large mixing bowl and slowly add lemon mixture, beating at high speed. Continue beating 20 minutes until the mixture is the consistency of whipped cream. Turn into baked shell. Cover with topping. Serves eight.

TOPPING

1 egg yolk, beaten
  until thick
⅓ cup sugar
1½ tablespoons lemon
  juice

3 tablespoons melted butter
¾ cup heavy cream,
  whipped

Place egg yolk in bowl. Add sugar. Stir in lemon juice and butter. Fold in whipped cream.

PERFECT MERINGUE

1 tablespoon cornstarch
2 tablespoons cold water
½ cup boiling water
1 teaspoon fresh lemon
  juice

3 egg whites
6 tablespoons sugar
1 9-inch pie crust

In small saucepan mix cornstarch and cold water until blended. Stir in boiling water, put over medium heat and bring to a boil, stirring constantly. Cook, stirring, 2 minutes or until thickened. Remove from heat and cool to room temperature. Add lemon juice to egg whites and beat until whites stand in soft peaks. Gradually add sugar, beating well after each addition. Then beat until whites stand up in firm glossy peaks. Add cornstarch mixture all at once and beat until well blended. Put cooled filling in cooled shell, spreading to sides. Top with meringue, spreading to edges. Bake in preheated 350-degree oven for 12 minutes or until lightly browned. Remove from oven and put in draft-free spot to cool 2 to 3 hours before cutting.

NAPOLEON PEACHIES

1 8-ounce package
  cream cheese
1 cup soft butter

2 cups sifted all-purpose
  flour
1½ cups peach jam

Beat cream cheese and butter together until well blended. Gradually stir in flour to blend. Shape into a ball, then into a rectangle. Chill in refrigerator about 1 hour. Divide in half. Roll out half of the dough at a time on a pastry cloth until very thin. Cut into 3-inch squares. Place a teaspoon of peach jam on each in the center and bring the points of rectangle to center so they overlap. Press to seal. Bake on greased cookie sheets in preheated 400-degree oven until lightly browned, 12 to 15 minutes. Place on cake rack. Makes 5 dozen.

Note: We sprinkle the tops with granulated sugar.

PLANTATION PEANUT PIE

1 9-inch pie crust
1 cup dark corn syrup
1 cup sugar
1 teaspoon vanilla

1 cup salted peanuts
¼ cup soft butter
2 tablespoons sugar

Preheat oven to 350 degrees. Beat eggs, corn syrup, 1 cup of sugar, and vanilla. Stir in peanuts. Pour filling into pie crust. Dot surface with butter. Bake about 45 minutes or until filling is firmly set. Serve with whipped cream and finely ground peanuts on top. Serves eight.

PEANUT BUTTER PIE

Gilbert Lenz is a friend who lives the best of many worlds. Musician, expert photographer, gourmet cook, and dedicated traveler, Gilbert does it all and keeps finding room for more adventures. One day he came over with this recipe for Peanut Butter Pie. We love it!

¾ cup powdered sugar
2 heaping tablespoons
   crunchy peanut butter
1 9-inch pie shell, baked
1 cup plus 6 tablespoons
   granulated sugar
1 well-rounded tablespoon
   cornstarch

½ teaspoon salt
2 cups milk
3 eggs, separated
½ cup finely chopped
   peanuts
1 teaspoon vanilla extract

Mix powdered sugar and peanut butter until it resembles coarse crumbs. Cover bottom of pie shell with this mixture, reserving ⅔ cup for later use. Mix together in saucepan the 1 cup of granulated sugar, cornstarch, and salt. Stir in milk and 3 beaten egg yolks until well mixed. Cook over medium heat, stirring constantly until mixture comes to a boil and thickens. Stir in peanuts and vanilla. Cool to room temperature and pour into pie shell. Beat three egg whites until foamy. Add the 6 tablespoons granulated sugar and beat until stiff. Spread meringue over filling and top with reserved crumb mixture. Bake at 350 degrees until lightly browned, 5 minutes or less. Serves eight.

ANDERSON HOUSE
PECAN PIE

6 eggs
1 cup sugar
1 teaspoon vanilla
2 tablespoons butter,
  melted

1½ cups dark corn syrup
½ cup maple syrup
1 cup pecans
1 9-inch pie crust
Whipped cream

Beat eggs and sugar together. Add vanilla to butter, then combine with egg mixture. Add syrups. Place pecans on the bottom of the crust. Pour liquid mixture into shell. Bake at 300 degrees for about 45 minutes. Serve with whipped cream. Serves eight.

Note: There are several pecan pie recipes available for the dedicated and adventuresome cook. Ours has more eggs than any I've seen, and we go to Georgia for our pecans. We serve the pies with whipped cream delicately flavored with bourbon. It's been on our menu for years and remains one of our most popular pies.

BLACK-BOTTOM PECAN PIE

An ingenious combination of favorite flavors—chocolate and pecan. Preparation time is about 30 minutes.

4 eggs
¾ cup dark corn syrup
½ cup sugar
¼ cup butter, melted
4 tablespoons rum (optional)
1 teaspoon vanilla extract
½ teaspoon salt

1½ cups pecan halves
1 6-ounce package semi-sweet chocolate morsels (preferably Nestle Toll House)
1 9-inch unbaked pie shell
1 cup heavy cream

Preheat oven to 350 degrees. Lighly beat together eggs, corn syrup, sugar, butter, 3 tablespoons of rum, vanilla, and salt. Do not overbeat. Stir in pecan halves and half the morsels; pour into pie shell. Cover edges with foil. Bake at 350 degrees for 25 minutes. Remove foil and bake 20 to 25 minutes more or until knife inserted in center comes out clean. Cool, then chill. Melt remaining morsels over hot (not boiling) water; stir until smooth. Cool. Whip cream and remaining 1 tablespoon rum until soft peaks form; gently fold in melted morsels. Serve with pie. Store pie and whipping cream in refrigerator. Makes one 9-inch pie.

CREAM CHEESE-PECAN PIE

1 8-ounce package cream cheese
4 eggs
⅓ cup plus ¼ cup sugar
2 teaspoons vanilla extract

1¼ cups coarsely chopped pecans
1 cup light corn syrup
¼ teaspoon salt

In a large bowl, beat together until smooth at medium speed of an electric mixer: the cream cheese, 1 egg, ⅓ cup sugar, and 1 teaspoon vanilla. Spread over the bottom of the pie crust. Sprinkle with pecans. In a large clean bowl, beat the remaining 3 eggs at medium speed until frothy. Add the corn syrup, ¼ cup sugar, salt, and 1 teaspoon vanilla; beat until blended. Gently pour the mixture over the pecans. Bake in a preheated 375-degree oven until a knife inserted halfway between the center and edge comes out clean, about 40 minutes. Place on wire rack to cool before cutting. Serves ten.

PRALINE-EGGNOG PIE

2 envelopes unflavored
　gelatin
¼ cup sugar
3 egg yolks
2 cups prepared eggnog
¼ cup praline liqueur
1 tablespoon rum

½ teaspoon vanilla extract
1 cup whipping or heavy
　cream, whipped
9-inch graham cracker crust
Ground nutmeg
Whole-berry cranberry
　sauce, drained (garnish)

In medium saucepan, mix gelatin with sugar. Beat egg yolks with 1 cup eggnog. Blend with gelatin and sugar. Let stand 1 minute. Stir over low heat until gelatin is completely dissolved, about 5 minutes. Stir in remaining eggnog, liqueur, rum, and vanilla. Pour into large bowl and chill, stirring occasionally, until mixture mounds slightly when dropped from spoon. Fold in whipped cream. Turn into prepared crust; sprinkle with nutmeg. Chill until firm. Garnish with cranberry sauce. Serves eight.

PUMPKIN MERINGUE PIE

1 unbaked 9-inch pie crust
3 egg yolks, lightly beaten
¼ cup light molasses
¾ plus ⅓ cup sugar
½ plus ¼ teaspoon salt
½ teaspoon nutmeg
½ teaspoon cinnamon
1 cup half-and-half

2 cups mashed cooked
 pumpkin
¼ cup plus 1 tablespoon
 bourbon
3 egg whites
¼ teaspoon cream of tartar
Grated orange rind
 (garnish)

Place pastry in 9-inch pie tin. Preheat oven to 400 degrees. Combine egg yolks, molasses, and ¾ cup of sugar. Beat well until sugar has dissolved. Add ½ teaspoon of salt, nutmeg, and cinnamon; add half-and-half. Blend in the pumpkin a bit at a time, stirring after each addition. Stir in the ¼ cup bourbon. Pour into pie shell, place in center of oven, and bake for 15 minutes. Lower heat to 350 degrees and bake until filling seems firm to the touch, about 35 minutes. Remove pie from oven and cool on cake rack. When cool, preheat oven to 350 degrees. Beat egg whites until light and frothy. Add cream of tartar and the ¼ teaspoon of salt and continue to beat until the egg whites hold peaks but are not dry. Beat in ⅓ cup of sugar slowly, beating well after each addition. Fold in the 1 tablespoon bourbon. Spread the meringue over entire pie to the edge. Swirl meringue up into little peaks. Return to oven and bake until delicately browned, 10 to 15 minutes. Sprinkle with grated orange rind. Serves eight.

RHUBARB PIE

1 9-inch pie crust,
 including lattice top
3 cups diced rhubarb
1½ cups sugar
1 tablespoon quick-
 cooking tapioca

Grated rind of ½ lemon
1/8 teaspoon salt
Nutmeg
1 tablespoon butter

Line a 9-inch pie pan with half of pastry and sprinkle with a little flour. Combine the rhubarb, sugar, tapioca, lemon rind, and salt, and turn into the pastry shell. Sprinkle with nutmeg and dot with butter. Then arrange a lattice of pastry strips on top. Sprinkle strips with sugar. Bake in a 350-degree oven for 1 hour. Serves six.

RASPBERRY MOUSSE MERINGUE PIE

4 egg whites (room
  temperature)
¼ teaspoon salt
1½ cups sugar
⅓ cup sliced almonds
2 10-ounce packages
  frozen raspberries,
  thawed

2 envelopes unflavored
  gelatin
1 cup amaretto
2 cups heavy cream,
  whipped
Fresh or frozen (thawed
  and drained) raspberries
  (garnish)

Place egg whites in a large bowl. Beat with salt until stiff. Beat in sugar, 1 tablespoon at a time, until meringue is stiff and glossy. Spread two-thirds of the mixture evenly over the bottom and sides of a greased 11-inch pie pan. Place remaining meringue into a pastry bag fitted with a star tip. Press rosettes of meringue on outer edge of pie pan. Sprinkle shell with almonds. Bake in preheated 275-degree oven for about 40 to 45 minutes, or until lightly browned and hard to the touch. Turn off oven and let shell cool in oven. Puree raspberries in a blender. Press puree through a sieve to remove seeds. Place puree in a saucepan. Add gelatin, and stir over low heat until gelatin is dissolved. Stir in amaretto. Chill until syrupy. Fold in whipped cream. Chill until mixture mounds. Turn filling into pie shell. Garnish with raspberries. Chill until ready to serve and filling is firm. Serves ten.

ETHYL FURNE'S
COCONUT RUM PIE

4 cups moist coconut
  (canned)
¼ cup butter, melted
2 cups whole milk
¼ teaspoon nutmeg
4 eggs, separated
⅔ cup sugar

¼ teaspoon salt
1 tablespoon unflavored
  gelatin
⅓ cup hot water
¼ cup rum
Topping (below)

Mix coconut and butter together to form pie crust. Carefully pack to line a 9-inch pie plate. Heat milk and nutmeg in a double boiler. Beat egg yolks with sugar and salt until eggs are light in color. Pour hot milk over egg mixture and return to double boiler to cook to the consistency of thick cream. Remove from heat and stir in gelatin dissolved in hot water. When custard is cool, add rum and fold in stiffly beaten egg whites. Fill coconut shell and refrigerate for 2 hours.

TOPPING

2 8-ounce milk chocolate
  bars
⅓ cup hot water
¾ cup whipping cream

⅓ cup rum
1 tablespoon powdered
  sugar

Melt milk chocolate in hot water, stirring constantly. Whip cream; flavor half of the whipped cream with rum. Add sugar to the rest of the whipped cream. Add rum-flavored whipped cream to cooled chocolate. Cover pie with layer of sweetened whipped cream. Spread chocolate mixture over all and return to refrigerator for 2 hours for further chilling. Serves ten.

Note: Ethyl Furne formerly supervised Grandma Anderson's Preserving Kitchens, our little plant that produced fruit cakes, plum puddings, jams, jellies, and fancy breads, until the business grew beyond our capacity to handle it in the space available. Ethyl is the best cook in town. To add to her talents, she finished the Minneapolis Marathon in the sum-

mer of 1985 at the age of seventy-six. She still works for us upon occasion, and we hope she never stops. She knows where every wild berry, every wild stalk of asparagus, and the first watercress of the season grows, and we are blissfully on the receiving line of all of it.

ANN POLISCHTAK'S UKRAINIAN RASPBERRY TARTS

When Grandma made tarts they came from leftover pie-crust dough. She rolled them thin, baked one with a hole on top and one without and spread her strawberry jam in between. We loved them! When Ann Polischtak worked for me at the Venetian Beach Hotel in Venice, Florida, she paraded out with these one night, and we all went into rhapsodies of delight. A long-time family recipe over from the Old Country, she said.

1 cup butter (no substitute, says Ann)
½ cup lard
2 cups sugar
4 egg yolks
1 teaspoon almond flavoring

6 cups flour
1 teaspoon baking powder
½ pint cream
1 jar preserves (any flavor)

Cream butter and lard until creamy. Add sugar gradually, then egg yolks and almond flavoring; mix until well blended. Sift flour with baking powder. Add alternately with cream. Add cream until you have a soft, easy-to-handle dough. (Flours will differ; you may not have to use all the cream.) Roll dough out quite thin. Cut out with doughnut cutter, then make a hole in half of the cut-outs. (Use bottle cap if you do not have a small enough cutter.) Place on greased cookie sheet. Sprinkle the halves with the hole in sugar. Bake at 350 degrees until lightly browned. Cool on cake rack. To serve, spread preserves between two tarts; the top tart will have the hole. We use raspberry and apple-geranium jelly that we make ourselves. Makes 3 to 4 dozen, depending on your cutter.

BELLE'S SHOO-FLY PIE

1½ cups brown sugar
3 tablespoons plus 3 cups
  flour
¾ cup sorghum or molasses
1 large egg, beaten
3 cups hot water
1½ teaspoons baking soda

¾ cup butter or margarine
1/8 teaspoon nutmeg
1/8 teaspoon ginger
1/8 teaspoon cloves
½ teaspoon cinnamon
2 8-inch pie crusts

Mix brown sugar, 3 tablespoons flour, sorghum or molasses, beaten egg, and hot water, and bring to a boil. Add baking soda. Let cool. Pour cooled liquid into shells. Combine 3 cups flour, butter or margarine, and spices; mix until it resembles coarse crumbs. Gently put crumbs on top of liquid and bake at 350 degrees for 30 minutes. Makes 2 pies.

SOUR CREAM-RAISIN PIE

1 packed cup raisins
½ cup sugar (or more if
  you like a sweeter pie)
¼ teaspoon salt
½ teaspoon cinnamon
1 cup sour cream

3 eggs, separated
½ teaspoon baking soda
1 baked 8-inch pie crust
2 tablespoons sugar
½ teaspoon cornstarch

Wash, drain, and pat raisins dry. Mix together the raisins, ½ cup sugar, salt, cinnamon, and sour cream. Let boil slowly about 20 minutes. Take off heat and add 3 beaten egg yolks, and cook until the yolks are thick. Remove from heat again and add baking soda. Let cool and pour into the baked pie crust. Beat the egg whites and add sugar and cornstarch (or make a Never-Fail Meringue). Spread on pie and bake in oven at 400 degrees, just long enough to brown meringue. Do not leave—watch constantly, and remove from oven as soon as pie is a beautiful light brown. Makes 1 pie.

ANDERSON HOUSE SPECIAL STRAWBERRY PIE

5 cups fresh strawberries, washed and hulled
½ cup plus 1 tablespoon Cointreau
1 10-inch baked pie crust, cooled
1 8-ounce package cream cheese, softened and whipped

1 cup water
1 cup sugar
3 tablespoons cornstarch
Red food coloring
1 tablespoon butter
1 cup whipping cream (optional)

Soak 4 cups of berries in Cointreau for 45 minutes, turning berries occasionally so all have a Cointreau bath. Spread the pie shell with cream cheese. Drain berries and place in pie shell. Cut up the remaining cup of berries and add to the water; simmer for 5 minutes. Combine sugar and cornstarch, and add to the cooked fruit. Cook over medium heat until the syrup is thick and clear, stirring constantly. Add food coloring for the desired shade, and add butter. Cool to lukewarm before pouring over the berries in shell. Be sure all berries are covered. Chill for 3 hours in coldest part of refrigerator before serving. Serve with whipped cream, if desired. You may fold a little of the Cointreau left over from soaking the berries into the whipped cream. Serves eight.

STRAWBERRY-BANANA PIE

1 8-inch pie crust,
  baked and cooled
1 large banana
1 #2 can (2 cups)
  strawberry pie filling
1 teaspoon grated lemon
  rind

2 egg whites
¼ teaspoon cream of tartar
¼ cup sugar
1 teaspoon grated lemon
  rind (additional)

Slice banana into cooled pastry shell. Combine strawberry pie filling and 1 teaspoon lemon rind and pour over bananas. Beat egg whites and cream of tartar until foamy. Gradually add sugar, a tablespoon at a time, beating until stiff but not dry. Fold in remaining lemon rind. Spread meringue over pie filling, sealing it to the crust all around. Bake in a 350-degree oven for 12 to 15 minutes, or until meringue is golden brown. Serves eight.

TOFFEE CHIFFON PIE

2 envelopes unflavored
  gelatin
½ cup cold water
3 eggs, separated
1½ cups milk
½ cup brown sugar, packed
½ teaspoon salt
1 teaspoon vanilla extract
1 cup (6 ounces) chopped
  Heath English Toffee
  candy bars

¼ cup sugar
1 envelope (2 ounces)
  whipped dessert topping
1 9-inch baked pie crust
  or favorite crumb pie
  crust, chilled

Soften gelatin in cold water. Beat egg yolks slightly. Add 1 cup milk, brown sugar, and salt; stir. Cook over low heat, stirring constantly until mixture coats a spoon. Add softened gelatin; stir until it dissolves. Blend in vanilla and ¾ cup candy bits. Chill until mixture starts to set. Beat egg whites until frothy; add sugar gradually, continuing to beat until stiff and glossy. Fold into candy mixture. Prepare dessert topping as directed on package using remaining ½ cup milk. Fold into candy mixture. Pour into chilled crust. Sprinkle with remaining ¼ cup candy bits, or more if desired. Chill until firm. Serves eight.

Cakes

The first cake ever made in the Anderson House by Grandma Anderson was a towering Sunshine Cake frosted with a delicate lemon frosting that was served at the first noon dinner. It was the first of many cakes that appeared every morning at breakfast and soon the workers at the button factory were stopping by every day on their way to work to buy a piece of fresh cake for their lunch buckets. Other pieces were carefully packed for box lunches for guests traveling by paddle-wheelers on the Mississippi. Since that time many new cakes have been produced and we probably taste every one of them. Some we never make a second time, others become a part of both our regular and party menus and will probably be made forever.

Since our little preserving kitchen makes fruitcakes for sale every year, we include a couple of our favorites, which until now were carefully cherished secrets. We have fun with them. We make them in July, pack them in stone crocks with a gallon of brandy, uncovered in the middle, and seal them until December. When we take them out we decorate them, wrap them, and send them all over the country. Our White Fruitcake flavored with rum is the favorite.

Also included here is our Milky Way Cake—a heavy, dense cake with a superb, light topping. We take it to every family reunion, and so do many of our customers. Our Chocolate Pound Cake is another delight.

Probably the best cake in the book is the Double Chocolate Marshmallow Cake, and its towering splendor is equalled only by the taste. It is a truly great cake. We urge you to try it!

We have stayed away from complicated cakes requiring much time, effort, and expense since we feel this is a family cookbook, and certainly the Anderson House has always been a family inn. We're sure you'll find our recipes fun and easy!

HOT APPLE CAKE WITH CARAMEL RUM SAUCE

1 cup butter (room
  temperature)
1 cup sugar
2 eggs, beaten
1½ cups all-purpose flour
1 teaspoon freshly grated
  nutmeg
1 teaspoon cinnamon

1 teaspoon baking soda
½ teaspoon salt
3 medium apples, cored
  and finely chopped
¾ cup walnuts
1 teaspoon vanilla extract
Vanilla ice cream (optional)
Caramel Rum Sauce (below)

Preheat oven to 350 degrees. Grease a 10-inch pie plate and set aside. Cream butter with sugar in large bowl. Add eggs and beat well. Sift flour, spices, baking soda, and salt. Blend into butter mixture. Add apples, nuts, and vanilla and mix thoroughly. Pour into prepared pie plate. Bake until lightly browned, about 45 minutes. Serve warm, topped with vanilla ice cream and Caramel Rum Sauce. Serves eight to ten.

CARAMEL RUM SAUCE

½ cup sugar
½ cup firmly packed
  brown sugar

½ cup whipping cream
½ cup butter
¼ cup rum

Combine sugars and cream in top of double boiler. Set over gently simmering water and cook 1½ hours, replenishing water in bottom of double boiler as necessary. Add butter and continue cooking 30 minutes. Remove from heat and beat well. Add rum and blend thoroughly. Serve warm over Hot Apple Cake.

BANANA GEM CAKES

½ cup chopped walnuts
1¼ cups sifted cake flour
1 teaspoon baking powder
½ teaspoon salt
¼ teaspoon baking soda
1/8 teaspoon mace
⅓ cup shortening

¾ cup sugar
1 egg
½ teaspoon vanilla extract
¾ cup mashed ripe banana
2 tablespoons milk
Frosting and walnut halves
(optional)

Chop walnuts medium-fine and set aside. Resift flour with baking powder, salt, baking soda, and mace. Cream shortening and sugar together until light and fluffy. Add egg and vanilla; beat until well blended. Add banana and beat until smooth. Blend in about half the flour mixture. Add milk, then remaining flour, mixing to a smooth batter. Stir in walnuts. Spoon into greased and floured gem pans, muffin tins, or individual gelatin molds. Bake at 350 degrees for about 20 to 25 minutes, just until cakes spring back when touched lightly in centers. Let stand 5 minutes, then invert onto wire rack to cool. Serve plain or swirl your favorite homemade or packaged frosting on top of cakes and decorate with a walnut half. Makes 12 to 14 small cakes.

BLUE RIBBON
BLACK WALNUT CAKE

1 cup coconut
⅓ cup ground black walnuts
¼ cup chopped black
    walnuts
2 cups sifted flour
1 teaspoon baking powder
1 teaspoon baking soda
1 teaspoon salt

1½ cups sugar
½ cup shortening
1 teaspoon vanilla extract
1 teaspoon black walnut
    flavoring
2 eggs
1 cup buttermilk
⅓ cup hot strong coffee

Mix coconut and ground and chopped walnuts. Set aside. Sift together flour, baking powder, soda, and salt. Cream the sugar and shortening together, and add the flavorings and eggs, one at a time, beating after each addition. Add the dry ingredients to the creamed mixture, alternately with the buttermilk, beginning and ending with dry ingredients. Blend thoroughly after each addition using low speed on mixer. Stir in the coffee and all but 2 tablespoons of the coconut-nut mixture (reserve remaining portion for topping). Blend thoroughly. Bake in two 8-inch square pans, greased and floured on bottoms only. Bake at 375 degrees for 30 to 35 minutes. Cool on cake rack. Do not frost until entirely cool.

CREAMY COFFEE ICING

**4 cups sifted confectioners'
 sugar
¼ cup butter, softened
1 egg
1 teaspoon black walnut
 flavoring**

**½ teaspoon vanilla extract
1/8 teaspoon salt
2 tablespoons melted butter
2 to 3 tablespoons hot
 strong coffee**

Combine sugar and softened butter, and add the egg. Beat well. Add the flavorings and salt. Add melted butter and coffee and mix until the mixture reaches a spreadable consistency. Spread icing on the cake and garnish with the 2 tablespoons of coconut-nut mixture reserved from the cake recipe. Serves eight.

MAHALA'S BLACK WEDDING CAKE

2 cups light brown sugar
2 cups sifted flour
½ teaspoon salt
2 1-ounce squares bitter
  chocolate
1 cup boiling water

½ cup butter
2 eggs, separated
½ cup buttermilk
1 teaspoon baking soda
1½ teaspoons orange
  extract

Mix brown sugar, flour, and salt together in large bowl. Melt chocolate, water, and butter together, and bring to a boil. Add to flour and sugar mixture. Beat egg yolks with buttermilk. Add orange flavoring and baking soda. Add to chocolate-and-flour mixture. Beat egg whites until stiff and fold in last. Bake in a greased and lightly floured 9 x 13 inch pan. Bake in a 350-degree oven for 30 to 40 minutes. Cool on cake rack. When completely cool, frost with Deluxe Chocolate Icing (see index). Serves twelve.

Note: Mahala was Grandma's sister, and like all Pennsylvania Dutch women, she lived a good life, always cooking, cleaning, and looking for more to do. She made this cake for a cousin who sniffed at pale, white wedding cakes. That day, it was baked in two pans, split, frosted with boiled frosting in between the layers, and then lavishly covered with chocolate and more white frosting swirled around the top in circles. What a cake!

BROWN VELVET CAKE

2 cups flour
1 teaspoon baking soda
¾ teaspoon salt
½ cup shortening
1½ cups firmly packed
  light brown sugar
2 eggs
3 squares (3 ounces)
  unsweetened chocolate,
  melted

1 cup plus 2 tablespoons
  milk
1 teaspoon vanilla extract
Quick Fudge Frosting
  (below)

Preheat oven to 350 degrees. Sift together flour, baking soda, and salt; set aside. Using an electric mixer, beat shortening and sugar in a large bowl. Beat in eggs. Blend until mixture is light and fluffy. Stir in chocolate. In a separate bowl combine milk and vanilla. Alternate milk mixture and dry ingredients to batter, beginning and ending with dry ingredients. After each addition beat until smooth. Pour mixture into 2 greased and floured 9-inch layer cake pans. Bake 25 minutes or until inserted toothpick comes out clean. Cool in pan 10 minutes. Remove from pan and cool thoroughly on rack. Frost with Quick Fudge Frosting.

QUICK FUDGE FROSTING

½ cup granulated sugar
2 tablespoons unsweetened
  cocoa
2 tablespoons butter
¼ cup milk
1 tablespoon light corn
  syrup

1/8 teaspoon salt
½ to ⅔ cups powdered
  sugar
½ teaspoon vanilla extract

In a small heavy saucepan combine sugar and cocoa. Add butter, milk, syrup, and salt. Heat mixture to boiling, stirring frequently. Boil 3 minutes, stirring occasionally. Cool slightly. Beat in powdered sugar and vanilla. Continue beating until thick enough to spread. Spread on cooled cake.

BURNT-SUGAR CHIFFON CAKE

Burnt sugar is another name for caramelized sugar. In making it, a heavy skillet and rapid stirring promote even browning, which should not go past the golden stage. The darker the sugar becomes, the less its sweetening power.

Burnt-Sugar Syrup (below)
2 cups all-purpose flour
1¼ cups sugar
1 tablespoon baking powder
1 teaspoon salt
½ cup oil

7 eggs, separated
¼ cup water
1 teaspoon vanilla extract
½ teaspoon cream of tartar
Burnt-Sugar Frosting (below)

Prepare Burnt-Sugar Syrup. In a small mixing bowl combine flour, sugar, baking powder, and salt. Add oil, egg yolks, water, ½ cup Burnt-Sugar Syrup, and vanilla. Beat at low speed until blended, then slowly increase to medium speed, and beat until very smooth, about 2 minutes. Wash and dry beaters. In large mixing bowl beat egg whites and cream of tartar at high speed until stiff but not dry, just until whites no longer slip when bowl is tilted. Gently but thoroughly fold yolk mixture into whites. Pour into ungreased 10-inch tube pan. Bake in preheated 325-degree oven until top springs back when lightly touched with finger, 1 hour and 10 to 20 minutes. Invert cake in pan on funnel or bottle neck. Cool completely, about 1½ hours. Cut cake in half horizontally and frost between layers, then on top and sides of cake with Burnt-Sugar Frosting. Serves twelve to sixteen.

BURNT-SUGAR SYRUP

¾ cup sugar

1 cup boiling water

In medium saucepan cook sugar, stirring constantly, over medium heat until melted and deep golden brown. Remove from heat. Very slowly pour in boiling water, stirring constantly until blended. Cool.

BURNT-SUGAR FROSTING

1 cup sugar
⅓ cup water
1 tablespoon light corn
 syrup
2 egg whites

1/8 teaspoon cream of
 tartar
1½ tablespoons Burnt-
 Sugar Syrup
1 teaspoon vanilla extract

In medium saucepan combine sugar, water, and corn syrup. Cover and cook over medium heat until boiling rapidly. Uncover. Boil until mixture reaches 240 degrees on candy thermometer, or until a 6- to 8-inch thread forms when mixture is dropped from a spoon. Meanwhile, beat egg whites and cream of tartar at high speed until stiff but not dry, just until whites no longer slip when bowl is tilted. Slowly pour hot sugar mixture in a thin stream into egg whites, beating constantly. Add Burnt-Sugar Syrup and vanilla. Beat at high speed until stiff peaks form and frosting reaches spreadable consistency, about 6 minutes.

Note: Leftover Burnt-Sugar Syrup may be stored in refrigerator.

CARAMEL
UPSIDE-DOWN CAKE

(Very rich — and it makes its own sauce!)

1½ cups sifted all-
   purpose flour
2 teaspoons baking powder
1 teaspoon salt
½ cup butter or margarine
⅔ cup sugar
1 cup milk

½ cup seedless raisins
Grated rind and juice of
   1 orange
Grated rind and juice of
   1 lemon
½ cup light molasses
1¼ cups water

Mix and sift flour, baking powder, and salt. Cream 4 tablespoons of the butter, gradually adding the sugar. Cream until light and fluffy. Add the milk alternately with the flour mixture, beating until smooth after each addition. Stir in the raisins and lemon and orange rinds. Spoon into a well-greased 9-inch square baking pan. Combine the lemon and orange juices with the remaining butter or margarine, the molasses, and the water in a saucepan. Bring to a boil. Remove from heat; pour gently and evenly over batter. Bake at 350 degrees for 45 to 50 minutes. To serve, spoon into dessert dishes, and cover with sauce from the bottom of the baking pan. Serves eight.

CARROT CAKE

2½ cups all-purpose flour
2 teaspoons baking powder
1 teaspoon cinnamon
½ teaspoon salt
¼ teaspoon ginger
¼ teaspoon nutmeg
1 cup butter, softened
2 cups sugar

5 eggs, separated
½ cup water
1½ cups shredded carrots
½ cup finely chopped
   pecans
½ teaspoon vanilla extract
½ teaspoon cream of tartar

Stir together flour, baking powder, cinnamon, salt, ginger, and nutmeg. Set aside. In large mixing bowl beat together butter and sugar at medium speed until light and fluffy. Add egg yolks, one at a time, beating well after each addition. Add ¾ cup flour mixture alternately with ¼ cup water, blending thoroughly after each addition. Repeat with remaining flour and water. Stir in carrots, pecans, and vanilla. Wash and dry beaters. In large mixing bowl beat egg whites and cream of tartar at high speed until stiff but not dry, just until whites no longer slip when bowl is tilted. Gently fold whites into yolk mixture. Pour into greased and floured 10-inch tube pan. Bake in preheated 375-degree oven until wooden pick or cake tester inserted in center comes out clean, about 1½ hours. Cool on wire rack 15 minutes. Remove from pan and cool completely. Makes one 10-inch tube cake or ten to twelve servings.

CHOCOLATE POUND CAKE

(An intensity of chocolate!)

2 cups sifted cake flour
3 cups sugar
1 cup cocoa
3 teaspoons baking powder
1 teaspoon salt

1 cup butter, softened
1½ cups whole milk
3 teaspoons vanilla extract
3 eggs
¼ cup light cream

Sift dry ingredients into mixing bowl. Make a well in the center and add softened butter, milk, and vanilla. Beat at low speed. Scrape bowl and beat at medium speed until mixed, about 8 minutes. Return mixer to low speed, and add eggs, one at a time, beating half a minute after each addition. Add light cream and beat at medium speed for about 2 minutes. Pour batter into a well-greased 10-inch tube pan and bake at 325 degrees for about 1 hour and 40 minutes or until done. Cool cake completely on a cake rack before removing from pan. Do not invert pan. A bundt pan makes a very pretty cake. Dust lightly with powdered sugar if you wish, and if you are a real chocoholic, frost with chocolate glaze. Serves ten.

CHERRY-CHOCOLATE CAKE

CHERRY FILLING

2½ cups (22-ounce can)   2 tablespoons cherry
   cherry pie filling   liqueur (kirsch)
2 tablespoons sugar

Combine pie filling, sugar, and cherry liqueur. Chill several hours.

DARK CHOCOLATE CAKE

1¾ cups all-purpose flour   1 cup buttermilk
2 cups sugar   ½ cup vegetable oil
¾ cup unsweetened cocoa   1 teaspoon vanilla extract
2 teaspoons baking soda   Chocolate Whipped Cream
1 teaspoon baking powder   (see index)
1 teaspoon salt
2 eggs
1 cup strong black coffee,
   or 2 teaspoons instant
   coffee dissolved in 1 cup
   boiling water

Combine flour, sugar, cocoa, baking soda, baking powder, and salt in large mixing bowl. Add eggs, coffee, buttermilk, oil, and vanilla. Beat at medium speed for 2 minutes. (Batter will be thin.) Pour batter into two greased and floured 9-inch cake pans. Bake at 350 degrees for 30 to 35 minutes or until done. Cool completely. To assemble, place one cake layer upside down on serving plate. Spread layer of Cherry Filling. Place remaining cake layer on top. Frost with Chocolate Whipped Cream. Fill center with remaining Cherry Filling. Chill at least 1 hour before serving.

CHOCOLATE-COCONUT CAKE

1 cup flaked coconut
½ cup milk
2 cups sifted cake flour
1 teaspoon baking soda
½ teaspoon salt
1 cup butter
2 cups sugar
2 squares unsweetened
 chocolate, melted and
 cooled

4 egg yolks
1 cup sour cream
1 teaspoon vanilla extract
1 cup chopped pecans
4 egg whites, stiffly beaten
Buttercream Frosting
 (below)

Add milk to coconut and allow to stand until ready to use. Sift flour once, measure, add soda and salt, and sift again. Cream butter and sugar until light and fluffy. Add chocolate and blend. Add egg yolks, one at a time, beating well after each addition. Add dry ingredients alternately with sour cream, beating after each addition until smooth. Add vanilla, nuts, and coconut with milk. Fold in egg whites. Pour into three greased and lightly floured 9-inch layer cake pans and bake in a 350-degree oven for about 30 minutes, or until a cake tester inserted in the center comes out clean. Remove from oven, allow to stand in the pans 5 minutes, then turn out onto wire racks. When completely cooled, spread Buttercream Frosting between the layers and on the top and sides.

BUTTERCREAM FROSTING

½ cup flour
1 cup milk
1 cup butter

1 cup sugar
½ teaspoon vanilla extract

Cook flour and milk together until thick and smooth. Cool. Cream butter and sugar until light and fluffy. Gradually add the cold flour mixture, a tablespoon at a time. Beat until smooth and light. Add vanilla and blend. Refrigerate cake after frosting.

MAGGIE'S CHOCOLATE CAKE

¾ cup shortening
1½ cups sugar
3 eggs, separated
2¼ cups sifted cake flour
3½ teaspoons baking
  powder
½ teaspoon salt
1 cup milk

3 1-ounce squares
  unsweetened chocolate,
  melted and cooled
1 teaspoon vanilla extract
Light Butter Icing (below)
Dark Chocolate Icing
  (below)

Cream shortening and sugar until light and fluffy. Add egg yolks; beat thoroughly. Sift together dry ingredients; add to creamed mixture in thirds alternately with milk, beating after each addition until smooth. Blend in chocolate and vanilla. Beat egg whites until stiff but not dry; fold into batter. Grease two 9 x 9 x 2 inch baking pans, line with waxed paper, and grease again. Turn batter into pans. Bake at 350 degrees for 35 minutes, or until done.

LIGHT BUTTER ICING

½ cup butter
2 cups plus ⅓ cup
  confectioners' sugar
2 egg whites, stiffly beaten

3 tablespoons cocoa
3 tablespoons hot water
  or hot coffee

Cream butter and sugar with electric mixer until mixture resembles coarse meal. Add egg whites; beat until blended. Mix cocoa and water or coffee until smooth; gradually beat into first mixture. Set aside.

DARK CHOCOLATE ICING

¼ cup butter
2 1-ounce squares
  unsweetened chocolate
1½ cups confectioners'
  sugar

2 to 3 tablespoons
  half-and-half

Melt butter and chocolate in top of double boiler. Stir in sugar; cook for 10 minutes. Remove from heat. Add half-and-half; beat until icing is smooth and glossy. Split cake layers horizontally. Spread generous layers of light icing between layers. Spread dark icing on top and sides of cake. Decorate with the remaining light icing, using a pastry tube. Serves twelve to sixteen.

CRANBERRY SPICE CAKE

½ cup shortening
1 cup sugar
1 egg, beaten
1 cup raisins
½ cup nuts
1¾ cups sifted all-purpose
  flour
¼ teaspoon salt

1 teaspoon baking soda
1 teaspoon baking powder
1 teaspoon cinnamon
½ teaspoon cloves
1 cup cranberry sauce
  (jellied or whole)
Cranberry-Cream Cheese
  Frosting (below)

Cream shortening and sugar, and add egg. Stir in raisins and nuts. Combine dry ingredients and sift; add to first mixture. Stir in cranberry sauce. Bake at 350 degrees for about 1 hour in greased tube pan, or for 30 to 40 minutes in greased 8-inch layer cake pans. Ice with Cranberry-Cream Cheese Frosting. Makes 1 cake.

CRANBERRY-CREAM CHEESE FROSTING

1 3-ounce package cream
  cheese
4 tablespoons cranberry
  sauce (jellied or whole)

1/8 teaspoon salt
1 pound confectioners'
  sugar

Soften cream cheese with cranberry sauce. Add salt. Gradually add sugar, beating until creamy.

DOUBLE-CHOCOLATE MARSHMALLOW CAKE
(Anderson House Specialty)

4 1-ounce squares
   chocolate, melted
¼ cup butter, melted
2 cups sugar
2 teaspoons baking soda
2 cups rich milk
4 egg whites, stiffly beaten

¼ teaspoon cream of tartar
3 cups sifted flour
¼ teaspoon salt
2 teaspoons vanilla extract
Creamy White Frosting
   (below)

Combine the chocolate and butter and add the sugar. Dissolve the soda in the milk. Beat egg whites with cream of tartar until stiff; set aside. Add salt to flour. Then add the dry ingredients and the milk alternately to the chocolate mixture, beating until smooth. Add the vanilla; beat well. Fold in the egg whites. Pour the batter into three greased 9-inch layer pans. Bake in a moderate oven, 350 degrees, for 20 to 25 minutes. When cool, frost with Creamy White Frosting. You may swirl chocolate over the frosting after it has been allowed to set. For the chocolate drip, melt 2 squares of chocolate with 2 teaspoons of butter.

CREAMY WHITE FROSTING

½ cup sugar
¼ cup egg whites (2 or 3)

1½ teaspoons corn syrup
Pinch cream of tartar

Place all the ingredients in the top of a double boiler. Heat over boiling water until mixture reaches 150 degrees or until it is hot to the touch, about six minutes. Remove from the heat and pour into a bowl. Beat with a rotary beater or in an electric mixer until the icing is of proper consistency. Ices one layer cake. If you wish, you can double frosting recipe and use an inch of frosting between layers. The result is a spectacular, high cake.

CHOCOLATE-RASPBERRY CAKE SUPREME

1 6-ounce package (1 cup)
   semi-sweet real
   chocolate morsels
½ cup butter, softened
½ cup sugar
6 eggs, separated

¾ cup unsifted flour
½ tablespoon cream of
   tartar
3 tablespoons brandy
¾ cup raspberry jam
Chocolate Glaze (below)

Preheat oven to 325 degrees. Melt over hot (not boiling) water the semi-sweet chocolate morsels; set aside. In large bowl, combine butter and sugar; beat until creamy. Blend in melted chocolate. Add egg yolks, one at a time, beating well after each addition. Gradually add flour and beat until smooth; set aside. In small bowl, combine egg whites and cream of tartar. Beat until stiff (not dry) peaks form. Gently fold beaten whites into chocolate batter. Pour evenly into two well-greased 8-inch round cake pans. Bake at 325 degrees for 20 to 25 minutes. Loosen edges of cake from pan. Remove immediately; cool completely. Slice each cake layer in half horizontally. Brush 1 tablespoon brandy on one layer. Spread ¼ cup raspberry jam over brandy layer. Place second layer on top. Repeat procedure with second and third layers. Top with plain layer. Spread top and sides of cake with Chocolate Glaze. Makes 1 layer cake.

CHOCOLATE GLAZE

1 6-ounce package semi-
   sweet real chocolate
   morsels

½ cup evaporated milk
Dash salt
1 teaspoon brandy

In small saucepan, combine evaporated milk and salt. Bring just to a boil over moderate heat. Remove from heat. Add chocolate morsels and brandy; stir until morsels melt and mixture is smooth. Makes 1 cup glaze.

COFFEE-RASPBERRY
RIBBON CAKE

Gold and chocolate cake
  layers (below)
½ cup raspberry jam
Coffee-Cream Filling
  (below)

Whipped cream and
  chocolate shavings
  (garnish)

Carefully split each cake layer in half crosswise to make a total of 4 layers. Place 1 gold cake layer on serving plate, spread with half the raspberry jam, then with a third of the coffee-cream filling. Follow with a chocolate layer and spread with a third of the coffee-cream filling. Follow with the second gold cake layer, the remaining jam, and remaining coffee-cream filling. Top with second chocolate layer. Whip ½ cup whipping cream and force through a decorating tube to make a lattice pattern on surface. Scatter shaved chocolate over all. Makes 1 cake.

GOLD CAKE LAYER

1¼ cups sifted cake flour
¾ cup sugar
½ teaspoon salt
1½ teaspoons baking
  powder

¼ cup butter or margarine,
  softened
⅔ cup milk
3 egg yolks
½ teaspoon vanilla extract

Sift flour, measure, and sift again with sugar, salt, and baking powder. Add butter or margarine and ⅓ cup milk, and beat 2 minutes. Add egg yolks, vanilla, and remaining milk and beat 2 minutes longer. Turn batter into a well-greased and floured 9-inch layer cake pan. Bake at 350 degrees for 35 to 40 minutes or until cake tests done. Cool in pan 10 minutes. Remove to wire rack to finish cooling.

CHOCOLATE CAKE LAYER

¼ cup sifted unsweetened
   cocoa
½ cup boiling water
1¼ cups sifted cake flour
¼ teaspoon baking soda
½ teaspoon baking powder
¼ teaspoon salt

¼ cup butter or margarine,
   softened
1 cup sugar
½ teaspoon vanilla extract
¼ cup buttermilk
3 egg whites

Combine cocoa and boiling water and mix well. Cool. Sift flour, measure, and sift again with baking soda, baking powder, and salt. Beat butter, sugar, and vanilla until light and fluffy. Blend in flour mixture alternately with combined buttermilk and cocoa mixture. Beat egg whites until stiff but not dry; fold through batter gently but thoroughly until no white flecks show. Turn batter into well-greased and floured 9-inch layer pan. Bake at 350 degrees for 25 to 30 minutes or until cake tests done. Cool in pan 10 minutes. Remove to wire rack to finish cooling.

COFFEE-CREAM FILLING

1½ cups whipping cream
⅓ cup sugar

3 tablespoons instant
   coffee granules

Combine all ingredients and chill thoroughly. When chilled, whip until stiff.

DAFFODIL CAKE

1 cup sifted cake flour
1¼ cups sugar
12 egg whites
1½ teaspoons cream of
tartar
½ teaspoon salt

1½ teaspoons vanilla
extract
½ teaspoon almond extract
6 egg yolks
2 teaspoons grated orange
rind

Sift together flour and ¾ cup sugar twice. Set aside. In large mixing bowl beat egg whites, cream of tartar, and salt at high speed until foamy. Add remaining ½ cup sugar, 1 tablespoon at a time, beating constantly until sugar is dissolved and whites are glossy and stand in soft peaks. Beat in vanilla and almond extracts. Sift ⅓ cup flour mixture over egg whites and gently fold in just until flour disappears. Repeat, folding in remaining flour mixture ⅓ cup at a time. Set aside. In small mixing bowl beat egg yolks and orange rind at high speed until thick and lemon-colored, about 5 minutes. Fold 1 cup egg white mixture into yolks. Spoon half of remaining egg white mixture into ungreased 10-inch tube pan. Alternately spoon tablespoons of yellow and white batter over batter in pan. Spoon remaining white batter over top. Gently cut through batter with narrow spatula or knife, swirling to marble. Bake in preheated 375-degree oven until top springs back when touched lightly with finger, 30 to 35 minutes. Invert cake in pan on funnel or bottleneck. Cool completely, about 1½ hours. Loosen cake from pan with narrow spatula or knife, and gently shake onto serving plate. Serve plain or frosted. Makes one 10-inch tube cake or ten to twelve servings.

DOUBLE DATE CAKE

1 cup dates
1 cup boiling water
1 tablespoon margarine
1 teaspoon baking soda
1 cup sugar
1 egg

1½ cups sifted all-purpose
   flour
½ cup finely chopped
   walnuts
Topping (below)

Pour water over dates; add margarine and baking soda. Cool. Mix sugar and unbeaten egg; beat thoroughly. Add flour; mix until mixture resembles coarse meal. Stir in date mixture and nuts. (Batter is thin.) Turn into a greased 11 x 7 x 2 inch pan. Bake at 375 degrees for 25 minutes. Cool. Spread topping on cake. Serves twelve to sixteen.

TOPPING

1½ cups chopped dates
1½ cups water

⅔ cup sugar
½ cup chopped walnuts

Cook ingredients in a heavy pan over low heat, stirring frequently, for 15 minutes. (Watch carefully to avoid scorching.) Cool.

DOUBLE-CHOCOLATE
FRUIT CAKE

1 cup candied cherries
1 cup raisins
2 cups walnuts
⅔ cup California brandy
1 cup butter
1⅓ cups sugar
3 ounces semi-sweet
   baking chocolate, melted
   and cooled

4 eggs
1½ teaspoons vanilla
   extract
2 cups flour
1 tablespoon cinnamon
1 teaspoon salt
1 cup chocolate morsels
Brandied Hard Sauce
   (below)

Marinate cherries, raisins, and nuts in brandy at least 2 hours or over-night. Cream butter and sugar; mix in chocolate and eggs, one at a time. Blend in vanilla. Sift together flour, cinnamon, and salt; mix into chocolate mixture. Fold in marinated fruit, nuts, and chocolate morsels. Pour into two round greased and papered 8-inch pans. Bake at 300 degrees for 1 hour and 10 minutes. Serve warm or at room temperature, topping with Brandied Hard Sauce. Makes 2 cakes. Each cake will serve eight.

BRANDIED HARD SAUCE

5 tablespoons butter
1 cup powdered sugar

3 tablespoons California
brandy

Cream butter thoroughly; beat in sugar gradually. Mix in brandy. Chill. Makes 1 cup sauce.

Note: We suggest you double sauce recipe.

FUDGE CAKE WITH FLUFFY PEPPERMINT ICING

2 1-ounce squares bitter chocolate
¼ cup butter
½ cup water
1 cup sugar
1 cup flour
½ teaspoon salt

½ teaspoon baking powder
1 egg
½ teaspoon baking soda
¼ cup buttermilk
1 teaspoon vanilla extract
Peppermint Icing (below)

Break chocolate into small pieces; set aside. Melt butter in top of double boiler, and add chocolate. When chocolate is melted, add water and sugar. Stir until well blended. Remove from heat and allow to cool. Sift flour, then add salt and baking powder. When chocolate mixture is cool, add unbeaten egg, and mix well. Then add sifted dry ingredients. Blend well. Dissolve soda in buttermilk and add to batter. Add vanilla. Pour into an 8-inch square pan, greased and lined with waxed paper. Bake in 350-degree oven for 30 to 35 minutes. When done, invert on wire rack and spread with Peppermint Icing.

PEPPERMINT ICING

1½ cups confectioners' sugar
¼ cup water

2 egg whites
2 drops peppermint extract

Boil sugar and water 10 minutes or until clear. Pour slowly over unbeaten egg whites, beating constantly. When mixture is stiff and holds shape (about 6 minutes with electric beater, 10 by hand), add peppermint extract. Ice cake.

FUDGE UPSIDE-DOWN CAKE

2 cups all-purpose flour
4 teaspoons baking powder
Dash salt
2 tablespoons plus ⅔ cup
cocoa
2½ cups sugar
¼ cup butter, softened

1 cup whole milk
½ cup chopped walnuts
or pecans
1 cup firmly packed
brown sugar
3 cups boiling water

Preheat oven to 350 degrees. Sift together the flour, baking powder, salt, and 2 tablespoons of cocoa. Cream 1½ cups of the sugar and butter until light and fluffy. Add the milk, then add sifted ingredients. Mix well, and add the chopped nuts. Spread evenly in a greased 9 x 13 inch pan. Combine the remaining cup of sugar, brown sugar, and ⅔ cup cocoa. Spread this evenly over the mixture in the pan and slowly pour the boiling water over all. Bake 40 minutes. Remove from the oven and place on cake rack. You may serve this warm with whipped topping or serve when cool. In dishing the dessert, be sure to cut down to the very bottom of the pan because the rich, fudge-like topping is there. Serve upside down or in squares with the whipped topping. Serves eight.

Note: We first made this dessert in high school home economics class, and it has always been one of our most popular desserts. Through the years, we have made some changes. Now and then we add a teaspoon of instant coffee to the boiling water for a mocha taste.

LAYERED LACE AND VELVET CAKE

1 cup butter
1 cup sugar
⅓ cup California brandy
⅔ cup milk
4 eggs, beaten

3¼ cups flour
1 teaspoon baking powder
1 teaspoon cinnamon
1 teaspoon allspice
2½ cups raisins

Cream butter and sugar. Combine brandy, milk, and eggs. Add alternately with sifted flour and baking powder to cream mixture. Spoon half of batter into two of four greased and floured 8-inch cake pans. Add spices and raisins to remaining batter; spoon into remaining pans. Bake all layers at 350 degrees for 30 to 35 minutes until done. Cool 10 minutes; remove and cool. Spread filling between layers and on top of cake, alternating light and dark layers. Serves sixteen to twenty.

FILLING

1 lemon and 1 orange,
  unpeeled, seeded, and
  chopped fine in food
  processor
1 cup sugar
1 cup flaked coconut

⅓ cup California brandy
½ cup water
2 tablespoons cornstarch
1 8¼-ounce can crushed
  pineapple, drained

To prepare filling, combine ingredients in saucepan. Cook over medium heat, stirring until mixture boils. Lower heat and simmer 15 minutes. Cool.

LEMON VELVET CAKE WITH PEACH GLAZE

1 lemon cake mix (without pudding)
1 small package instant lemon pudding
4 eggs
¾ cup oil
1 cup fresh orange juice
½ cup butter
¾ cup peach brandy
1 12-ounce jar peach preserves
¼ cup real lemon juice

Mix together cake mix, pudding mix, eggs, oil, and ½ cup orange juice. Grease an angel-food pan or bundt pan. Pour mixture in and bake 45 to 55 minutes at 350 degrees. Several minutes before the cake is due to come out of the oven, melt butter, last ½ cup orange juice, and peach brandy. Remove cake from oven, and place on wire cake rack. Pierce cake all over and pour the brandy mixture over at once. Melt preserves with lemon juice, and when cake has cooled, brush glaze over the top. If you are serving cake intact, we suggest you fill center with sweetened whipped cream, pre-slice it, and have your guests serve themselves with whipped cream over the top. This is definitely a special occasion cake and can be handled by beginners very easily. Serves twelve.

MILKY WAY CAKE

6 Milky Way bars
1 cup butter
2 cups sugar
4 extra large eggs
1 teaspoon vanilla extract
2½ cups pastry flour
½ teaspoon baking soda
1¼ cups buttermilk
1 cup chopped pecans

In a medium saucepan combine candy and ½ cup of the butter. Melt, stirring until smooth. In a large bowl, cream remaining ½ cup butter and sugar. Add eggs, one at a time, beating well after each addition. Continue beating until light and fluffy, about 5 minutes. Sift flour and combine with baking soda. Add alternately with buttermilk to batter. Beat in vanilla and melted candy until well mixed, about 5 minutes. Fold in nuts. Pour into greased bundt pan. Bake at 350 degrees for 1 hour and 20 minutes. Remove from oven and place on a cake rack. Allow to set for 10 minutes. Remove to cake plate. It will take a long time to cool properly before frosting, but it is well worth the wait. Serves twelve.

Note: This is a somewhat heavy, dense cake. It will burn easily in your oven. We suggest placing the pan on a cookie sheet and baking on the highest rack. Watch it carefully. Ovens differ and in some the cake will be done before the time is up. Frost with a doubled recipe of Deluxe Chocolate Icing (see index).

QUEEN OF CAKES

½ cup cocoa
½ cup boiling water
¾ cup buttermilk
1 tablespoon cider vinegar
1 teaspoon vanilla extract
2 cups unsifted flour
1 teaspoon baking powder

1 teaspoon salt
8 tablespoons butter,
  softened
2 cups dark brown sugar
2 eggs
Filling (below)
Frosting (below)

Preheat oven to 350 degrees. Lightly butter and flour bottom and sides of two 8-inch layer cake pans. Mix cocoa and boiling water to make a paste in a small bowl. Cool to lukewarm, then stir in buttermilk, vinegar, and vanilla. Combine the flour, baking soda, and salt, and sift them together into a small bowl. In a larger bowl, cream butter and dark brown sugar until mixture is light and fluffy. Beat in eggs, one at a time. Add about 1 cup of flour mixture, and when mixed beat in ½ cup cocoa mixture. Add remaining flour and beat in the rest of cocoa mixture. Pour batter into pans and bake about 45 minutes or until an inserted toothpick comes out clean. Bake in center of oven. Remove, cool on cake rack, and gently remove from pan. Cover with filling when cool. Cover filling and sides with fluffy frosting. Serves ten.

ORANGE GÉNOISE CAKE

6 eggs (room temperature)	1 cup sugar
2 teaspoons grated orange rind	1 cup sifted cake flour
1 teaspoon orange extract	¼ cup butter, melted

Preheat the oven to 350 degrees. Warm mixing bowl by running hot water into it, then drying thoroughly. Beat the eggs, orange rind, and extract in the warm bowl until fluffy. Slowly add the sugar, about 2 tablespoons at a time, beating well after each addition at the highest speed of the mixer. When thoroughly beaten, the egg mixture should stand in stiff peaks. Divide the flour into 6 portions and sift over the egg mixture, a portion at a time. After each addition, fold the flour in gently with a rubber spatula. Cool the melted butter to lukewarm. Fold the butter gently, a teaspoon at a time, into the cake mixture. Turn the batter into two 9-inch cake pans that have been greased, lined with waxed paper, and greased again. Bake for 30 to 35 minutes or until done. When done, the cake will spring back when touched lightly with finger. Turn cake out onto cooling rack and remove paper. Cool.

FILLING

1 cup whipping or heavy cream	2 tablespoons sugar
2 teaspoons grated orange rind	

Whip the cream until stiff. Fold in orange rind and sugar. Makes 3 cups.

GLAZE

1 8-ounce can mandarin orange sections	1 cup orange drink
	1 tablespoon cornstarch

Drain the mandarin orange sections. Combine the orange drink and cornstarch in a small saucepan. Place over medium heat; cook and stir until the sauce is clear and thickened. To assemble cake, cut each layer in two horizontally. Spread each with the filling. Garnish top layer with orange sections and pour glaze over top and sides of cake. Makes 1 cake.

FILLING

1 5.3-ounce can evaporated milk	**1 cup dates, chopped**
¾ cup sugar	**1 teaspoon vanilla extract**
	1 cup nuts, chopped

Combine milk, sugar, and dates. Cook over medium heat about 10 minutes until thick. Remove from heat, and add vanilla and nuts. Cool.

FROSTING

6 ounces chocolate chips   **½ cup sour cream**

Melt chocolate chips, fold in sour cream, and let stand for 5 minutes until spreadable.

STRAWBERRIES IN THE SNOW

(A delightful, light dessert)

1 package lemon cake mix
1⅓ cups orange juice
4 egg yolks
1½ teaspoons grated
  orange or lemon rind
4 egg whites
¼ teaspoon cream of tartar
1¼ cups sugar

1 16-ounce package
  individually frozen
  strawberries, or 1 quart
  fresh strawberries
2 cups whipping cream,
  whipped
Strawberry Syrup (below)

Combine the first four ingredients. Beat about 5 minutes in electric mixer. Pour into two greased, floured 9-inch cake pans. Beat egg whites with cream of tartar until they form a soft peak. Gradually add 1 cup of sugar, and beat until the egg whites form a stiff peak. Divide the meringue into two equal parts and spread carefully over the batter. Bake at 350 degrees for 40 minutes. Cool on a cake rack. Remove from pans, being careful to run a knife around the cake several times as the meringue will have spread over the sides. This should be broken off and discarded. Turn the cake meringue side up carefully onto the plate from which it will be served. Mash 1 cup of berries, add ¼ cup sugar, and fold gently into whipped cream. Frost the bottom layer about 1 inch high with whipped cream and berries. Gently place the second layer on top of this. Frost the sides and top of the cake. Take half of the remaining berries and slice or place whole over the top of the cake. (Reserve remaining berries for Strawberry Syrup.)

STRAWBERRY SYRUP

Reserved strawberries
  (above)

¾ cup sugar
¾ cup water

Place the remaining berries in a bowl with sugar and water. Bring to a boil. Strawberries will disintegrate in the liquid. Boil about 10 minutes or until thickened drops from the spoon indicate syrup has formed.

Remove from heat. Cool. When completely cool, pour slowly around the sides of the cake on top so that it will drizzle slowly down the sides. Pour balance over the top. We place the cake in our freezer after it is frosted and before we pour the strawberry syrup over the top.

RUM CAKE

½ cup butter, softened
½ cup shortening
2 cups sugar
4 eggs
3 cups unsifted self-rising
   cake flour

1 cup buttermilk
3 teaspoons rum extract
2 teaspoons vanilla extract

GLAZE

1 cup sugar
½ cup water

2 teaspoons rum extract
1 teaspoon vanilla extract

Preheat oven to 325 degrees. Grease and flour a 10-inch tube pan. In a large bowl, with electric mixer at medium speed, beat butter, shortening, and 2 cups sugar until light and fluffy. Beat in the 4 eggs, one at a time. With rubber scraper or wooden spoon, stir in flour (in fourths) alternately with buttermilk (in thirds), beginning and ending with flour. Stir in 3 teaspoons rum extract and 2 teaspoons vanilla just to combine. Turn into prepared pan. Bake 1 hour and 20 minutes, or until cake tester inserted near center comes out clean. Cool in pan on wire rack 15 minutes. Meanwhile, make glaze: in small saucepan, combine sugar and water; bring to boiling, stirring until sugar is dissolved. Remove from heat; add extracts. Cool slightly. Remove cake from pan. Brush top with glaze. Cool thoroughly on wire rack. Serves ten to twelve.

KATIE'S TOP-SECRET CAKE

⅔ cup butter
1¼ cups sugar
2 eggs
½ fresh cake yeast
¾ cup lukewarm water
2 cups sifted cake flour
⅔ cup ground chocolate

1 teaspoon cinnamon
¼ teaspoon cloves
½ teaspoon salt
⅔ cup coarsely chopped
   nuts
1 teaspoon baking soda
1 tablespoon hot water

Cream butter and sugar until light and fluffy. Add eggs to one side of mixing bowl and beat well; stir into creamed mixture. Dissolve yeast in lukewarm milk. Sift together flour, chocolate, spices, and salt. Add alternately to batter with milk, beating well after each addition. Stir in nuts. Cover bowl, let sit in cool place overnight. In morning, combine baking soda and hot water and stir into batter. Pour into a greased and floured 8-inch square pan and bake at 350 for 30 minutes. Cool on rack. Frost with fluffy white frosting.

IDA'S WHITE FRUIT CAKE

½ pound sugar
1 cup butter
6 eggs, well beaten
1 cup plus 2 tablespoons
   flour
¼ teaspoon baking powder
¼ teaspoon nutmeg
½ pound preserved citron

½ pound candied cherries
½ pound candied pineapple
3 ounces candied orange
   rind
½ pound blanched almonds
¼ pound pecans
½ pound white raisins
1 cup chopped coconut

Cream sugar, butter, and eggs alternately with the sifted dry ingredients. Dust chopped fruit with flour, and add to the batter. Add nuts and coconut. Grease an angel-food pan. Cut butcher's paper to fit bottom and sides. Line pan with paper, then grease paper. (This procedure is necessary to avoid burning fruit.) Pour batter. Bake 2 to 3 hours in 300-degree oven.

GRANDMA ANDERSON'S
SUNSHINE CAKE

1 cup sifted cake flour
1¼ cups sugar
4 egg yolks, beaten
8 egg whites

⅓ teaspoon cream of tartar
½ teaspoon salt
1 teaspoon vanilla
Lemon Frosting (below)

Sift the flour three times after measuring. Sift the sugar five times. Beat the egg yolks until thick and lemon-colored. Whip the egg whites to a foam and add the cream of tartar, whipping until stiff. Fold the sugar into the egg whites gradually. Add the salt and vanilla and then fold in the egg yolks. Next lightly fold in the flour. Bake in an ungreased 9-inch tube pan in a moderate oven, 350 degrees, for about 45 minutes. Place a small pan of water in the oven with the cake. Cover with Lemon Frosting.

LEMON FROSTING

3½ cups powdered sugar
¼ cup melted butter
2 tablespoons heavy cream

¼ cup lemon juice
Grated rind of 1 lemon

Combine 2 cups of the sugar, the butter, and the cream and beat. Then add the lemon juice. When smooth, add the remaining cup and a half of the sugar, or more, until it reaches spreading consistency. Add the grated lemon rind or sprinkle the rind on top of the frosted cake. Frosts one layer cake.

Icings
and Toppings

I have never forgotten Grandma Anderson the day the clerk came screeching into her kitchen and yelled hysterically, "There are two buses out in front with forty-five people in each bus. Something is broken in one bus, and the part won't be delivered until almost midnight. They want dinner right now!"

Ninety unexpected persons might not be a cause for concern in a larger town but our little village had a population of less than two thousand at the time. Furthermore, the Anderson House is small by some standards.

Grandma Anderson was a very cool lady. She served the guests homemade tomato cream soup, chicken and dumplings, mashed potatoes, carrots julienne in a fruit glaze, wilted lettuce salad, and bread pudding. The latter was a delight topped with a bourbon sauce served hot out of the saucepan with a dollop of thick whipped country cream. The entire meal was great, but that dessert sent people scrambling for the recipe. It taught me how important toppings and sauces can be in turning a simple dish into something impossible to forget.

For your own memorable desserts, try any one of our icings or toppings. We think our recipe for Elegant Butterscotch Sauce is the best we have ever encountered. Our Perfect Chocolate Fudge Sauce is equally good. Fresh Strawberry Sauce served over strawberry ice cream in a strawberry meringue is very festive; we serve it at every one of our New Year's Day buffets.

Although toppings and icings don't require much skill or preparation time, they can easily be the key to a successful meal. So next time you need a special touch, turn to this section.

BROWN SUGAR FROSTING

⅔ cup firmly packed dark
  brown sugar
¼ teaspoon salt
⅓ cup water

1 pound confectioners'
  sugar
¼ cup butter or margarine,
  softened

In a 1½-quart saucepan over high heat stir together the brown sugar, salt, and water until mixture comes to a full rolling boil; remove from heat and cool until bottom of pan feels lukewarm, about 10 minutes. In a medium mixing bowl stir the syrup into the confectioners' sugar; add butter and beat until soft and smooth. Will frost a two-layer cake.

BUTTERCREAM ICING

½ cup butter
4 egg yolks
1 teaspoon vanilla extract
½ cup cream

½ teaspoon salt
5½ cups confectioners'
  sugar

Place butter and eggs in a bowl. Beat until light and fluffy. Add vanilla, cream, and salt. Beat until well blended, stopping now and then to scrape bowl. Add one-third of confectioners' sugar and beat until combined. Continue adding sugar until frosting reaches the proper consistency, about 2 to 3 minutes. Icing should be thick enough to hold its shape when a spoonful is placed on cake. Will frost three 8-inch layers amply.

NEVER-FAIL CARAMEL
CHIFFON FROSTING

2 cups light brown sugar
1 cup melted and cooled
butter

1 cup whipping cream
Pinch salt

Combine sugar, butter, cream, and salt. Mix together with wooden spoon. Place in blender, and blend until it thickens. Remove from blender and frost a 13 x 9 cake or two-layer cake. Sprinkle grated chocolate over the top or swirl three tablespoons of chocolate syrup through the frosting if you are frosting a chocolate cake.

CARAMEL FILLING

2 cups brown sugar
½ cup light cream
¼ cup butter

¼ teaspoon salt
1 cup confectioners' sugar

Mix the first four ingredients. Boil two minutes. Add confectioners' sugar. Beat until thick enough to spread. If too hard, add a little cream to soften mixture.

DELUXE CHOCOLATE ICING

This is Aunt Belle's chocolate icing. Belle was a former Fannie Farmer cooking school pupil, and she used this on everything—so do we!

⅓ cup butter, softened
1½ cups powdered sugar
1 teaspoon vanilla extract

1 egg, unbeaten
2 1-ounce squares
chocolate, melted

Combine all ingredients and beat until smooth and of proper consistency for spreading. Ices one two-layer cake. Double the recipe for three layers and filling.

CHOCOLATE WHIPPED CREAM

1½ pints whipping cream **6 tablespoons cocoa**
6 tablespoons sugar **1/8 teaspoon salt**

Whip cream, add sugar, cocoa, and salt. Place in refrigerator for 1 hour or more. Remove from refrigerator and whip mixture again. Will frost one angel food or a two-layer cake.

NEVER-FAIL DELICATE
WHITE FROSTING
(From Grandma Anderson's
Primer for Brides)

2 cups sugar **½ cup salt**
⅔ cup water **4 egg whites, unbeaten**
½ teaspoon cream of tartar **1 teaspoon vanilla extract**

Combine all ingredients except egg whites and vanilla and place over medium heat. Stir constantly until the sugar dissolves. After it comes to a rolling boil, add very slowly to the unbeaten egg whites in mixing bowl. As you beat, the volume will increase until finally it stands in stiff peaks. Add the vanilla and continue beating for a few seconds. This will frost a three-layer cake. If you are baking a two-layer cake we suggest that you spread the frosting one inch thick between layers and the same amount on top. This will make your cake look much higher than a normal two-layer cake.

KAHLUA FROSTING

5 1-ounce squares
  unsweetened chocolate
3 tablespoons hot milk
1½ cups powdered sugar
2 eggs

½ cup sweet butter,
  softened
2 tablespoons Kahlua
Pinch salt
1½ teaspoons cocoa

Melt chocolate over hot water. Add 3 tablespoons of hot milk and powdered sugar, and stir until just barely mixed. Add eggs, beating with a spoon after each addition until smooth. Flavor with Kahlua and salt. Cool, stirring occasionally. Spread on sides and top of cake, and sprinkle top with cocoa in a shaker to ensure even distribution. Will frost a two-layer cake.

NO-COOK
MARSHMALLOW FROSTING

¼ teaspoon salt
2 egg whites
¼ cup sugar

¾ cup light corn syrup
1½ teaspoons vanilla
  extract

Beat together the salt and egg whites until frothy. Gradually add the sugar and beat until smooth and glossy. Slowly beat in the syrup and continue beating until peaks form. Fold in vanilla. Will frost a two-layer cake or a 13 x 9 inch cake.

PEPPERMINT ICING

1½ cups confectioners'
  sugar
¼ cup water

2 egg whites
2 drops peppermint extract

Boil sugar and water 10 minutes until clear. Pour slowly over unbeaten egg whites, beating constantly. When mixture is stiff and holds shape (about 6 minutes with electric mixer, 10 by hand), add peppermint extract. Will frost a two-layer or 9 x 13 inch cake.

SOUR CREAM TOPPING

1½ cups sour cream
2 tablespoons honey
1/8 teaspoon nutmeg

2 tablespoons light brown
  sugar

Combine all ingredients in small bowl; blend thoroughly. Serve the sauce at room temperature. Good with fruit. Makes 1⅔ cups.

BING CHERRY SAUCE

⅔ cup sugar
3 tablespoons flour
Pinch salt
2 tablespoons lemon juice
1½ cups cherry juice and
  water

2 cups cherries
4 tablespoons butter
¼ cup rum

Blend sugar, flour, salt, lemon juice, and cherry juice. Add cherries. Cook over medium heat until thick, about 10 to 15 minutes. Remove from heat and add butter and rum.

BLUEBERRY SAUCE

⅔ cup sugar
3 tablespoons flour
Pinch salt
2 tablespoons lemon juice

2 cups hot water
2 cups blueberries
4 teaspoons sweet butter
¼ cup rum

Combine sugar, flour, salt, and lemon juice with hot water, and cook over medium heat until mixture thickens, about 10 to 15 minutes. Add berries, and remove from heat. Add butter and rum.

PERFECT CHOCOLATE
FUDGE SAUCE

(Wickedly decadent!)

1¾ cups cocoa
2 cups sugar
1 cup whole milk
¾ cup light corn syrup

2 cups whipping cream
¼ teaspoon salt
½ tablespoon vanilla
  extract

Mix cocoa, sugar, and milk together. Place in medium saucepan, and heat until barely warm. Then add remaining ingredients and cook in double boiler until thick. Makes about 1 quart of sauce.

Note: We use this in our ice cream parlor, on steamed puddings, desserts, tortes. We swirl it in frosting and do all manner of things with it. We are chocoholics at the Anderson House!

ELEGANT
BUTTERSCOTCH SAUCE

1¾ cups light corn syrup
2 cups sugar
1 cup butter (no substitutes)

2 cups cream
1 teaspoon vanilla extract

Cook syrup, sugar, butter, and 1 cup of the cream together until it reaches the soft-ball stage. Add the remaining cup of cream and cook until the candy thermometer reads 218 degrees. Remove from the heat, and add vanilla. Serve hot or cold. Makes about 3 cups.

TUTTI-FRUTTI
SUNDAE SAUCE

1 cup sugar
1 cup brandy
1 cup apple juice

1 cup cubed fresh pineapple
1 cup cubed fresh pears
1 cup cubed fresh peaches

Mix sugar, brandy, and apple juice in blender. Remove, add fruits. Place in glass jar in refrigerator for several days. Serve on ice cream, bread puddings, or other desserts. Makes 3 pints.

Note: You may substitute other fruits.

CINNAMON BUTTER

1½ cups butter, softened
1 teaspoon cinnamon

6 teaspoons powdered
sugar

Mix well, transfer to blender, and beat until smooth and creamy. We serve it with hot biscuits.

RUM-RAISIN SAUCE

1 cup raisins
1 cup brown sugar
1 tablespoon cider vinegar
1 tablespoon flour
½ cup water, or ¼ cup dry
  sherry and ¼ cup water

Dash salt
1 teaspoon rum
2 tablespoons butter

Into a 3-cup heavy saucepan, put raisins and brown sugar. Mix vinegar, flour, and liquid and add to pan. Cook over medium heat, stirring constantly, until sauce begins to thicken. Add salt and rum, and cook for 1 minute. Remove from heat and stir in butter. Serve hot. Makes 2 cups.

STRAWBERRY SAUCE

1 12-ounce package frozen
  strawberries, thawed

2 teaspoons cornstarch
1 teaspoon lemon juice

Drain strawberries, reserving liquid. In medium saucepan, combine 1 tablespoon strawberry liquid and the cornstarch, then stir until smooth. Add remaining ingredients; bring to a boil, stirring. Sauce will be slightly thickened and translucent. Serve the sauce warm. Makes about 1½ cups.

HONEY BUTTER

½ cup honey
½ cup butter, softened

1 teaspoon grated orange
  rind

Beat honey into butter. Add orange rind, and continue beating until light and fluffy. Makes about 1 cup.

DATE BUTTER

 pitted dates   Dash salt
 water   ½ cup butter
spoon lemon juice

 small saucepan cook dates, uncovered, with water, lemon juice,
alt over medium heat until mixture is thick. Cool. Whip butter un-
ht and fluffy; gradually beat into thickened date mixture. Turn into
l, cover, and chill. Makes about 1 cup.

WHIPPED
ORANGE HONEY BUTTER

½ cup butter or margarine,   Grated rind of 1 orange
  softened   ½ cup honey

Beat butter with grated orange rind until light and fluffy. Gradually
beat in honey. Great on pancakes. Makes 1 cup.

COFFEE SYRUP

1 cup sugar   ¾ cup strong coffee
½ cup light corn syrup

Combine all ingredients in saucepan. Boil gently for 5 minutes. Remove
from heat. Serve hot. Good on pancakes, puddings, cake, or ice cream.
Makes 2 cups.

MAPLE SYRUP
(From Grandma Anderson's
Primer for Brides)

1 cup light corn syrup   **Maple flavoring to taste**
½ cup brown sugar   **1 tablespoon butter**
½ cup water

Combine syrup, sugar, and water. Stir and cook over medium heat until sugar dissolves. Add flavoring to taste and butter. Use on pancakes. Makes 2 cups.

Desserts

When Grandma Anderson went back to Pennsylvania for a visit a few years before she died, she returned pensive and sad. Some of the early inns had closed, so there were very few places serving real Dutch food. She felt the families weren't as close as they had been, and that the young ones going out into the world were not using their language or home customs.

How I wish I had paid more attention to the stories of my family's origins. It all began when Benjamin Franklin issued an invitation to the inhabitants of the Rhine Valley to come to a new world free of religious persecution. It was a very real chance for them to live their lives as they wanted. Nevertheless, it seems incredible that people would pack up entire families for a chance to be strangers in a new land.

When they arrived in Pennsylvania, the Dutch came as experienced and thrifty farmers. Almost overnight, their farms blossomed with fruit trees and vegetable gardens they referred to as market gardens; this was the start of the wonderful markets in so many Pennsylvania towns. Off-shoots from the original families went into business, and many of them had restaurants and country inns where Pennsylvania Dutch food was served as a matter of course. The women of the family were dedicated to their families' well being. They canned or dried or smoked everything within their grasp. People began to come to their markets from as far away as New York. Produce was divided. Half for the family, half for the market. The large farms and some of the small ones had their own smokehouses, and wonderful sausages were made in them. Ladies spun their own wool, made their own soap, and had hundreds of recipes for all ills and ailments—even the weeds in the fields were used. Trees were sapped, and roots were dug and used. Thrifty and creative were the best words to describe the Pennsylvania Dutch.

The wonderful markets are prevalent today, and there are still restaurants in Pennsylvania serving the food so well loved by the Dutch. Some of the recipes are in this book; Grandma would have loved knowing another cookbook from her little country inn was going out into the world.

OLD-FASHIONED
APPLE DESSERT

2 cups flour	1 cup sugar
1 cup shortening	1 teaspoon cinnamon
2 tablespoons sugar	Pinch nutmeg
Pinch salt	Pudding (below)
3 to 4 cups sliced apples	Meringue (below)

Combine flour, shortening, 2 tablespoons sugar, and salt as for crust and pat in a 9 x 13 inch pan. Combine apples, 1 cup sugar, and spices, and place over first mixture. Bake 45 minutes at 350 degrees.

PUDDING

2 tablespoons sugar	3 egg yolks
Pinch salt	2 cups milk
2 tablespoons cornstarch	

Cook all ingredients over medium heat until thickened. Pour cooked pudding mixture over baked apple mixture.

MERINGUE

3 egg whites	½ teaspoon vanilla
½ cup sugar	

Beat all ingredients until stiff peaks form. Spread over pudding mixture and brown 8 to 10 minutes in oven at 350 degrees. Serves about twenty-five.

BRANDY ALEXANDER SOUFFLÉ

Brandy and crème de cacao, the winning team in the Alexander cocktail, work the same magic for this wonderful dessert.

Butter
Sugar
Shaved chocolate
½ cup sugar
1½ tablespoons unflavored
 gelatin
½ cup water
6 eggs, separated

2 3-ounce packages cream
 cheese, softened
⅓ cup brandy
⅓ cup crème de cacao
¼ teaspoon cream of tartar
2 cups whipping cream
Chocolate curls (optional)

Butter and sugar bottom and sides of 1½-quart soufflé dish. Make 4-inch band of triple-thickness aluminum foil long enough to go around dish and overlap 2 inches. Butter one side of band and sprinkle with shaved chocolate. Wrap around outside of dish with buttered side in. Fasten with tape, paper clip, or string. Collar should extend 2 inches above rim of dish. Set aside. In medium saucepan, combine ¼ cup sugar and gelatin. Stir in water and let stand 1 minute. Cook, stirring constantly, over low heat until gelatin dissolves, 5 to 8 minutes. Remove from heat. In small mixing bowl beat egg yolks at high speed until thick and lemon-colored, about 5 minutes. Blend a little of hot gelatin mixture into yolks. Blend yolk mixture into gelatin mixture in saucepan. Cook, stirring constantly, over low heat 2 to 3 minutes longer. Remove from heat. Blend in cream cheese, brandy, and crème de cacao. Chill, stirring occasionally, until mixture mounds slightly when dropped from a spoon, 30 to 45 minutes. Wash and dry beaters. Beat egg whites and cream of tartar at high speed until foamy. Add remaining ¼ cup sugar, 1 tablespoon at a time, beating constantly until sugar is dissolved (rub just a bit of meringue between thumb and forefinger to feel if sugar is dissolved), and whites are glossy and stand in soft peaks. Set aside. Beat 1½ cups whipping cream until stiff (reserve remaining cream to whip for serving). Gently but thoroughly fold cream cheese mixture and whipped cream into egg whites. Pour into prepared dish. Chill until firm, several hours or overnight. Just before serving, carefully remove foil band. Garnish soufflé with chocolate curls, if desired. Whip remaining cream until stiff. Serve with soufflé. Serves six.

CANTALOUPE ICE CREAM

2 cups cantaloupe pulp
1 cup sugar
Juice of ½ lemon

1 cup cream
1 egg, beaten
1 cup whipping cream

Chop cantaloupe in blender or food processor; add ½ cup sugar and lemon juice. Beat egg until lemon-colored, and add ½ cup sugar. Fold into cantaloupe and add cream. Freeze about 1 hour to a mushy consistency. Whip whipping cream to a soft custard consistency. Fold into frozen mixture. Complete freezing (about 4 hours). Serves eight.

CHEESY APPLE SQUARES

1½ cups flour
1½ cups graham cracker
  crumbs
1 cup firmly packed
  brown sugar
½ teaspoon baking soda
¾ cup butter or margarine
8 slices (8 ounce package)
  American or cheddar
  cheese

1 20-ounce can pie-sliced
  apples, drained; or 2½
  cups peeled and sliced
  cooking apples sweetened
  with ¾ cup sugar
½ cup chopped nuts

Preheat oven to 350 degrees. Combine flour with cracker crumbs, brown sugar, and baking soda. Cut in butter until crumbly; reserve 1½ cups crumb mixture for topping. Press remaining crumbs into ungreased 13 x 9 inch baking pan. Place cheese slices over crumbs. Spoon apples evenly over cheese slices. Sprinkle with reserved crumb mixture and nuts. Bake for 45 minutes to 1 hour. Serves twelve to fifteen.

CHOCOLATE-FILLED
SNOWBALLS

1 cup butter or margarine,
  softened
½ cup sugar
1 teaspoon vanilla
2 cups sifted all-purpose
  flour

1 cup finely chopped
  walnuts
1 5¾-ounce package
  chocolate kisses
Confectioners' sugar

Beat butter, sugar, and vanilla until light and fluffy. Add flour and nuts; blend well. Chill dough. Remove foil from kisses. Shape dough around kisses, using about 1 tablespoon dough for each; roll to make ball. Be sure to cover kiss completely. Bake on ungreased cookie sheet at 375 degrees for 12 minutes, or until set but not brown. Cool slightly; remove to wire rack. While still warm, roll in confectioners' sugar; cool. Store tightly covered. Roll in sugar again before serving, if desired. Makes about 4 dozen.

CHOCOLATE-PEPPERMINT ICEBOX DESSERT

2 cups crushed chocolate
  wafers (cookies)
½ cup butter, melted
1 13-ounce can evaporated
  milk
1 3-ounce package lime-
  flavored gelatin
1 cup boiling water
1 8-ounce package cream
  cheese

1 cup sugar
Several drops green
  food coloring
1 4-ounce package instant
  chocolate pudding
1⅓ cups milk
¼ cup finely crushed
  peppermint candy

Combine crushed wafers and butter; reserve ⅓ cup for topping. Press remainder over bottom of 9 x 13 x 2 inch pan. Freeze evaporated milk in freezer until crystals form around edges. Meanwhile, dissolve gelatin in boiling water; let stand 30 minutes. Beat together cream cheese and sugar; gradually beat in gelatin and coloring. Whip evaporated milk to soft peaks; fold in cheese mixture. Spread half over crust; chill 1 hour. Keep remaining mixture at room temperature. Beat together pudding mix and milk; stir in candy. Let stand 2 minutes; spoon over layer in pan. Top with remaining cheese mixture, then add wafers. Chill at least 1 hour. Serves twelve.

CARAMEL UPSIDE-DOWN PUDDING

1½ cups all-purpose flour
2 teaspoons baking powder
1 teaspoon salt
½ cup butter
⅔ cup sugar
1 cup whole milk

Grated peel and juice of
  1 lemon
½ cup light corn syrup
1¼ cups water
Whipped cream

Mix and sift flour, baking powder, and salt. Cream 4 tablespoons of the butter with the sugar, adding sugar gradually. Cream until light and fluffy. Add the milk alternately with the flour mixture, beating smooth after each addition. Stir in the lemon peel. Spoon into a well-greased 9-inch square baking pan. Combine the lemon juice with the remaining butter, the syrup, and the water in saucepan. Bring to a boil. Remove from heat and carefully pour evenly over the batter. Bake at 350 degrees for 45 minutes. The syrup will form on the bottom, so be sure you spoon this over the pudding. Serve with whipped cream. Serves six.

COCONUT REFRIGERATOR DESSERT

4 teaspoons (1 envelope)
  plain gelatin
¼ cup cold water
3 egg yolks, slightly beaten
½ cup sugar
¼ teaspoon salt
1 cup hot milk

1 teaspoon vanilla
½ cup shredded coconut
3 egg whites, stiffly beaten
1 9-inch graham cracker
  crust, chilled
Toasted coconut (optional)

Soak gelatin in cold water for 5 minutes. Combine egg yolks, sugar, and salt; gradually stir in milk. Cook in double boiler over hot, not boiling, water, stirring constantly, until mixture coats a spoon. Remove from heat. Add gelatin mixture. Stir to dissolve. Chill until partially set. Add vanilla and ½ cup coconut. Fold in egg whites. Pour into pie crust and chill until serving time. Sprinkle with toasted coconut if desired. Serves eight.

WHITE HOUSE COCONUT TORTE

1 cup butter	1 cup whipped topping
2 cups flour	2 packages coconut
1 tablespoon sugar	instant pudding mix
1 8-ounce package cream	2½ cups cold milk
cheese	Whipped topping
1 cup powdered sugar	1 cup toasted coconut

Mix butter, flour, and 1 tablespoon sugar as for pie crust. Press into a 9 x 13 inch pan. Bake 20 minutes at 350 degrees. Cool. Place cream cheese, powdered sugar, and 1 cup whipped topping in bowl and mix well. Fold in pudding mix and milk. Beat until thickened, then spread mixture over the cooled crust. Top with whipped topping and cover with coconut. Serves eight.

Note: This is a very easy, delightfully light dessert that looks fancier than it really is. The recipe originally came from Washington—it was said to have been served at a President's daughter's wedding in the Rose Garden.

FROSTED COFFEE JELLY

2 envelopes unflavored
  gelatin
⅔ cup sugar
¼ teaspoon salt
¼ cup instant coffee
  granules

3 cups water
¼ cup plus 1 tablespoon
  crème de cacao
1 cup whipped cream
Shaved chocolate (garnish)

Mix gelatin, sugar, salt, and instant coffee in saucepan. Add 1 cup of the water, and place over low heat. Stir constantly until the gelatin and sugar are dissolved. Remove from heat and stir in remaining 2 cups water and the ¼ cup crème de cacao. Pour into 8 stemmed glasses or individual molds. Chill in refrigerator until firm. Serve with whipped cream flavored with 1 tablespoon of crème de cacao. Sprinkle lightly with shaved chocolate. Serves eight.

FROZEN CRANBERRY LOAF

1 16-ounce can cranberry
  sauce (jellied or whole)
2 tablespoons lemon juice
½ pint heavy cream,
  whipped

¼ cup powdered sugar
1 teaspoon vanilla
⅔ cup chopped nuts

If jellied cranberry sauce is used, crush with a fork. Add lemon juice to cranberry sauce, and pour into 9-inch square pan. Combine whipped cream, sugar, vanilla, and nuts. Spoon whipped-cream mixture over cranberry layer and freeze until firm. Slice to serve. Serves six to eight.

Note: A delicious and striking dessert with ribbons of red and white. Excellent to serve at a party because it can be made well in advance, then sliced when it is time for refreshments.

NEW ENGLAND
INDIAN PUDDING

1 quart milk, scalded
⅔ cup yellow cornmeal
1 teaspoon salt
1 large cup chopped beef
   kidney suet
1 cup molasses
1 cup sugar
1 large egg
1 large orange, chopped
   (rind, pulp, and juice)

½ teaspoon cinnamon
½ teaspoon allspice
½ teaspoon cloves
1 cup raisins
½ cup currants
½ teaspoon nutmeg
1 teaspoon baking powder
1 cup cold milk

In double boiler, scald milk; gradually stir in the cornmeal, salt, and kidney suet. Cook in double boiler for 20 minutes. Remove to very large bowl and add remaining ingredients except baking powder and cold milk. Mix thoroughly. Just before putting into baking dish, stir in baking powder and cold milk. Bake in large well-buttered stoneware pan or crock in a slow oven of about 300 degrees for about 3 hours or more, until firm. (An old-fashioned range is ideal.) Serve warm with vanilla ice cream. Serves eight to ten.

Note: This recipe is a family heirloom from five generations of the Scranton family, who first came to America in 1637 and founded Guilford, Connecticut, and several surrounding communities. The recipe is still a tradition for New England Thanksgiving and many good cooks have had a finger in it. The whole house is permeated with a wonderful aroma while it is baking.

STEAMED FIG PUDDING
(From Poplarville, Mississippi)

1 pound figs, chopped
1 tablespoon flour
1 cup butter
1 cup brown sugar
3 eggs, separated
2 cups soft bread crumbs

1 tablespoon molasses
½ teaspoon baking soda,
  dissolved in 1¼ cups
  hot water
½ teaspoon cinnamon

Sprinkle figs with flour. Cream butter and sugar. Add egg yolks, beat well. Then add bread crumbs, molasses, baking soda, and cinnamon. Lastly, fold in stiffly beaten egg whites. Steam in a greased 2-quart mold over hot water for 3 hours.

SAUCE

2 eggs, separated
1 cup powdered sugar
½ pint whipped cream

1 teaspoon vanilla
1 tablespoon sherry

Beat yolks with powdered sugar until creamy. Add whipped cream and vanilla. Add sherry. Pour over individual servings of pudding. Serves six.

ITALIAN CHOCOLATE ICEBOX DESSERT

Margaret McCaffrey Kappa, my youngest sister, was at the Greenbrier Hotel in White Sulpher Springs, West Virginia, for twenty-six years. Several times she was loaned to other companies out of the country and as a consequence brought back some interesting and delightful recipes. This one came from Italy and, being a family of chocoholics, we seized it with delight.

1 envelope unflavored
  gelatin
2 tablespoons strong
  coffee, cold
2 squares unsweetened
  chocolate
1 cup milk
2 egg yolks
¾ cup sugar
2 ounces raspberry
  preserves
¼ teaspoon salt
¼ cup Cointreau or
  amaretto
½ cup finely chopped
  pecans
Chocolate Whipped Cream
  (see index)
Shaved chocolate (garnish)

Sprinkle gelatin over cold coffee to soften. Melt chocolate in double boiler over hot water. Add milk, remove from water, and put over low heat. Heat until a film forms over top of milk (do not boil). Mix together the yolks, sugar, preserves, salt, and Cointreau or amaretto. Stir the hot milk into the sugar mixture very slowly, stirring continuously until mixture comes to a boil. Remove from heat, stir in gelatin, add pecans and pour into a 1-quart ring mold. Chill several hours until solid. When ready to serve, remove from mold and serve with Chocolate Whipped Cream. Sprinkle with shaved chocolate, if you wish. Serves four to six.

LEMON FLUFF SQUARES

1 cup rolled oats
⅓ cup sifted flour
½ cup brown sugar,
  firmly packed
½ teaspoon salt
½ teaspoon cinnamon

½ cup flaked coconut
⅓ cup melted butter
Slightly sweetened
  whipped cream
Filling (below)

Combine oats, flour, brown sugar, salt, cinnamon, and coconut in baking pan. Pour melted butter over the top and toss lightly to blend. Toast this mixture in a 375-degree oven until golden brown, about 8 to 10 minutes, then cool, stirring occasionally. While crumb mixture is cooling, prepare filling.

FILLING

1 envelope (1 tablespoon)
  unflavored gelatin
¼ cup water
4 egg yolks, beaten
1 cup sugar

¼ teaspoon salt
Grated rind of 1 lemon
½ cup lemon juice
4 egg whites

Soften gelatin in water. Combine egg yolks, ½ cup sugar, salt, lemon rind, and juice in a saucepan. Cook, stirring constantly, over very low heat until the mixture boils, about 7 minutes. Remove from the heat, add softened gelatin, and stir until dissolved. Cool. Beat egg whites until foamy throughout, then beat in ½ cup sugar a tablespoon at a time until the mixture stands in soft peaks. Fold into the cooled egg mixture. Pack half the crumb mixture into the bottom of a buttered 8-inch square pan. Gently spoon in filling and sprinkle remaining crumbs on top. Chill until firm. Cut into squares and serve with a topping of whipped cream. Serves eight.

HOT LEMON SOUFFLÉ

This dessert is said to have originated two centuries ago at the LaGrande Taverne de Londres in Paris. Served today, it makes a spectacular appearance with flavor to match.

Butter
Sugar
⅓ cup sugar
1½ teaspoons grated
  lemon peel

3 tablespoons lemon juice
¼ teaspoon salt
⅓ cup butter
4 eggs, separated
¼ teaspoon cream of tartar

Butter and sugar bottom and sides of 1½-quart soufflé dish. Make a 4-inch band of triple-thickness aluminum foil long enough to go around dish and overlap 2 inches. Lightly butter 1 side of band and sprinkle with sugar. Wrap around outside of dish with sugared side in. Collar should extend 2 inches above rim of dish. Fasten with paper clip or string. Set aside.

In medium saucepan beat together ⅓ cup sugar, lemon peel, juice, and salt until well blended. Add butter. Cook, stirring constantly, over medium-high heat until mixture boils. Boil, stirring constantly, 1 minute. Remove from heat.

In small mixing bowl beat egg yolks at high speed until thick and lemon-colored, about 5 minutes. Blend a little of the hot mixture into yolks. Stir yolk mixture into hot lemon mixture.

Wash and dry beaters. In large mixing bowl beat egg whites and cream of tartar at high speed until stiff but not dry, just until whites no longer slip when bowl is tilted. Gently but thoroughly fold yolk mixture into whites. Carefully pour into prepared dish.

Bake in preheated 350-degree oven until the soufflé is puffy, delicately browned, and shakes slightly when oven rack is gently moved back and forth, about 25 to 30 minutes. Carefully remove foil band. Serve immediately. Serves six.

Note: 3 tablespoons frozen lemonade concentrate may be substituted for lemon peel and juice.

MAPLE FRANGO

I thought it was incredible going to a girls' boarding school my senior year in high school. Holy Angels Academy was more fun than Derham Hall where I had been the preceding three years, but we all thought it was prison. However, when my mother came up to Minneapolis and took me out on a shopping spree, we always had fun. We stayed at the Radisson, and had great formal dinners in the Flame Room. The most fun of all was being taken to Donaldson's for Maple Frango, which I thought was food for the gods. These probably aren't the recipes used by Donaldson's for their famous dessert, but they're a pretty fair substitute!

4 egg yolks
¾ cup real maple syrup

2 cups whipped cream

Beat egg yolks until light and frothy. Heat syrup in the top of a double boiler. When it becomes hot, stir in the egg yolks; stir constantly until thickened. Remove from heat and cool. When completely cool, fold into whipped cream. Pour into a mold and chill in refrigerator. Place in freezer after ½ hour. Serves four.

ALTERNATE RECIPE

1 pint maple syrup
1 tablespoon maple
flavoring

3 egg yolks
6 cups whipping cream

Heat syrup to boiling point, but do not boil. Beat egg yolks until foamy. Slowly pour the hot syrup over the egg yolks, stirring while you pour. Return to the stove and cook at medium heat until thick, stirring continuously. As soon as it is thick, remove from stove. Add maple flavoring. Strain and cool completely. Whip cream; when it holds a soft point add the maple mixture and whip together. When it is thoroughly mixed, freeze in 9 x 5 inch bread-loaf tins. Cut in slices and serve on frosted plates, or you may scoop it out, but this is difficult since frango has an unusual grain. Serves twenty.

MELON BALLS JON-MAR

A friend of mine had just left the Air Force after a flying career that included some wild escapades against the enemy; I had just completed the restoration of a country inn, and we both wanted some planning time before we decided what to do next. Another friend who owned an agency informed us that there were job openings for a cook and a butler on a delightful estate in Fort Dodge, Iowa, occupied by a father and two grown sons who operated Brady Coast-to-Coast Truck Lines. I'm afraid we misrepresented our past experiences somewhat, or we probably wouldn't have been hired. But we were, and it was great fun. It taught me an enormous lesson about being an employee instead of a boss. I had a marvelous kitchen to cook in, and we had great respect and liking for the people for whom we worked. Every time I see a Brady truck on the road I have a real nostalgia for those twelve months at Jon-Mar estate.

Cantaloupe, watermelon,
Persian or Catawba
melons, and mangoes,
if in season

2 cups sugar
2 cups water
½ cup Cointreau
2 fresh limes, quartered

Using a melon-ball scoop, make watermelon, cantaloupe, Persian or Catawba melon, and mango balls. Make a simple syrup by cooking sugar and water together until thick. Cool syrup. Add to watermelon balls and then add Cointreau. Store in coldest part of the refrigerator for at least 6 hours. Store glass dishes in your freezer. Remove at last minute before serving this as a first course or dessert. Fill with melon balls and serve with a lime wedge on the edge of each dish. Serves eight.

MAPLE-WALNUT TAPIOCA

1 pint milk
¼ cup tapioca
⅔ cup maple syrup

½ teaspoon salt
1 egg, separated
½ cup chopped walnuts

Scald milk in a double boiler. Add tapioca, syrup, and salt. Cook 15 minutes, stirring frequently. Cool a few spoonfuls, then add to them a well-beaten egg yolk. Combine mixture, remove from heat, and stir for 5 minutes. Cool; add walnuts, then fold in stiffly beaten egg white. Serve with whipped cream. Serves four.

PECAN PIE BARS

Just like pieces of pie and just the right size.

1 cup plus 1 tablespoon
    flour
½ cup quick-cooking
    rolled oats
¾ cup packed brown sugar
½ cup butter

3 eggs
¾ cup light or dark
    corn syrup
1 cup broken pecans
1 teaspoon vanilla
¼ teaspoon salt

Mix together 1 cup flour, ¼ cup brown sugar, and butter until particles are fine. (With mixer, use low speed.) Press into a greased 9-inch square pan. Bake at 350 degrees for 15 minutes. Beat together eggs, syrup, pecans, vanilla, salt, ½ cup brown sugar, and 1 tablespoon flour. Pour over partially baked crust. Bake 25 to 30 minutes. Serves eight.

PINEAPPLE TORTE

½ cup shortening
½ cup sugar
4 egg yolks, well beaten
½ cup plus 2 tablespoons
  cake flour

1 teaspoon baking powder
¼ teaspoon salt
4 tablespoons milk

Cream shortening; gradually add sugar. Add yolks. Sift dry ingredients. Fold in alternately with milk. Grease bottoms of two 8-inch layer cake pans. Pour in mixture. Spread with meringue topping (below).

TOPPING

4 egg whites
1 cup sugar
1 teaspoon vanilla

A few chopped pecans
  or almonds
Coconut

Beat egg whites until frothy; gradually add sugar. Beat until meringue holds a point. Add vanilla. Spread over mixtures in cake pans. Sprinkle with chopped nuts and coconut. Bake at 325 degrees for 25 to 30 minutes. Cool; remove from pans. Place meringue side down on torte plate; spread with Pineapple Filling (below).

PINEAPPLE FILLING

½ cup cream, whipped
½ cup crushed pineapple
1 tablespoon powdered
  sugar

1 teaspoon vanilla

Gradually fold pineapple, sugar, and vanilla into whipped cream.

ELLIE CONCIDINE'S PINEAPPLE DELIGHT

3 eggs, separated
Pinch salt
¾ cup sugar
1 9-ounce can crushed
  pineapple, drained
  (reserve juice)

2 tablespoons lemon juice
1 cup heavy cream or
  evaporated milk, whipped
2 cups vanilla wafer crumbs

Beat the egg yolks. Add the salt and ½ cup of the sugar. Add the reserved juice from the canned pineapple and the lemon juice. Cook in a double boiler over hot, not boiling, water until the mixture coats a spoon. Stir constantly. Remove from the heat and add the crushed pineapple. Cool. Beat the egg whites with the remaining sugar until stiff. Fold into the pineapple mixture and add the whipped cream. Line the sides and bottom of the deep buttered 9-inch square pan with half of the crumbs. Pour the custard mixture into the pan and cover with the remaining crumbs. Freeze 4 to 6 hours. Serves eight.

Note: Ellie Concidine was my college roommate when we both went away to study home economics. This recipe came from Ellie's mother-in-law. We've used it for years. It can also be poured into a 9-inch pie tin and served in wedges—with pineapple sundae sauce on top.

PINEAPPLE-RUM-COCONUT BALLS

These were served to us in San Juan at a celebration dinner for Nathan Leopold and his charming wife. Leopold persuaded the waitress to give us the recipe, and we've been making these ever since.

1 quart vanilla ice cream
(French, if possible)
1 8-ounce can crushed
pineapple
4 ounces flaked coconut

¼ cup coconut syrup (in
the foreign foods section
of grocery store)
¼ cup light rum
Lightly toasted coconut

Soften ice cream until it can be stirred quite easily. Meanwhile, blend the pineapple, coconut, syrup, and rum. Set aside for 1 hour. When ice cream is soft enough and the pineapple mixture has stood long enough, fold the pineapple mixture into the ice cream. Freeze for 6 hours. Remove from freezer and soften so that you can scoop out balls of the mixture. Roll in lightly browned coconut and serve with chocolate sauce or strawberry sauce. Serves six.

RASPBERRY DESSERT

2 10-ounce packages frozen
red raspberries
(with syrup)
1 cup water
½ cup sugar
Juice of 1 lemon
2 teaspoons cornstarch
¼ cup cold water
50 large marshmallows

1 cup milk
2 cups heavy cream,
whipped, or 2 packages
dessert topping mix
(prepared)
1¼ cups graham cracker
crumbs
¼ cup chopped walnuts
¼ cup butter, melted

Heat raspberries with water, sugar, and lemon juice. Dissolve cornstarch in cold water. Stir into raspberries and cook until thickened and clear. Cool. Melt marshmallows in milk over boiling water. Cool thoroughly. Fold whipped cream or prepared topping into marshmallow mixture. Mix graham cracker crumbs, nuts, and butter and press firmly into bottom of 9 x 13 inch pan. Spread marshmallow mixture over crumbs. Spread raspberry mixture over top. Refrigerate until firm. Serves twenty to twenty-five.

VINARTERTA

½ cup butter, softened
1 cup sugar
¼ cup cream
2 eggs
½ teaspoon vanilla extract

3 cups flour
½ teaspoon baking soda
½ teaspoon baking powder
1 teaspoon cardamom

FILLING

1 pound prunes
¾ cup sugar

¼ cup brandy or rum

FROSTING

1 cup powdered sugar
1 tablespoon melted butter
½ tablespoon cream
¼ teaspoon brandy, wine,
   rum, or almond extract

Whipped cream or brandy
   (topping)

Cream butter and sugar; add cream, eggs, and vanilla. Mix thoroughly but do not overbeat. Add flour, baking soda, baking powder, and cardamom to make a soft dough. Turn out onto floured surface and knead lightly, 5 minutes or less. Divide dough into 5 parts; pat each part into a separate greased layer cake pan (preferably with loose bottom). Bake at 350 degrees for 15 minutes; cool. (The 5 layers will be crisp like a cookie before they soften with the filling.) Prepare filling by removing pits from prunes and simmering in water until soft. Put through a food mill or grinder or mash through a colander. Mix well with sugar and cook until spreadable consistency. Add brandy or rum; cool. To assemble torte, spread about 4 tablespoons filling over each of 4 layers, arranging one on top of the other. Combine frosting ingredients, mix well, and spread over top. When frosting is firm, wrap the torte in foil and let stand at room temperature for 3 days. It then may be refrigerated or frozen. To serve, cut in slices or strips across the torte and top with whipped cream or brandy. Makes one 5-layer torte.

Note: This recipe first appeared in the Women's Home Companion *years and years ago. We have made it often and found other fillings to be as good as the original prune filling. It is a truly unusual dessert, and a very impressive one.*

PUMPKIN CAKE DESSERT

1 cup all-purpose flour
2 teaspoons baking powder
¼ teaspoon salt
½ teaspoon cinnamon
¼ teaspoon nutmeg
1/8 teaspoon cloves
¼ cup shortening (heaping),
   half butter and half lard
   or vegetable shortening

⅔ cup sugar
1 egg
½ cup canned pumpkin
2 tablespoons milk
Sauce (below)

Sift flour, measure, add baking powder, salt, and spices; sift twice. Cream shortening, and add sugar gradually, beating until light. Add egg, beat well. Add dry ingredients alternately with combined pumpkin and milk. Beat well after each addition. Turn into well-greased 8-inch square pan or baking cups. Bake at 375 degrees 20 to 25 minutes. Serve hot with sauce. Serves six.

SAUCE

½ cup sugar
1 tablespoon cornstarch
1 cup boiling water
Pinch salt
2 tablespoons butter

1½ tablespoons lemon juice
1½ tablespoons orange
   juice
Pinch grated nutmeg

Mix sugar and cornstarch, and add water gradually, stirring constantly. Boil 5 minutes, remove from heat, and add other ingredients. Stir well, and pour over Pumpkin Cake Dessert.

KUNGSHOLM
SWEDISH PUDDING WITH
RASPBERRY SAUCE

1 envelope unflavored
gelatin
¼ cup cold water
1 cup boiling water
¾ cup sugar
¼ cup lemon juice

1 tablespoon grated lemon
rind
3 egg whites, stiffly beaten
½ pint whipping cream,
whipped
Sauce (below)

Soak gelatin in cold water for 5 minutes to soften. Add boiling water and stir until gelatin is dissolved. Stir in sugar, lemon juice, and rind. Chill gelatin mixture until it is the consistency of unbeaten egg whites. Beat until frothy. Fold in egg whites and whipped cream. Turn into serving dish or individual fancy molds. Chill overnight, well covered. Serve sauce over pudding. Serves eight to twelve.

SAUCE

1 12-ounce package frozen
raspberries
1 cup sugar

2 tablespoons butter,
melted
2 tablespoons cornstarch

Place raspberries and sugar in saucepan. Cook over low heat. Add melted butter. Place cornstarch in ¼ cup liquid from raspberry mixture, mix thoroughly, and gently add to raspberries. Cook slowly until mixture begins to thicken. Remove from stove, cool, and serve over pudding.

ALTERNATE CUSTARD SAUCE

2 tablespoons sugar
1 tablespoon flour
1¼ cups milk
3 egg yolks, slightly beaten

½ teaspoon vanilla
½ cup whipping cream,
whipped

Mix the sugar and flour together in a small saucepan. Stir in milk and cook, stirring constantly, until sauce thickens. Turn down heat until sauce bubbles only occasionally. Add several tablespoons of the hot sauce to egg yolks to warm them, stir well, and then add to the sauce. Continue cooking about 2 minutes, stirring constantly. Remove from heat and add vanilla. Cool quickly. Serve plain or fold whipped cream into the cold sauce just before serving.

Note: Our recipe comes from the famous Kungsholm Restaurant in Chicago. In packing and moving, it became lost somewhere in our possessions at any one of three places. We were delighted to find a version of it in the "Tastes Good!" column in the Northfield News *by Jean Mohrig, who is a Carlton College faculty wife with a wide knowledge of food. She serves her Swedish Pudding with Custard Sauce, which we also offer in case you prefer it. You might be daring and use the Raspberry Sauce over the Custard Sauce. Kungsholm always used the Raspberry Sauce.*

Alas, the beautiful Chicago Kungsholm is no more. Once located in a lovely mansion on the Near North side, it was a mecca for those who appreciated its magnificent and spectacular noon and evening buffets. On our last trip before it closed, our waiter obtained the recipe for our favorite dessert.

Cookies

Grandma didn't have the heart to take employees away from their homes on Christmas, so the Anderson House has always closed at four o'clock on Christmas Eve and opened again for breakfast on December 26, the unofficial start of the Christmas house party. If anyone chanced to stray our way on Christmas Eve or Christmas Day, Grandma had enormous and very festive food baskets packed for them, and the cookie jar on the upper floor was loaded with cookies, and of course, the coffee pot was always on. We follow Grandma's directives, and we too have the food baskets just in case.

It's the most beautiful time of the year at the Anderson House. We have enormous Christmas trees in the dining rooms and lobby, in the Lost Dutchman (our pub), and in some of the upstairs rooms. We have a beautiful old stairway that we decorate with garlands of greenery. We pass trays and trays of Christmas cookies, and we think our Dark and Light Fruit Cake is the best ever. We make it in August, stack it unwrapped in sealed twenty-gallon jugs containing open bottles of good brandy, and don't take it out until early December.

When the trees are etched in frost outside the Garden Room window there isn't a more beautiful scene anywhere. Most Decembers, our hordes of white squirrels are in for the winter, as are the black ones, but occasionally one will zip down from his tree to check the weather or the tourist peanut offerings, which are excellent in the spring, summer, and fall.

We have sleigh rides all winter long and serve hot grog when the sleighers return. There is special entertainment in the Lost Dutchman during the Christmas house party, but best of all is the food! We feature wonderful stuffed hams cooked in applejack, thick steaks grilled outside...yes, John Hall actually does the steaks outside, winter or not! We stuff turkeys with oyster, mushroom, and rosemary dressing, sauté pheasants in cream, cook pork roasts wrapped in apple butter, and serve our famous pumpkin-mince pie, as well as our steamed chocolate pudding with rum sauce, which is habit-forming—all of this and more. We love Christmas, and the Anderson House shows that the minute you step in our door.

You'll find some of our favorite cookies here, although we haven't duplicated any from our earlier books; we have excluded other popular Christmas cookies because we are sure you already have the recipes. In another part of the book you will find our famous Holiday Conserve, and recipes for our special Christmas beverages.

AMMONIA COOKIES

The ammonia called for in this recipe is not the household ammonia! You get this at your local drug store. It is called Baker's Ammonia. (Does some wonderful things to this cookie recipe!)

2 teaspoons dry cooking or baker's ammonia
2 cups butter or margarine, softened

2¼ cups sugar
3 cups unsifted flour
1 teaspoon almond extract

Crush ammonia finely between two pieces waxed paper with rolling pin or hammer. Cream butter and sugar together until light and fluffy. Stir in flour and ammonia. Beat well. Blend in extract. Form into small balls; bake on greased and floured cookie sheets at 350 degrees for 10 to 12 minutes or just until golden. Makes 5 to 6 dozen.

CHOCOLATE COOKIE SANDWICHES

Everyone loves Oreo cookies; this is one we make that isn't quite as professional, but almost as good.

1 cup butter
2 cups sifted flour
½ cup powdered sugar

4 tablespoons cocoa
1 teaspoon vanilla

Put all ingredients in medium-sized mixing bowl. Do not use mixer; blend with your hands as you would dough. Roll into balls the size of a marble and flatten very thin. Bake in 300-degree oven until done. A little time-consuming, but worth the work. Cool on cake rack, and when cool put together with your favorite frosting, white or chocolate. The amount will depend on the size of your ball.

WALNUT FUDGE
BROWNIES SUPREME

⅔ cup butter
4 1-ounce squares
  chocolate
1½ cups flour
½ teaspoon salt
4 eggs

2 cups sugar
1 teaspoon vanilla extract
1/8 teaspoon cinnamon
Frosting (below)
¼ cup chopped walnuts

In a double boiler melt and cool butter and chocolate. Sift in flour and salt. Whip eggs until they are very light and fluffy. Add sugar slowly, then add vanilla and cinnamon. Add to flour and chocolate. Put in two buttered 8-inch square pans and bake at 350 degrees for about 25 minutes. Let cool and top with frosting. Sprinkle nuts over top.

FROSTING

3 cups powdered sugar
1/8 teaspoon salt
4½ tablespoons cocoa
4½ tablespoons butter

4½ tablespoons coffee
1½ teaspoons vanilla
  extract

Beat all ingredients until very smooth and spread over brownies.

CANDIED CHERRY
CHRISTMAS COOKIES

1 cup margarine
1 cup powdered sugar
1 egg
1 teaspoon vanilla extract
¼ teaspoon cream of tartar
2½ cups flour

1 cup chopped nuts
½ cup red candied cherries,
  cut up
½ cup green candied
  cherries, cut up

Combine margarine, sugar, and egg; add remaining ingredients. Form mixture into 2 rolls. Roll dough in a little flour for easier handling. Place in freezer overnight. Slice and bake at 350 degrees for 10 minutes or until brown. Makes 25 to 30 cookies.

BOOZERS

½ cup margarine, room
   temperature
2 1-pound boxes
   confectioners' sugar
1 15-ounce can sweetened
   condensed milk

3 tablespoons whiskey
4 cups finely chopped
   pecans
Dipping Chocolate (below)

Mix all ingredients except Dipping Chocolate together. Shape into 1-inch balls. Place in single layer on waxed paper. Let dry several hours or overnight. Reshape and dip in chocolate mixture.

DIPPING CHOCOLATE

12 ounces chocolate chips   ¾ block paraffin wax

Melt chocolate chips and paraffin in top of double boiler. Drop one ball at a time into chocolate mixture. Retrieve with a fork and shake off excess chocolate. Place on waxed paper. Let cool and harden. Store in tin in cool place. Makes 12 dozen.

Note: The first time we had these was at the Kentucky Derby in Louisville. We took several boxes home and became addicted. I talked about it to a home economist one day, and she sent us this recipe. Sometimes at Christmas we add finely chopped glazed red and green cherries.

CANDY-BAR COOKIES

2½ cups fork-stirred
  all-purpose flour
1¼ cups firmly packed
  dark brown sugar
1 cup butter
⅓ cup crunchy peanut
  butter

1 large egg yolk, slightly
  beaten with 1 teaspoon
  vanilla extract
Topping (below)

Combine flour and sugar. Cut the butter and peanut butter into flour mixture until particles are fine. Add egg-yolk mixture, and mix well. Press over bottom of ungreased 15 x 10 x 1 inch jelly-roll pan. Bake in preheated 350-degree oven 25 minutes. Remove from oven; leave on oven control. Cool crust about 5 minutes. Drop Topping over crust at intervals; return to oven for about 2 minutes, then remove and immediately spread topping evenly. While still warm, loosen edges; chill until just firm enough to cut into bars. Remove bars to wire rack and cool completely.

TOPPING

½ cup crunchy peanut
  butter
½ cup chopped roasted
  peanuts

1 cup semi-sweet chocolate
  pieces

Mix together peanut butter, peanuts, and chocolate pieces.

CHINESE CHEWS
(Rich Cookies)

2 cups flour
4 tablespoons sugar

1 cup butter
Topping (below)

Mix all ingredients except for topping as for pie crust. Put in a 9 x 13 inch pan and bake at 375 degrees until brown, 30 to 35 minutes. Cover with topping and bake for 30 minutes or until topping is nicely browned.

TOPPING

4 eggs
3½ cups brown sugar
1 cup nuts

1 cup coconut
Few grains salt

Beat eggs and add other ingredients; mix well.

QUICK CHOCOLATE CRISPS

2 cups all-purpose flour
¾ teaspoon baking powder
½ cup butter or margarine,
  softened
¼ cup shortening

1 cup sugar
2 3¾-ounce packages
  instant chocolate
  pudding
3 eggs, slightly beaten

Preheat oven to 375 degrees. Sift together flour and baking powder. In a medium bowl, cream together butter or margarine and shortening. Add sugar and pudding mix, blending until light and fluffy. Add eggs and mix well. Add sifted ingredients; beat until blended. Drop by teaspoonful onto greased cookie sheets, spacing drops 2½ inches apart. Bake 8 to 10 minutes. Let cool on wire racks. Makes 4 dozen.

Note: This recipe is wonderful because it is interchangeable. You may substitute orange, lemon, coffee, coconut, or other instant puddings to change flavors. The only one that doesn't seem to be especially appealing is pistachio. In using other flavors, we add a teaspoon of orange, lemon, or maple flavoring, depending upon which cookie we are making.

MRS. GUENTHER'S CHOCOLATE-CHERRY COOKIES

This was a prize-winning cookie in the cooking school sponsored by the Oshkosh *Daily Northwestern* when we had the Athearn Hotel in that city. The cookie has been part of our Christmas celebration ever since. People who come to the Christmas house party always find a cookie jar in the hallway filled with these delights.

½ cup butter, softened
¾ cup powdered sugar
1 teaspoon vanilla extract
1 square chocolate, melted
1½ cups flour

1/8 teaspoon salt
20 to 25 maraschino
  cherries with stems,
  well drained
Icing (below)

Preheat oven to 350 degrees. Combine butter, sugar, vanilla, and chocolate. Blend in flour and salt. If this seems dry, add 1 to 2 tablespoons cream. Wrap one teaspoon of dough around each cherry. Place one inch apart on ungreased cookie sheet. Bake 12 to 15 minutes. Cool. Dip in icing and cool on cake rack until icing has set. Makes 25 to 30 cookies.

ICING

1 cup powdered sugar
¼ cup cream
2 teaspoons vanilla extract

2 squares melted chocolate
  or sweet chocolate

Mix ingredients together; blend well.

CHOCOLATE KISSES

4 egg whites
1 cup sugar
½ pound almonds, blanched
and chopped

¼ pound bitter chocolate,
grated
1 teaspoon vanilla extract

Whip egg whites until they stand in peaks. Add sugar and beat for 15 minutes. Fold in the almonds, chocolate, and vanilla. Drop by teaspoonsful on greased cookie sheet and bake in slow 250-degree oven about 60 minutes. Makes about 90 small, dainty cookies.

CHOCOLATE PFEFFERNUESSE

2½ cups flour
½ teaspoon ground
cinnamon
½ teaspoon ground cloves
¼ teaspoon ground
allspice
¼ teaspoon ground
black pepper
¼ teaspoon salt
½ cup chopped almonds

½ cup semisweet
chocolate chips
¼ cup candied orange peel,
finely chopped
2 tablespoons finely
chopped candied citron
3 eggs
½ cup sugar
1 cup powdered sugar

Sift together flour, cinnamon, cloves, allspice, pepper, and salt. Mix in almonds, chocolate chips, orange peel, and citron. Beat eggs until foamy; add sugar gradually and continue to beat until thick and lemon-colored. Add flour, nuts, and fruit; mix thoroughly. Cover and chill several hours. Dust hands lightly with flour and form dough into balls using about 1½ teaspoons for each cookie. Arrange on well-greased cookie sheet, and bake at 350 degrees about 20 minutes or until browned. Remove from pan and roll in powdered sugar while still warm. Store in covered container. Makes about 5 dozen cookies.

COCOA CLOUD COOKIES

3 egg whites (room
    temperature)
½ teaspoon cream of tartar

1/8 teaspoon salt
1 cup super-fine sugar
¼ cup unsweetened cocoa

Preheat oven to 275 degrees. In a small mixing bowl, beat egg whites, cream of tartar, and salt at high speed until foamy. Gradually add the sugar, beating until stiff but not dry. Fold in cocoa. Drop by teaspoonfuls 2 inches apart onto cookie sheets lined with brown paper. Bake for 20 minutes. Let stand 5 minutes before removing to a wire rack to cool. Makes about 7 dozen.

COCONUT MACAROONS

To the Italians goes credit for the creation of these sweet morsels. Macaroon comes from the same Italian verb that gave us macaroni. It refers to the mashing of ingredients. In macaroons, an egg white meringue provides the framework for the mashed food—coconut.

3 egg whites
¼ teaspoon salt
¼ teaspoon cream of tartar
½ cup sugar

1 teaspoon vanilla
1½ cups (3½-ounce can)
    flaked coconut

In large mixing bowl beat egg whites, salt, and cream of tartar at high speed until foamy. Add sugar, 1 tablespoon at a time, beating constantly until sugar is dissolved and whites are glossy and stand in soft peaks. (Rub just a bit of meringue between thumb and forefinger to feel if sugar has dissolved.) Beat in vanilla. Fold in coconut. Drop by rounded tablespoons onto greased and floured cookie sheets.

Bake in preheated 325-degree oven until lightly browned, 18 to 20 minutes. Cool slightly before removing to wire rack. Cool completely. Store in airtight container between sheets of foil or waxed paper. Makes about 3 dozen.

COFFEE-RUM CRISPS

2 cups sifted all-purpose
    flour
2 tablespoons instant coffee
1/8 teaspoon baking soda
½ teaspoon baking powder
½ teaspoon salt
⅔ cup butter

½ cup firmly packed
    brown sugar
⅓ cup granulated sugar
1 egg
1 teaspoon rum flavoring
2 cups small pecan halves

Sift together flour, coffee, soda, baking powder, and salt. Cream butter; add brown and granulated sugars, and cream until light. Add egg and flavoring, and mix well. Blend in sifted dry ingredients and form into 2 rolls about 2 inches in diameter. Wrap in waxed paper; chill several hours. Slice thin, place on ungreased baking sheets, and center each cookie with a pecan half. Bake in preheated 350-degree oven for 10 to 12 minutes. Makes 5 to 6 dozen.

DATE-NUT CHEWS

2 eggs
¾ teaspoon salt
¼ teaspoon almond extract
½ cup sugar
½ cup light corn syrup

¾ cup sifted flour
1 cup finely chopped dates
½ cup chopped nuts
Confectioners' sugar

Blend all ingredients well except for confectioners' sugar, adding dates and nuts last. Pour into a well-greased 9-inch square pan (we use waxed paper in bottom of pan). Bake in 375-degree oven for 20 to 25 minutes. Remove from oven, and cut into 1-inch squares at once; form into balls as soon as they can be handled in palm of hand, and roll in confectioners' sugar. Makes 2 dozen.

FIG-NUT SQUARES

2 eggs
½ cup sugar
1 teaspoon vanilla extract
½ cup flour
½ teaspoon baking powder

½ teaspoon salt
1½ cups dried figs, cut up
1 cup chopped nuts
Fig Sauce (below)
Whipped cream

Beat eggs until foamy. Beat in sugar and vanilla. Stir in flour, baking powder, and salt. Add figs and nuts. Place in a greased 9-inch square pan and bake 25 minutes in a 350-degree oven. Cut into squares and serve with fig sauce and whipped cream.

FIG SAUCE

Sugar and water for
   simple syrup

¾ cup dried figs, cut up
1 tablespoon lemon juice

Cook figs in simple syrup until thickened. (To make simple syrup, heat equal parts of sugar and water until thickened.) Add lemon juice. Serve over fig squares.

Note: This recipe came from Poplarville, Mississippi, where figs grow in nearly every yard.

FLORENTINES

¾ cup candied orange rind
5 tablespoons flour
1 cup slivered almonds,
   coarsely chopped
½ cup whipping cream

½ cup sugar
Pinch salt
¼ teaspoon almond extract
3 1-ounce squares
   semi-sweet chocolate

Mix orange rind with 1 tablespoon flour so it isn't sticky; chop fine. Mix all ingredients except chocolate; drop by teaspoonsful about 4 inches apart on well-greased cookie sheets. Flatten slightly with wet knife blade. Bake at 350 degrees 9 or 10 minutes. Allow to cool on cookie sheet 1½ to 2 minutes, then loosen with spatula and invert on wire racks to cool. (Keep spatula clean to prevent tearing the cookies.) Melt chocolate in saucepan over hot water; spread onto flat sides of cookies. Makes 2½ dozen.

FORGOTTEN COOKIES

A meringue is the basis for these confection-like cookies which are filled with chocolate bits, coconut, cherries, or nuts. They are baked, then left, or forgotten, in the cooling oven so that they will dry thoroughly.

6 egg whites
½ teaspoon cream of tartar
1½ cups sugar
1 3½-ounce can flaked coconut
½ teaspoon vanilla extract
1 6-ounce package semi-sweet chocolate pieces
¼ teaspoon mint extract
Few drops green food coloring
1 cup chopped nuts
½ cup finely chopped drained maraschino cherries
Few drops red food coloring

Beat egg whites and cream of tartar at high speed until foamy. Add sugar, 2 tablespoons at a time, beating constantly until sugar is dissolved (to test, rub a bit of meringue between thumb and forefinger to feel if it is dissolved) and whites are glossy and stand in soft peaks. Divide egg whites equally among 3 bowls. Fold coconut and vanilla into mixture in first bowl. Fold chocolate, mint extract, and green food coloring into mixture in second bowl. Fold nuts, cherries, and red food coloring into mixture in third bowl. Drop by rounded teaspoons onto greased cookie sheets. Place in preheated 350 degree oven. Immediately turn oven off. Let cookies stand in oven until dry and crisp, several hours or overnight.

REFRIGERATOR COOKIES

1 cup shortening
1 cup sugar
2 egg yolks
3 cups all-purpose flour

3 teaspoons baking powder
¾ teaspoon salt
6 tablespoons milk
1 teaspoon vanilla extract

Cream shortening and sugar together. Add yolks and beat well. Add a portion of dry ingredients sifted together, then milk and remainder of the dry ingredients, then vanilla. Make rolls and chill until firm enough to slice. Slice thin and evenly, and bake at 400 degrees about 10 minutes. Makes 7 dozen cookies.

Variations: Add 2 squares chocolate to half the dough. Divide the dark and light doughs in half and make 4 rolls ½ to 1 inch wide, depending on size desired. Lay a dark and a light roll side by side and press them together. Lay 2 more rolls on top of these alternating colors so as to form a checkerboard. Press together firmly. For Halloween, use orange coloring for the white parts. Liquid or paste colorings may be added to the dough to carry out color schemes. Striped and circular designs are also attractive.

FRUIT JEWELS

1½ cups flour
1½ cups quick-cooking
  rolled oats
1 teaspoon baking powder
⅓ cup coconut

1 cup brown sugar
¾ cup butter
1 12-ounce jar raspberry,
  apricot, or peach
  preserves

Mix flour, oats, baking powder, coconut, and brown sugar; cut in butter as for pie crust until mixture is crumbly. Pat two-thirds of mixture into ungreased 9 x 13 inch pan. Press down firmly. Pour preserves evenly over surface and spread to corners of pan. Crumble remaining ⅓ flour mixture over top of preserves. Bake at 350 degrees for about 35 minutes.

While baking, the preserves will bubble through the top somewhat. Cut when cool. Makes 2 dozen squares.

JOHNNY APPLESEED BARS

1 cup sifted all-purpose
    flour
½ teaspoon salt
½ teaspoon baking soda
1 teaspoon cinnamon
1½ cups uncooked oats
    (quick or old-fashioned)
⅔ cup packed brown sugar

½ cup shortening, melted
1 egg
1 teaspoon vanilla
¼ cup coarsely chopped
    pecans
2 cups thinly sliced pared
    apples
Confectioners' sugar

Mix and sift flour, salt, baking soda, and cinnamon. Add oats, sugar, shortening, egg, and vanilla; beat until smooth, about 2 minutes. Press half of dough in bottom of greased 9-inch square baking pan. Sprinkle pecans over dough. Arrange apple slices over pecans. Roll remaining dough between 2 sheets of waxed paper to form a 9-inch square. Remove top sheet of waxed paper; place dough over filling. Remove other sheet of paper; press lightly around edges. Bake at 350 degrees for 25 to 30 minutes. When cool, sprinkle with confectioners' sugar. Cut into bars. Makes 18 bars.

BESSIE'S GOLD BRICKS

2 eggs
½ cup cold water
1 cup sugar
1 teaspoon vanilla
Pinch salt

1 cup flour
2 teaspoons baking powder
Frosting (below)
Nuts, ground
Flaked coconut

Beat eggs, then add water and sugar. Beat well. Add vanilla, salt, and flour plus baking powder. Beat until batter forms bubbles. Bake in a 9 x 13 inch pan at 350 degrees for about 45 minutes. Remove from oven and cool on cake rack. Cut in small squares and frost on all sides, top and bottom. Mix nuts and coconut. Roll squares in mixture so that all sides are covered. Makes 3 dozen squares.

FROSTING

2 cups powdered sugar
Enough cream to make
  spreading consistency

1 teaspoon vanilla

Mix frosting ingredients. Consistency should be fairly thin, but adequate for spreading.

Note: Bessie Hansch fled Wabasha for New Orleans several years ago and has lived there in the French Quarter ever since, so the recipe comes from the South. Bessie is a top-notch cook, and anything in her recipe box is bound to be great.

JOHANNA HALL'S
VERY LEMON COOKIES

1 cup butter
1 cup sugar
3 eggs
3 cups flour
1 teaspoon baking soda

1 6-ounce can lemonade
  concentrate, thawed
¼ cup finely ground pecans
Sugar

Heat oven to 375 degrees. Cream butter and sugar until fluffy. Add eggs and beat after each egg. Mix flour and soda, and add to butter mixture alternately with ½ cup of the lemonade concentrate. Add pecans. Beat well. Drop cookies 2 inches apart onto a greased cookie sheet. Bake 8 to 10 minutes, depending on your oven. Remove from the oven and brush cookies with leftover concentrate. Sprinkle with sugar and cool on wire rack. Makes 4½ dozen cookies.

Note: These cookies do not brown while baking except around the edges. They are done when the edges turn light brown.

LEMON DIAMONDS

2 cups plus 3 tablespoons
  flour
1 cup butter
½ cup powdered sugar
4 eggs

2 cups sugar
1 teaspoon baking powder
Juice and grated rind of
  2 lemons

Mix 2 cups flour, butter, and powdered sugar as for pie crust. Pat firmly into bottom of 13 x 9 inch pan and bake about 20 minutes at 350 degrees. Now beat eggs, adding sugar slowly. Add 3 tablespoons flour, baking powder, juice, and grated rind. Pour over crust and bake 15 to 25 minutes, only until custard is set. Cool and cut into diamond shapes. Makes 4 dozen.

MINCEMEAT COOKIES

¾ cup shortening
1 cup granulated sugar
½ cup brown sugar
3 eggs
1½ cups flour
1 teaspoon baking soda

1 teaspoon salt
1½ cups quick oatmeal
1 9-ounce package
   dry mincemeat
3 tablespoons hot water
1 cup nut meats

Cream shortening and sugars, add eggs, and beat until light. Sift dry ingredients together, add oatmeal, and add to creamed mixture. Add finely crumbled mincemeat and water and stir until blended. Add nut meats. Drop on greased cookie sheet. Bake at 350 degrees for 10 to 12 minutes. Makes 4 to 5 dozen.

SWEDISH NUT BALL COOKIES

½ cup butter
½ cup powdered sugar
2¼ cups flour
¼ teaspoon salt

¾ cup nuts, finely chopped
1 teaspoon vanilla
Powdered sugar

Cream butter and sugar thoroughly. Sift flour and salt; add to creamed mixture. Work in with hands. Add nuts and vanilla. Chill dough. Form into small balls. Place on greased cookie sheet and bake at 375 degrees about 15 minutes or until very light brown. While hot, roll in powdered sugar. When cool, roll again in powdered sugar. Makes 5 dozen.

OATMEAL CRISPIES

½ cup sugar
½ cup brown sugar
½ cup shortening
1 egg
½ teaspoon baking soda

½ teaspoon salt
¾ cup flour
1½ cups quick oats
½ cup chopped nuts
½ teaspoon vanilla extract

Cream together sugars and shortening. Add egg. Combine soda, salt, and flour and add to creamed mixture. Blend in oats, nuts, and vanilla. Drop on cookie sheet, flatten with fingers dipped in cold water. Bake at 350 degrees for 10 to 12 minutes. When baked, remove immediately with spatula. Makes 3 dozen.

ORANGE SQUARES

½ cup butter or margarine
1 tablespoon grated
   orange rind
¼ cup sugar
1 egg
1¼ cups sifted flour
1½ cups brown sugar
2 eggs, beaten

⅔ cup nuts, chopped
⅔ cup shredded coconut
2 tablespoons grated
   orange rind
2 tablespoons orange juice
2 tablespoons flour
½ teaspoon baking powder
Confectioners' sugar

Cream butter with 1 tablespoon orange rind and ¼ cup sugar. Add egg, and 1¼ cups flour; blend well. Spread mixture in bottom of a buttered 9-inch square pan. Bake at 350 degrees for 15 minutes. Beat brown sugar and 2 eggs well. Stir in nuts, coconut, orange rind, and orange juice. Add flour and baking powder, stirring just to blend. Spread mixture over baked bottom layer. Bake at 350 degrees for 20 to 30 minutes or until cake tester inserted into center comes out clean. Dust with confectioners' sugar and cut into squares. Makes about 20 cookies. (Keep in an airtight container or freeze.)

OATMEAL BROWNIE DROPS

½ cup shortening, softened
¾ cup brown sugar
1 egg
½ cup milk

⅓ cup cocoa
1 teaspoon vanilla
1 cup pancake mix
1 cup rolled oats, uncooked

Combine all ingredients in bowl except rolled oats. Beat with rotary beater about 1 minute. Fold in rolled oats. Drop by teaspoon on greased baking sheet. Bake in moderately hot oven (375 degrees) 10 to 12 minutes. Makes 3 dozen cookies.

PEANUT BALLS

2 cups crunchy peanut
   butter
½ cup margarine
1 box powdered sugar
3 to 6 cups rice cereal

1 giant chocolate bar
1 6-ounce package
   chocolate chips
½ bar paraffin wax

Melt and cream together the chunky peanut butter and margarine. Add powdered sugar and rice cereal. Roll into balls and put in freezer to chill. Melt giant chocolate bar in double boiler, then add chocolate chips and wax. Dip balls in chocolate and place on waxed paper. Makes 4 dozen.

PECAN MERINGUES

1 cup butter
1 cup granulated sugar
3 eggs, separated
1 teaspoon orange extract
2¼ cups all-purpose flour

¼ teaspoon salt
Granulated sugar
½ cup light brown sugar
¼ cup finely chopped
   pecans

Cream butter and granulated sugar. Beat in the egg yolks and orange extract. Combine the flour and salt. Add this to the butter mixture, and beat until just mixed. Shape into 1-inch balls, dip in granulated sugar and place on ungreased cookie sheet. Flatten slightly with a glass. Beat egg whites until they begin to hold their shape. Gradually add brown sugar, then beat until egg whites are stiff. Place one teaspoon of meringue on top of each cookie. Sprinkle with pecans. Bake at 325 degrees for about 20 minutes. After a few minutes remove to cake rack to cool. Makes about 4 dozen.

PEANUT BUTTERSCOTCH BARS

1 egg
1 egg white, well beaten
¼ cup milk
1 teaspoon vanilla extract
1½ cups brown sugar
½ cup peanut butter

¼ cup melted fat
2 cups sifted flour
2 teaspoons baking powder
½ teaspoon salt
Peanut Butter Topping
  (below)

Mix first seven ingredients with beater. Sift dry ingredients, and add to mixture, stirring until blended. Spread in greased 10 x 15 inch pan. Bake at 350 degrees for 25 minutes. While warm, brush with peanut butter topping. When cool cut into bars. Makes 64 1 x 2½ inch bars.

PEANUT BUTTER TOPPING

½ cup confectioners'
  sugar
1 egg yolk

2 tablespoons peanut
  butter
1 tablespoon water

Beat all ingredients until smooth.

DOUBLE-GOOD
PEANUT BUTTER COOKIES

¾ cup firmly packed
  dark brown sugar
½ cup corn oil
½ cup crunchy peanut
  butter
1 egg
1 cup shredded carrot
1 cup quick oats

¾ cup whole wheat flour
½ cup instant non-fat
  dry milk
½ cup raisins
¾ teaspoon salt
½ teaspoon cinnamon
½ teaspoon baking powder

Stir together sugar, corn oil, peanut butter, and egg until mixed; stir in carrots. Mix together oats, flour, milk, raisins, salt, cinnamon, and baking powder. Stir into peanut butter mixture. Place by heaping tea-spoonsful on ungreased cookie sheet. Bake in 350-degree oven 15 minutes or until lightly browned; cool on rack. Makes 3 dozen 2-inch cookies.

POTATO CHIP COOKIES

2 cups butter
1 cup sugar
2 teaspoons vanilla extract
3 cups flour

1½ cups crushed potato
  chips
Powdered sugar

Beat butter until light and fluffy—a long time! Add sugar and beat well. Add vanilla and flour gradually. Add potato chips last. Drop from teas-poon onto cookie sheets. Bake in 350-degree oven until slightly brown. Sprinkle with powdered sugar. These keep well in a tightly closed tin—they actually taste better the second or third day. Makes 9 to 10 dozen.

PINK MERINGUE CLOUDS

2 egg yolks
2½ cups flour
1 teaspoon salt
½ teaspoon baking powder
¾ cup sugar

⅔ cup shortening
¼ cup milk
1 teaspoon vanilla extract
Peppermint Meringue
(below)

Blend ingredients well with mixer. Chill while preparing meringue.

PEPPERMINT MERINGUE

2 egg whites
¼ teaspoon salt
½ cup sugar
½ teaspoon vanilla extract
½ teaspoon vinegar

1 cup (6 ounces) semisweet
chocolate chips
1 cup coarsely crushed
peppermint candy

Beat egg whites with salt until soft peaks form. Fold in remaining meringue ingredients. Shape cookie dough into balls using a rounded teaspoon for each. Place on ungreased cookie sheets. Flatten with bottom of glass dipped in sugar. Top each cookie with a rounded teaspoon of meringue. Bake at 325 degrees for 20 to 25 minutes. Makes 5 dozen.

PECAN PIE COOKIES

1 cup flour
½ cup brown sugar
½ teaspoon baking powder

⅓ cup butter or margarine,
   melted
Topping (below)

    Mix flour, sugar, and baking powder; add melted butter. Mix well and put into a greased 11 x 7 x 1½ inch baking pan. Bake 10 minutes at 350 degrees. While baking, combine topping ingredients; pour topping over baked mixture while still hot. Bake at 350 degrees for about 30 minutes or until a knife comes out clean. Cool and cut into 40 squares.

TOPPING

2 eggs, beaten
½ cup brown sugar
2 tablespoons flour
¾ cup corn syrup

1 teaspoon vanilla extract
½ teaspoon salt
1 cup coarsely chopped
   pecans

    Mix all ingredients and pour over crust mixture as directed above.

BLANCHE EAVES'S PINEAPPLE CHEESECAKE BARS

½ cup cold butter
1¼ cups all-purpose flour
⅓ plus ¼ cup sugar
1 8-ounce package cream
   cheese, softened

1 egg
1 tablespoon lemon juice
1 cup crushed pineapple,
   drained

    Preheat oven to 350 degrees. In mixing bowl, cut butter into chunks; add flour and ⅓ cup sugar. Beat at low speed, scraping sides of bowl several times until well mixed. Reserve ½ of crumb mixture for later use. Press remaining crumb mixture into ungreased 8-inch square pan. Bake on middle rack for 12 to 18 minutes, or until edges are slightly brown.

To make filling, combine cream cheese, ¼ cup sugar, egg, and lemon juice, and beat at medium speed until mixture is light and fluffy. Stir in pineapple. Spread filling over hot crust; sprinkle with remaining crumb mixture. Return to oven and bake 15 to 20 minutes or until edges are completely browned. Cool on cake rack. When cool, cut into bars. Makes about 2 dozen.

RASPBERRY WALNUT DIAMONDS

2 cups sifted all-purpose
   flour
1 teaspoon baking powder
¼ teaspoon salt
1 cup sugar
⅔ cup butter

4 eggs, separated
2 tablespoons milk
1 teaspoon lemon extract
1 cup raspberry jam
1 cup ground walnuts

Sift together flour, baking powder, salt, and ½ cup sugar. Cut in butter with pastry blender as for pie crust. Slightly beat egg yolks; mix with milk and lemon extract. Add liquid ingredients to dry ingredients; mix thoroughly. Press in bottom and about ½ inch up sides of a 13 x 9 inch pan. Spread jam over pastry layer. Beat egg whites until stiff; gradually beat in remaining ½ cup sugar. Fold in nuts; pile lightly over top of jam layer; bake at 350 degrees for 30 minutes. Cool. Cut into small diamond shapes. Makes 3 to 4 dozen.

TOFFEE COCONUT BARS

½ cup margarine, softened
½ cup brown sugar
1 cup sifted flour
2 eggs
1 cup brown sugar
1 teaspoon vanilla extract

2 tablespoons flour
1 teaspoon baking powder
½ teaspoon salt
1 cup moist coconut
1 cup fine nuts

Combine margarine and ½ cup brown sugar, and mix well. Stir in sifted flour. Press into ungreased 13 x 9 inch pan. Bake 10 minutes at 350 degrees. Beat eggs until very light. Add 1 cup brown sugar and vanilla. Mix together 2 tablespoons flour, baking powder, and salt; add to egg mixture. Stir in coconut and nuts. Spread in pan and return to oven and bake at 350 degrees for 25 minutes until top is golden brown. Cool and cut into bars. Makes 24 bars.

WHISKEY SNAPS

½ cup corn syrup
½ cup butter
1 cup sifted flour
⅔ cup plus 2 tablespoons
  sugar

¼ cup whiskey
1 cup heavy cream

Heat corn syrup to boiling, remove from heat, and stir in butter. Mix flour and ⅔ cup sugar, and add to syrup mixture. Blend thoroughly and add 1 tablespoon whiskey. Cool slightly and drop by half teaspoons on greased cookie sheets about 3 inches apart. Bake in preheated 300-degree oven 10 minutes or until golden brown. Working quickly, roll each cookie around the handle of a wooden spoon to shape into tubes. Beat heavy cream and 2 tablespoons sugar until stiff. Add remaining whiskey and continue beating until very stiff. Spoon filling into cooled whiskey snaps, wrap in foil, and set in freezer until ready to serve. Makes 20 or more filled snaps. (They could become the cream of your cookie recipe collection!)

Candy

Candy isn't something you would normally find on a country-inn menu, and it doesn't appear on ours. But when Christmas approaches, our test kitchen busily engages in a search for the perfect candy to deck our trays of goodies that are passed around following each holiday meal.

Like almost every custom here, Grandma Anderson started the hunt for unusual holiday goodies. Just before Christmas, she made popcorn balls with real Vermont and Wisconsin maple syrup; one year she tried dozens of different chocolate popcorn balls and red and green popcorn balls. They were all marvelous. On Christmas Day the boarders and roomers were summoned to a taffy pull. There was so much fun and merriment that most of them forgot they weren't in a traditional family setting. There was a different kind of taffy for each two persons; peppermint, chocolate, lemon, strawberry, raspberry, and orange were popular flavors. When it was time to wind the taffy into a rope and cut it with scissors, everyone waited expectantly for it to harden. They drank hot apple cider with cinnamon sticks and gathered near the lobby fireplace, which had been crackling and burning for hours.

Now we have a cookie jar at the front desk all year, but during the holidays there are two jars. One jar is for cookies and one for candy. We make pralines, divinity fudge, jellied Turkish candy, hand-dipped chocolate-covered cherries, and Pennsylvania Dutch sugar candy. We even drop molasses in snow, which is another Pennsylvania Dutch custom. Peanut brittle is a prime favorite; sometimes we make brittle with other nuts if they are plentiful. Our special Christmas candy, which everybody loves, is a white fudge with red and green candied cherries.

And let's not forget Belle Ebner's Famous Fudge. Belle Anderson Ebner was a graduate of Fannie Farmer's cooking school, and her recipe for fudge is priceless. The recipe is long, but there just isn't any fudge like it anywhere.

For holidays or any other special time, look to our candy recipes for the sweetest delights around.

BRANDY CANDY

2 cups sugar
½ cup butter
1 cup evaporated milk
1 12-ounce package
   chocolate bits
1 7-ounce jar marshmallow
   creme

1 tablespoon instant coffee
2 teaspoons concentrated
   orange juice or orange
   flavoring
2 teaspoons brandy
   (preferably apricot)

Combine sugar, butter, and milk in 2½-quart saucepan. Bring to a boil, stirring occasionally. Continue boiling 10 minutes, stirring constantly. Remove from heat; stir in chocolate pieces until they are melted. Add marshmallow creme, nuts, instant coffee, and flavorings. Beat at high speed until well mixed. Pour into a 13 x 9 inch pan. Cool on cake rack at room temperature. Cut into squares. Makes about 50 pieces.

CHOCOLATE BRITTLE

1½ cups sugar
¼ cup light corn syrup
Dash salt
½ cup water
1 1-ounce square semi-
   sweet chocolate, melted

2 tablespoons butter or
   margarine
¾ cup chopped, shelled,
   unsalted peanuts

Butter an 8 x 11 x 2 inch pan; line with waxed paper and butter again. Combine sugar, corn syrup, salt, and water in heavy saucepan. Cook over medium heat, stirring constantly, until sugar is dissolved and mixture comes to a boil. Boil until candy thermometer registers 300 degrees (hard-crack stage). Watch carefully, and stir frequently toward end of cooking. Remove from heat. Add chocolate, butter, and peanuts. Pour into prepared pan. Let stand until firm. Break into irregular pieces. Makes approximately 2 pounds.

COCONUT BRITTLE

3 cups sugar
3 tablespoons light corn
  syrup
1 tablespoon water
½ teaspoon salt

1 teaspoon vanilla flavoring
3 tablespoons butter or
  butter substitute
½ teaspoon baking soda
1 cup coconut

Combine sugar, syrup, water, and salt. Boil to hard-crack stage (285 to 290 degrees). Remove from heat. Add flavoring, butter or butter substitute, baking soda, and coconut. Stir until blended. Pour quickly into well-buttered jelly-roll pan. Let cool. Break into pieces.

CHOCOLATE TRUFFLES

½ cup butter or margarine
2 cups sifted confectioners'
  sugar
1/8 teaspoon salt
2 egg yolks
4 1-ounce squares
  unsweetened chocolate,
  melted

3 tablespoons rum
¼ cup whipping cream,
  whipped
4 ounces chocolate shot

Cream butter, sugar, and salt until light and fluffy. Add egg yolks; beat. Add cooled melted chocolate and rum; blend thoroughly. Fold in whipped cream. Chill several hours. Form into ½-inch balls; roll in chocolate shot. Work with small amounts, chilling remainder. Let stand several hours in refrigerator to dry. Store in covered container in refrigerator. Makes 1½ dozen.

BELLE EBNER'S FAMOUS FUDGE

2 1-ounce squares unsweetened chocolate	**¾ cup rich milk**
2 cups fine granulated sugar	**1 tablespoon butter**
	1 teaspoon pure vanilla

Melt chocolate in double boiler. Slowly add the sugar, stirring well. Add milk slowly while stirring. Place saucepan over low heat. Stir constantly. Wash down the sides of your saucepan with damp pastry brush so that no sugar crystals form. Test back of spoon with your finger to be sure you don't feel any. Increase heat, bring candy to a boil, and boil without stirring until the candy thermometer registers 232 degrees. When candy reaches the soft-ball stage remove from heat. Remove from pan, being careful not to scrape out pan, and then pour onto your working slab (preferably marble). Place butter on hot fudge, letting it melt into candy. Let fudge stand on slab until barely warm to the touch (about 15 minutes). Work fudge with a spatula turning edges of the fudge to center. Keep spatula clean and do not include any scrapings that might be grainy. Add 1 teaspoon pure vanilla to fudge as you work it. When it seems to be completely creamy move to another surface covered with waxed paper. It should make 36 squares of fudge (about ½ ounce each) after you have patted it out into a square.

Note: Belle Ebner had a candy kitchen in Grandma's basement—a long, bright room with windows that she kept as spotless as an operating room. She took many candy courses, and her greatest creation was her fudge. This can be rolled into balls and rolled again in cocoa, finely chopped nuts, or vanilla wafer crumbs.

DIVINITY FUDGE

It's the beaten egg whites that make this candy different from others that start with boiled syrup. A candy thermometer is a helpful guide for accurate cooking. The resulting candy is as white and airy as an angel's wing.

2½ cups sugar
½ cup light corn syrup
½ cup water

¼ teaspoon salt
3 egg whites
1 teaspoon vanilla

In medium saucepan combine sugar, corn syrup, water, and salt. Cook, stirring constantly, over medium heat until sugar is dissolved. Bring to a boil, and without stirring continue cooking until mixture reaches 260 degrees, or the hard-ball stage, on a candy thermometer.

Meanwhile, in large mixing bowl beat egg whites at high speed until stiff but not dry, just until whites no longer slip when bowl is tilted. Continue beating at high speed and slowly pour hot syrup over egg whites. Do not scrape saucepan. Beat at high speed until mixture holds its shape when dropped from a spoon, about 4 to 5 minutes. Beat in vanilla.

Working quickly, drop by teaspoons onto waxed paper, aluminum foil, or greased cookie sheets. Cool. Makes about 4½ dozen.

Note: If desired, ¾ cup chopped nuts, toasted coconut, raisins, chopped pitted dates, or candied fruits may be stirred into candy just before dropping onto waxed paper.

ALICE BRUNER'S
NEVER-FAIL FUDGE

⅔ cup evaporated milk
1 7-ounce jar marshmallow
  creme
1⅓ cups sugar

¼ cup butter
1½ cups chocolate chips
1 teaspoon vanilla extract
1 cup nuts

Mix first four ingredients in saucepan. Stir constantly. Heat to boiling, and boil 5 minutes. Remove from heat, add chocolate chips, and stir until melted. Stir in vanilla and nuts. Spread in 8-inch square pan. Chill until firm. Makes 3 dozen squares.

Note: This fudge won the first fudge competition we had at the Anderson House. We continued that custom for several years and stopped it when sugar became so expensive. However, we have had so many requests that we hope to start it again in the near future.

PEANUT BUTTER FUDGE DREAMS

1 cup granulated sugar
1 cup brown sugar
2 tablespoons butter
½ cup milk
Few grains salt

¼ pound (½ cup) peanut butter
1 cup marshmallows
1 teaspoon vanilla extract

Cook sugars, butter, milk, and salt to soft-ball stage, 234 degrees. Add marshmallows and peanut butter just before removing from heat. Cool at room temperature. Add flavoring. Beat until well mixed, thick and creamy. Pour into buttered 9-inch square pan. Chill until firm. Cut into squares. Makes 24 1-inch pieces.

GERMAN CHOCOLATE FUDGE

3 cups sugar
¾ cup margarine
⅔ cup (5⅓-ounce can)
   evaporated milk
3 4-ounce packages
   German sweet chocolate,
   broken into pieces

1 7-ounce jar marshmallow
   creme
1 teaspoon vanilla extract
Topping (below)

Combine sugar, margarine, and milk in a heavy 2½- to 3-quart saucepan; bring to a full rolling boil, stirring constantly. Continue boiling for 45 minutes over medium heat, stirring constantly to prevent scorching. Remove from heat; stir in chocolate until melted. Add marshmallow creme and vanilla; beat until well blended. Pour into greased 13 x 9 baking pan. Chill several hours.

TOPPING

⅔ cup (5⅓-ounce can)
   evaporated milk
⅔ cup sugar
¼ cup margarine

1 egg
1 teaspoon vanilla extract
1⅓ cups flaked coconut
1 cup chopped pecans

Combine milk, sugar, margarine, egg, and vanilla. Cook, stirring constantly, 8 to 12 minutes over low heat or until thickened. (Keep heat low or it will scorch no matter how religiously you stir.) Remove from heat; stir in coconut and nuts. Cool, beating occasionally. Spread over fudge; chill until firm. Makes 3 dozen.

VICTORIA FUDGE

¾ cup sweet cream
¼ cup butter
3 cups sugar
¼ cup chopped candied
   cherries
¼ cup chopped candied
   pineapple

¼ cup chopped figs
1 cup coconut
1 teaspoon almond or
   rose flavoring

Combine cream, butter, and sugar. Boil to soft-ball stage (234 to 238 degrees). Remove from heat. Cool to room temperature. Beat until creamy. Add chopped fruit and coconut. Add flavoring. Pour into well-buttered shallow 9-inch square pan. Chill until firm. Cut into squares.

BELLE EBNER'S
WALNUT-PECAN TOFFEE

1 cup chopped pecans
1 cup chopped walnuts
1 cup butter (no substitutes)

1½ cups light brown sugar
1 12-ounce package real
   chocolate chips

Spread nuts over the bottom of a cookie sheet with sides. Combine butter and sugar in a pan and bring to a boil for 8 minutes, stirring constantly. Pour immediately over the nuts, and sprinkle chocolate chips evenly over the mixture. Cover the pan with another pan the same size (or foil) to keep in the heat for about 5 minutes. Remove cover and spread the chocolate mixture over nuts evenly. Keep in refrigerator as is for about 4 hours. Turn pan over and break into pieces. If you do not have a cookie sheet you may use two 8-inch square pans, being careful to divide everything evenly.

FUDGIES

We've never been able to figure out if this is a cookie or a candy!

1 cup butter
2 1-ounce squares
  unsweetened chocolate
½ cup sugar
1 teaspoon vanilla extract
2 eggs, beaten
4 cups graham cracker
  crumbs
2 cups coconut

1 cup pecans, finely
  chopped
½ cup butter
¼ cup cream
4 cups powdered sugar
1 teaspoon vanilla extract
3 1-ounce squares
  chocolate, melted

Melt the 1 cup of butter and the 2 squares of chocolate in a saucepan over low heat. Add sugar, 1 teaspoon vanilla, eggs, graham cracker crumbs, coconut, and nuts, and mix thoroughly. Press into 9 x 13 inch pan. Place in refrigerator while you are working on the balance of recipe. Cream ½ cup butter with cream, powdered sugar, and 1 teaspoon vanilla. Spread over the crumb mixture. Chill in refrigerator. Pour melted chocolate over the chilled mixture in pan, and spread evenly with spatula. Return to refrigerator. Cut into squares before the chocolate becomes firm. Makes about 28 squares.

Note: The guest who brought us this recipe calls it another goodie from the Yum-Yum Tree! She sends a box a month to each of her four sons in college.

Beverages

We're not sure how Grandma Anderson would feel about the Lost Dutchman Cocktail Lounge. In her time there was never a bar in the Anderson House and the suggestion that there should be one was always met with icy silence on her part. As a matter of fact, she sent her three daughters away to boarding school at an early stage since hotels in those days were occupied mostly by male transients, and she wanted no temptations in anybody's path. In the summer the girls were put to work in the kitchens, and if that didn't keep them busy, they were hustled to the laundry where the day's wash was done and hung out in the sun to dry.

At any rate, we finally found room for a bar by using the 150-year-old cellar that had magnificent limestone walls and big, heavy, rustic tree trunks holding up the upper floors. It made a great lounge; private, quiet, sort of mysterious, and very colorful. The iron stairway leading down was perfect.

Wabasha is as beautiful in the winter as it is in the summer. The snowcapped bluffs surrounding us are spectacular, and in milder winters the Mississippi stays open. The cross-country ski trails are geared for all manner of skill. Swooping down through the hardwood forests is a breathtaking experience! We have a farmer friend who takes our guests sleigh-riding under the winter moon. (One man comes from New York just for that.) After these outside challenges are over, the Lost Dutchman serves hot grog, hot cider, and all manner of heart-warming brews. In the summer, white sangria is a favorite.

Our favorite drinks are included here, and we hope you like them as much as we do. The Lost Dutchman is on our lower level, but it was also the basement of a hotel that was in existence long before the Anderson House was—and our inn opened in 1856. So, the Lost Dutchman was in business while the Indians were still roaming the valley.

ANNIVERSARY PUNCH

2 32-ounce cans pineapple
  chunks
1 pint bourbon or rye
  whiskey
1 large piece of ice

3 or 4 bottles champagne,
  or ½ champagne and
  ½ soda water, or ⅔ Rhine
  wine and ⅓ soda

Place pineapple chunks in punch bowl. Cover with whiskey and let stand 1 hour. Place ice in center and add champagne as desired.

BANANA PUNCH

4 cups sugar
6 cups water
Juice of 5 oranges, or
  12 ounces frozen orange
  juice concentrate
Juice of 2 lemons

5 bananas, very ripe
1 46-ounce can pineapple
  juice
3 liters 7-Up
  (approximately)

Boil the sugar and water for 5 minutes and cool. Put orange juice, lemon juice, and bananas into a blender, and blend completely. In a large container blend cooled syrup, banana mixture, and pineapple juice. Pour into 1- to 2-quart plastic containers and freeze. The sides of the containers should be straight so contents can be removed easily. Remove from freezer at least 1 hour before you plan to use the punch, but do not allow it to become softer than slush. To serve, remove from plastic containers and in individual glasses, put half slush and half 7-Up, or empty frozen punch into a large punch bowl and add half 7-Up. This punch is very refreshing. Serve it at receptions with sandwiches, cookies, and small cakes. Serves about 15, allowing 2 cups per person. For a large number of people, increase the recipe and allow at least 2 to 3 small punch glasses per person, more if there are growing, hungry children.

CHRISTMAS EVE PUNCH

½ cup real lemon juice
¾ cup sugar
½ cup curaçao

1 large block of ice
1 fifth good bourbon
2 quarts soda water

Mix lemon juice, sugar, and curaçao in punch bowl until dissolved. Add block of ice to fit bowl you are using. Add the bourbon and soda water. Serves twenty (two punch cups each).

COFFEE LOVER'S DELIGHT

½ cup tapioca
½ cup sugar
1/8 teaspoon salt
3¾ cups cold strong coffee

¼ cup rum
Whipped cream lightly
    flavored with rum

Mix all ingredients and let stand for 15 minutes. Boil until thick, stirring continuously. Chill for 2 hours before serving. Serve in parfait glass, well chilled, and place a dollop of whipped cream on top. Serves six or eight.

Note: All the fancy new coffees give you a wide choice in creating this delightful dessert.

DERBY DAY MINT JULEP

1 teaspoon sugar
4 mint sprigs
2 jiggers Kentucky bourbon

Shaved ice
½ teaspoon water

Make a syrup with sugar and water and set aside. Bruise three of the mint sprigs and rub them around the rim of a 12-ounce frosted julep cup. Discard mint. Fill cup three-fourths full of shaved ice. Add bourbon, followed by syrup. Stir gently. Fill cup with shaved ice. Garnish with mint sprig. Makes 1 drink.

SOUTH AMERICAN FROSTED COCOA

Coffee (amount desired)　　**Whipped cream (garnish)**
Cocoa (amount desired)

Pour coffee into ice cube trays. Freeze. Make cocoa according to directions. Chill in refrigerator. When ready to serve, remove from refrigerator, scoop out light scum from the top. Pour 1 cup into a 12-ounce glass and fill with coffee ice cubes. Serve with whipped cream on top if desired.

Note: You may put the coffee ice cubes (about 7) in the blender with 1 cup of cocoa and blend until cubes are dissolved.

HOSPITALITY INN HOT SPICED CIDER

1 gallon apple juice　　　**½ cup orange juice**
½ cup applejack　　　　 **½ cup lemon juice**
1 teaspoon grated lemon　**1 cinnamon stick**
rind　　　　　　　　　　**4 whole cloves**
1 teaspoon grated orange　**¼ cup sugar**
rind

Combine ingredients and bring to a boil. Let stand a day so flavors will blend thoroughly. Strain. Discard spices. Serve hot. Serves twenty.

HOT SPICED WINE

½ teaspoon cinnamon
1 gallon apple cider
1 teaspoon cloves

6 cinnamon sticks
1 quart Burgundy wine

Add cinnamon to ½ cup cider and mix until dissolved. Slowly bring all ingredients except wine to a boil. Add Burgundy. Cover and simmer until the flavor of the spices begins to be evident. Strain to remove spices. Serve hot. Serves sixteen.

ICED CHOCOLATE VIENNESE

6 ounces double-strength
  coffee
6 double-strength coffee
  ice cubes
Dash cinnamon
¼ cup chocolate syrup

1 small scoop vanilla
  ice cream (or coffee
  ice cream)
1 tablespoon whipped
  cream
Shaved chocolate (garnish)

Blend all ingredients except whipped cream and shaved chocolate in your blender. Blend until ice has disintegrated. Serve in tall, frosted glass. Top with whipped cream and shaved chocolate. Serves one. Multiply for additional servings.

Note: When our sister Margie was on the executive staff of the Plaza Hotel in New York, we visited her whenever possible. We became addicted to their wonderful Coffee Viennese. We came home and tried to duplicate it for our ice cream parlor. We never quite managed a duplicate, but this, we think, is close. We think about those lovely, lazy afternoons in the Palm Court and wish we were back there right now.

OLD-FASHIONED EGG COFFEE

Scandinavians take special pride in making coffee this old-fashioned way; campers find it convenient. The clarifying effect of the egg white helps the coffee to sparkle.

4½ quarts water
1½ cups regular grind
  coffee

1 egg, beaten
½ cup cold water

In large saucepan, saucepot, or big coffee pot bring 4½ quarts water to boil. Combine coffee and egg, reserving shell. Stir coffee-egg mixture and shell into boiling water. Return to boil. Remove from heat and let stand 2 minutes. Slowly pour in cold water to help settle grounds. Strain, if desired. Makes 8½ cups or 11 6-ounce servings.

PEACH-BRANDY EGGNOG

3 egg yolks
1 cup confectioners' sugar
1⅔ cups peach brandy
1 cup cold milk

1 pint heavy cream,
  whipped
Freshly ground nutmeg

In large bowl, with electric mixer at medium speed, beat egg yolks until light. Gradually beat in sugar. Slowly pour in brandy while beating constantly. Let stand about 10 minutes. Gradually beat in milk. Refrigerate, covered, until very well chilled—3 hours or longer. To serve: Pour brandy mixture into chilled punch bowl. Gently fold in whipped cream just to blend. Grate or sprinkle nutmeg over top. Makes 10 to 12 punch-cup servings.

PRAIRIE OYSTER

A first-rate bracer any time, this drink is called the imbiber's breakfast. Making it properly may be tricky, the morning after, as the yolk should be intact before serving. Then, swallow it down in one gulp.

2 tablespoons (1 ounce)
brandy
1 tablespoon
Worcestershire sauce
½ to 1 tablespoon vinegar
1 teaspoon catsup

1 to 2 drops hot pepper
sauce
Dash salt
1 egg yolk
Cayenne pepper

In 4-ounce wine or cocktail glass, mix brandy, Worcestershire sauce, vinegar, catsup, hot pepper sauce, and salt. Gently slide yolk into glass so yolk remains intact. Sprinkle with cayenne pepper. Serves one.

PUNCHBOWL EGGNOG

This frothy mixture of eggs, milk, rum, and sugar was the customary drink of American colonists before setting out on a journey. It's still popular and has a special place in holiday festivities.

6 eggs, slightly beaten
1 quart milk
¼ cup sugar
¼ teaspoon salt
1 cup whipping cream,
whipped

1 teaspoon vanilla extract
¾ to 1 cup rum, brandy,
or whiskey
Nutmeg (optional)

Blend together eggs, milk, sugar, and salt. Fold in whipped cream and vanilla. Pour into bowl or pitcher. Cover and refrigerate until thoroughly chilled, several hours or overnight. Stir in liquor just before serving. Sprinkle with nutmeg, if desired. Makes about 8 cups.

SUMMER SANGRIA

2 oranges
2 lemons
2 pears
2 cups white grapes
½ cup sugar

2 bottles white wine
1 quart sparkling water
1½ cups vodka or light
    rum (optional)

Slice oranges and lemons in thin slices. Remove seeds. Peel pears and dice, removing the core. Wash grapes, cut in half and add to the mixture. Add sugar, pour in wine, and chill several hours. Add sparkling water and vodka or rum, if you wish. Serves six.

Miscellaneous

Into this chapter goes everything that doesn't fit anywhere else. For instance, Grandma said bacon should be done in an oven preheated to 400 degrees. Lay the strips on your broiler pan so you can collect all that good bacon grease, and cook 10 to 12 minutes. You don't have to worry about turning them, and if you have company or a big family, you can do many strips at once.

Other odds and ends that belong here include putting a few teaspoonful of horseradish in mashed potatoes, adding a heaping tablespoonful of cocoa to your coffee grounds (South Americans do it that way), and adding a tablespoon of chocolate syrup to your cola. (Ah, shades of 1932, when that and cherry coke were the "in" thing!) And you mustn't forget a tablespoon of whipped cream, a light dusting of paprika, and finely chopped parsley on top of any creamed soup. It will raise canned tomato soup to heights of delight!

You'll find other items tucked in this chapter, which if properly used, will amuse you and bring you joy.

APPETEASERS

A concoction of corned beef, ham, and kraut made into bite-sized balls and deep fried to a crisp, golden brown will whet the most jaded appetites.

3 tablespoons butter or margarine
1 medium onion, finely chopped
1 cup finely chopped cooked ham
1 cup finely chopped cooked corned beef
½ medium clove garlic, crushed
6 tablespoons flour
1 egg, beaten
2 cups well-drained sauerkraut, finely chopped

1/8 teaspoon salt
1/8 teaspoon monosodium glutamate
1/8 teaspoon Worcestershire sauce
1 tablespoon chopped parsley
½ cup beef stock or bouillon
2 cups milk
2½ cups sifted flour
2 cups fine dry bread crumbs

Melt butter, add onion, and cook over low heat 5 minutes. Stir in ham, corned beef, and garlic; cook 10 minutes, stirring occasionally. Blend in flour and egg. Stir in sauerkraut, seasonings, and stock. Cook over low heat, stirring occasionally, until thickened. Chill. Shape into walnut-sized balls. Thoroughly combine milk and 2½ cups flour; coat balls with this mixture. Roll in bread crumbs. Deep fry in hot fat (375 degrees) 2 to 3 minutes, or until lightly browned. Drain on absorbent paper. Serve warm on cocktail picks. Makes 54 balls.

APPLE BUTTER

4 lemons
4 quarts sliced apples
6 cups sugar
½ teaspoon ground cloves

½ teaspoon ground
cinnamon
½ teaspoon ground
allspice

Slice lemons and cover with water. Let stand overnight. In morning place in kettle with apples, which have been cored, pared and sliced. Cook 1 hour. Add sugar and cook slowly 1½ hours longer. Stir often to prevent burning or sticking. Add spices and place in jars.

GLAZED MINT APPLES

2 cups sugar
2 cups water

6 large apples
2 dozen mint sprigs

Boil sugar and water together for 15 minutes. Pare and core apples, and place in shallow saucepan. Pour syrup over them and add 18 mint sprigs tied in a bunch and simmer slowly until apples are clear. Turn often to prevent them from becoming mushy. Remove carefully, and place a sprig of fresh mint in the hole of each apple. Serve hot or cold with roast ham or pork—this is a delicious meat accompaniment.

GRANDMA'S APPLES

8 tart apples
½ cup butter

¾ cup sugar

Core apples. Leave skins on. Place in 12-inch skillet with a little water. Boil about 5 minutes over high heat. Remove and place in large pan and cover with sugar. Put in 350-degree oven, and bake until brown and clear. Occasionally spoon sugar back on top of slices as they bake. 3 slices to an apple should serve eight.

CANDIED APPLESAUCE

12 apples
3 cups sugar
2 cups water

4 whole cloves
¼ teaspoon cinnamon
1/8 teaspoon nutmeg

Cut apples in eighths. Add all spices to sugar and water. Place apples in water, cover, and bring slowly to a boil. Simmer uncovered, gently lifting apples from time to time. Stir only once in a while. When apples are transparent, sauce is done. Serves eight.

Note: You may add a little red food coloring if you wish.

JELLIED APPLESAUCE

2 cups strained applesauce
2 tablespoons gelatin
2 tablespoons cold water
1 teaspoon lemon juice

¼ cup sugar
2 tablespoons red
  cinnamon candies
¼ teaspoon nutmeg

Heat applesauce to boiling point. Meanwhile, dissolve gelatin in water and lemon juice. Add sugar, cinnamon candies, nutmeg, and gelatin to applesauce when it begins to boil. Turn into individual molds or one large mold. Makes a good garnish for pork dishes. Serve on beds of watercress for color. Serves eight.

SPICED APPLESAUCE

1 19-ounce can applesauce
½ cup brown sugar

½ teaspoon cinnamon
3 whole cloves

Simmer all ingredients for 1 hour. Serves eight as a garnish.

CHOW CHOW

4 carrots
2 large heads cabbage
9 red peppers
9 green peppers
8 medium onions
¼ cup salt

2 pints vinegar
4 cups sugar
2 tablespoons celery seed
2 tablespoons mustard seed
Dash red pepper

Chop vegetables in blender or food processor, then add salt and mix thoroughly. Add the rest of the ingredients, mix thoroughly, and seal in jars. Do not cook. Makes about 2 quarts.

Note: This may be served with ham.

HOLIDAY CONSERVE

2 30-ounce cans apricot
  halves
½ cup glazed mixed fruits
½ cup quartered glazed
  red cherries
½ cup quartered glazed
  green cherries
1½ cups sugar

¼ teaspoon salt
¼ teaspoon nutmeg
1 tablespoon grated
  lemon rind
1 tablespoon grated
  orange rind
1½ cups finely chopped
  pecans

Drain apricots, reserving 1½ cups syrup. Coarsely chop apricots. Place apricots, the 1½ cups apricot syrup, and all remaining ingredients except the pecans in a 6-quart pot. Bring to a boil, stirring occasionally. Reduce heat; simmer uncovered about 25 minutes or until thickened and of desired consistency. Stir in pecans, ladle into hot sterilized jars and seal with lid or paraffin according to manufacturer's directions. Save remaining syrup for your gelatin desserts. Makes about 6 cups.

Note: Twenty years ago we opened Grandma Anderson's Preserving Kitchens in a building in back of the inn and made our jams, jellies, salad dressings, and fruit cakes for sale. The demand was just greater than our ability to supply. Going into a huge operation would take our products out of the homemade class, so we reluctantly closed our little factory. While we were struggling to supply our guests, we found the bestsellers, next to our fruitcakes, were the two Holiday Conserves we made. We hope you will like this one!

PLUM CONSERVE

5 pounds blue plums,
  cut in small pieces
5 pounds sugar
1 pound raisins

½ cup nuts
Rind and juice of 2 oranges
Rind and juice of 1 lemon

Boil until thick, about 20 minutes. Put nuts in at the last minute. Store in refrigerator. Makes 4 to 5 pints.

RAINBOW CONSERVE

1 pint strawberries
1 pint red cherries
1 pint red raspberries

1 pint currants
3 pounds sugar

Wash, mix, and mash fruits. Add just enough water to start cooking. Cook over low heat until tender, about 15 to 20 minutes, stirring frequently to prevent sticking. Add sugar and continue to cook very slowly until thick. Store in refrigerator. Makes about 5 pints.

RHUBARB CONSERVE

6 cups diced rhubarb
1 cup chopped raisins
1 cup canned crushed
   pineapple
1 cup orange juice
½ cup grated orange rind

Juice and grated rind of
   1 lemon
4 cups sugar
1 teaspoon salt
1 cup coarsely chopped
   nuts

Mix all ingredients except nuts together, and bring to a boil. Cook slowly for 4 or 5 hours until it becomes very thick. Add nuts about 30 minutes before it is done. Seal in hot jars. Makes about 5 pints.

CORN RELISH

12 ears corn, cut raw
2 quarts ripe tomatoes,
   peeled and sliced
1 quart vinegar
4 cups sugar
4 tablespoons salt
4 cups finely chopped
   cucumbers

4 cups finely chopped
   onions
6 green peppers, finely
   chopped
2 tablespoons turmeric
2 tablespoons mustard
2 teaspoons celery seed

Mix corn and tomatoes well. Add remaining ingredients. Cook over medium heat about 1 hour and 15 minutes. Seal hot. Makes about 3 gallons.

CUCUMBER-CARROT RELISH

6 to 8 cucumbers (5¼ cups
  ground)
2 ounces pimiento
9 medium carrots (2¼ cups
  ground)
2 medium onions (1½ cups
  ground)

3 tablespoons salt
3¾ cups sugar
2¼ cups vinegar
2¼ teaspoons celery seed
2¼ teaspoons mustard seed

Put cucumbers, pimiento, carrots, and onions in blender or food processor and coarsely grind. Combine vegetables and salt. Let stand for 3 hours, then drain well. Combine sugar, vinegar, celery seed, and mustard seed. Bring to a boil, then add vegetables; simmer uncovered for 20 minutes. Seal at once in hot sterilized jars. Chill before serving. Makes 4 pints.

DILLY BEANS

2 pounds green beans,
  trimmed
1 teaspoon cayenne
4 cloves garlic

4 heads dill
2½ cups water
2½ cups vinegar
¼ cup salt

Pack beans into four hot jars, leaving ¼-inch head space. To each pint, add ¼ teaspoon cayenne, 1 clove garlic, and 1 head dill. In a medium saucepan, combine remaining ingredients and bring to a boil. Pour, boiling hot, over beans, leaving ¼-inch head space. Adjust caps. Process 10 minutes in water-bath canner. Let beans stand 2 to 4 weeks to allow flavor to develop. Makes 4 pints.

POPLARVILLE, MISSISSIPPI, FIG JAM

5 pounds fresh figs,
  peeled and cut in bits
2 lemons, thinly sliced,
  discarding seeds

4 pounds (8 cups) sugar
1 teaspoon salt
¼ cup Cointreau

Combine the figs and lemon with water to cover. Place in kettle and cook over medium heat for 1 hour. Add sugar and salt, and cook until figs are clear and the syrup is thick. Add Cointreau. Pour into hot, sterilized glasses and seal. Makes 6 pints.

PENNSYLVANIA DUTCH ONION EASTER EGGS

Onion peelings
Eggs

1 tablespoon salt
1 tablespoon vinegar

Take any kind of kettle and fill it up with onion peelings. Then fill with lukewarm water and let soak overnight. In the morning, put in eggs, but be sure your eggs are well covered with water. Boil slowly for 30 to 45 minutes. Add 1 tablespoon salt and 1 tablespoon vinegar. This gives them a beautiful color. Take eggs out and wipe with a clean cloth. This gives them a shine. You won't have two eggs alike, and the onions give them different designs.

PICKLED EGGS

In Pennsylvania Dutch Country, pickled eggs are a sign of summertime. Vary the flavor by substituting pineapple juice or canned beet liquid for the vinegar. The latter gives them a rosy look.

2 cups white vinegar
2 tablespoons sugar
1 medium onion, sliced and
separated into rings

1 teaspoon salt
1 teaspoon whole mixed
pickling spice
12 hard-cooked eggs

In medium saucepan combine all ingredients except eggs. Simmer over low heat, uncovered, until onion is tender, about 10 minutes. Arrange eggs in each of two 1-quart jars with tight-fitting lids. Pour 1 cup vinegar mixture over eggs in each jar. Cover and refrigerate several hours or overnight to blend flavors. Eggs may be stored in refrigerator up to 2 weeks. Makes 12 appetizers.

DUTCH PICKLED EGGS

2 cups white vinegar
2 tablespoons mild
prepared mustard
½ cup water
1 cup sugar
1 tablespoon salt

1 tablespoon celery seed
1 tablespoon mustard seed
6 whole cloves
12 hard-cooked eggs
2 onions, sliced

Mix all ingredients except eggs and onions together, and simmer 10 minutes. Cool; pour over shelled hard-cooked eggs and 2 sliced onions. Cover; refrigerate overnight.

SEASONED SALT

1 cup coarse sea salt
2½ teaspoons paprika
2 teaspoons dry mustard
1½ teaspoons dry crushed
  oregano
1½ teaspoons garlic
  powder

1 teaspoon dry crushed
  thyme
1 teaspoon curry powder
½ teaspoon onion powder
¼ teaspoon dry dill weed

Combine all ingredients and mix well. Pour into airtight containers and seal.

SHERRY WINE JELLY

2 cups ultra-dry sherry
2 cups Sauterne
3 cups sugar

½ bottle fruit pectin
Paraffin

In a large saucepan, combine sherry and Sauterne. Add sugar, and cook over medium heat, stirring until mixture comes to a boil. Reduce heat and simmer 2 minutes. Remove from heat, and quickly stir in fruit pectin. Immediately pour into sterile 8-ounce jelly glasses. Cover at once with 1/8 inch hot paraffin. Fills 6 8-ounce jars.

BLUE-RIBBON
STRAWBERRY PRESERVES

2 pints California straw-
berries, destemmed and
washed
7 cups sugar (3 pounds)

¼ cup lemon juice
3 ounces liquid pectin
(half of a 6-ounce bottle)

Measure 5 cups whole ripe berries (a packed measurement, but without crushing). Layer in broad, heavy pan with sugar; let stand 10 minutes. Bring slowly to boil, stirring gently to keep fruit whole. Remove from heat. Cool at room temperature 4 hours. Add lemon juice. Bring mixture to full rolling boil over high heat; boil hard 2 minutes, stirring gently. Remove from heat; at once, stir in liquid pectin. Skim off foam with metal spoon, and stir for 10 minutes to prevent floating fruit. Ladle into sterilized jars. Seal, or cover at once with hot paraffin. Makes 7 cups.

Note: All preserves need to be stored about 2 weeks before eating to reach perfect consistency.

ANN'S ZUCCHINI PICKLES

2 pounds zucchini (about
4 10-inch zucchini)
½ pound onions, thinly
sliced
½ cup salt
2 cups cider vinegar

1 teaspoon celery seeds
1 teaspoon ground turmeric
4 teaspoons prepared
mustard
2 teaspoons mustard seeds

Wash zucchini and cut into thin slices. Cover zucchini and onion with water and salt mixture. Let stand 2 hours. Bring to a boil the remaining ingredients and pour over zucchini. Let stand 2 hours. Boil whole mixture 5 minutes, and pack in sterilized jars. Seal and process or freeze in plastic containers. Makes 4 pints.

Index

Appeteasers, 363

Apple(s): and onion pork chops, 126; beet and, salad, 43; butter, 364; cake, hot, with caramel rum sauce, 247; cheesy, squares, 296; dessert, old-fashioned, 293; Grandma's, 364; mint, glazed, 364; molasses bread, 194; squash-, bisque, 38; tart, Dutch, Ann's special, 223

Applesauce: candied, 365; jellied, 365; spiced, 365

Apricot: dressing, 42; pie, blue-ribbon, 224; salad, 42

Avocado: bread, Santa Barbara, 194; mold, 41

Bacon: and potato chowder, Ann's, 17; cheese-, strips, 200; creamed browned potatoes with, 181; potato salad, 58; Canadian, roasted, 98

Banana: calico bread, 196; coffee cake, 195; dressing, 45; gem cakes, 248; punch, 355; salad, frozen, 41; strawberry-, pie, 244

Barbecue sauce, 65, 136

Barley: -and-mushroom casserole, 159; casserole, 162; mushroom-, soup, 28

Batter: fish, secret, 84; puff, 216

Bean(s): and ribs, John Hall's moose hunter's, 166; baked, elegant, 160; baked, Josephine Senderhauf's wonderful, 164; city-slicker, 163; dilly, 369; green, Pennsylvania-Dutch, 164; lamb and, Loren's, 112; outdoor camp-town, 163; potato and, soup, 33; red, and rice, Duke Ellington's, 160; soup, Senate, 17

Beef: roll, stuffed, 98; sauce, 99; sauce, golden cornmeal ring with, 99; tongue, Anderson style, 138; vegetable-, salad, 62. See also Corned Beef; Ribs; Steak

Beer: and cheese soup, Anderson House, 20; cabbage slaw, 44

Beet: and apple salad, 43; and egg salad, Nora Hoffman's, 42; mold, Ann's, 44

Beverages: Derby Day mint julep, 356; Hospitality Inn hot spiced cider, 357; hot spiced wine, 358; iced chocolate Viennese, 358; South American frosted cocoa, 357; summer sangria, 360. See also Coffee; Eggnog; Punch

Biscuits, 209; and gravy, Jacksonville, 208; honey-filled, 206; mix, homemade, 208

Bisque, squash-apple, 38

Black cherry salad, jellied, 45

Black Russian pie, 224

Black walnut cake, blue ribbon, 248

Bleu cheese coleslaw, 48

Blockbusters, 196

Blueberry(ies): sauce, 286; streusel, 197

Bourbon pie, 225

Bran, cheddar, bread, 200

Brandy: Alexander soufflé, 294; candy, 345

Bread(s): apple-molasses, 194; banana calico, 196; blueberry streusel, 197; brown, 198; cheddar bran, 200; cheese-bacon strips, 200; cranberry-orange, 204; Creole breakfast cakes, 204; ginger tea, 205; high-calcium, 207; Loren's garlic, 205; Mexican breakfast, 211; Mexican spoon, 207; onion squares, 212; orange-cream cheese, 212; Santa Barbara avocado, 194; Swiss pear, 218; tropical peanut, 220; whole wheat fig-honey, 203; zucchini, 219. See also Biscuits; Buns; Coffee cake; Corn bread; Doughnuts; Muffins; Pancakes; Rolls

Brittle: chocolate, 345; coconut, 346

Broccoli, cream of, soup, 18

Broilers, baked stuffed, 141

Brown bread, 198

Brown sugar frosting, 281

Brownie(s): oatmeal, drops, 336; walnut fudge, supreme, 320

Buns: chocolate sour cream, 202; sweet potato, 216

Burnt-sugar: chiffon cake, 252; frosting,

253; syrup, 252

Butters: apple, 364; cinnamon, 287; date, 289; dill, 74; honey, 288; whipped orange honey, 289

Buttercream: frosting, 257; icing, 281

Butterscotch sauce, elegant, 287

Cabbage: rolls, Ann Polischtak's Las Vegas, 100; beer, slaw, 44; slaw, Ann's, 45; soup San Juan, 18. *See also* Red cabbage

Caesar salad, 47

Cake(s): banana gem, 248; blue ribbon black walnut, 248; brown velvet, 251; burnt-sugar chiffon, 252; caramel upside-down, 254; carrot, 254; cherry-chocolate, 256; chocolate-coconut, 257; chocolate pound, 255; chocolate-raspberry, supreme, 261; coffee-raspberry ribbon, 262; cranberry spice, 259; daffodil, 264; double-chocolate fruit, 266; double-chocolate marsh-mallow, 260; double date, 265; fudge upside-down, 268; fudge, with fluffy peppermint icing, 267; Grandma Anderson's sublime, 277; hot apple, with caramel rum sauce, 247; Ida's white fruit, 276; Katie's top-secret, 276; layered lace and velvet, 269; lemon velvet, with peach glaze, 270; Maggie's chocolate, 258; Mahala's black wedding, 250; Milky Way, 270; orange Génoise, 272; Queen of, 271; rum, 275; strawberries in the snow, 274

Calico snow, 226

Candied cherry Christmas cookies, 320

Candy: brandy, 345; fudgies, 352. *See also* Brittle; Fudge; Toffee; Truffles

Cantaloupe: ice cream, 295; salad, jellied, 46

Caramel: chiffon frosting, never-fail, 282; filling, 282; -nut rolls, emergency, 199; rum sauce, 247; upside-down cake, 254; upside-down pudding, 298

Carrot(s): Anderson, 167; cake, 254; chips, French-fried, 167; circles and pineapple, 170; cucumber-, relish, 369; muffins, 193; -potato scallop, 170

Casserole(s): barley, 162; barley-and-mushroom, 159; chicken, 142; chicken 'n' potato, 150; crab, deluxe, 80; Dutch sauerkraut, 182; Mississippi scalloped crab, 83; Perry County fresh corn, 169; Playboy Guesthouse wild rice, 190; rutabaga en, 179; sauerkraut and Polish sausage, 125

Cassoulet, 101

Cheddar bran bread, 200

Cheese: and pineapple salad, 49; and spinach soup, 20; -bacon strips, 200; -olive muffins, 201; soufflé with fresh mushroom sauce, 168; beer and, soup, Anderson House, 20; spinach and-, squares, 184; tomato-, muffins, 220

Cheeseburger chowder, 21

Cheesecake, pineapple, bars, Blanche Eaves's, 340

Cheesy apple squares, 296

Cherry(ies): Bing, sauce, 285; -chocolate cake, 256; chocolate-, cookies, Mrs. Guenther's, 324; filling, 256

Chicken: à la King, 142; and dumplings, Grandma Anderson's, 143; and rice, 151; and sweetbread salad, 48; baked stuffed broilers, 141; casserole, 142;-corn soup, 21; dumpling soup, 22; giblet soup, Shorty Piotter's, 22; gizzards, pickled, 145; ham and, shortcake, Belleweather Plantation, 106; liver sauté, 144; loaf, 144; mold, 146; Muriel Humphrey's special occasion dish, 154; noodle soup, Anderson House, 24; oven-fried, quick and easy, 145; pie, baked, 146; pie, country-crust, 148; piquant i a pancake shell, 148; plum-glazed, 149; 'n' potato casserole, 150; ribs and, hoedown, 131; rolls, 152; spaghetti, 153

Chili, barnburner, 103

Chocolate: bar pie, 226; brittle, 345; cake, Maggie's, 258; cherry-, cake, 256; -cherry cookies, Mrs. Guenther's, 324; -coconut cake, 257; cookie sandwiches, 319; crisps, quick, 323; dark, icing, 258; dipping, 321; double-, fruit cake, 266; double-, marshmallow cake, 260; -filled snowballs, 296; filling, 203; fudge sauce, perfect, 286; German, fudge, 350; glaze, 261; icebox dessert, Italian, 302; icing, deluxe, 282; kisses, 325; mocha crunch pie, 227; -peppermint icebox dessert, 297; petal crust, 226; pfeffernuesse, 325; pound cake, 255; -raspberry cake supreme, 261; sour cream buns, 202; truffles, 346; Viennese, iced, 358; whipped cream, 283

Chow chow, 366

Chowder(s): Ann's bacon and potato, 17; Biloxi, 25; cheeseburger, 21; corn, Pennsylvania Dutch, 26; Dutch, 'n' dumplings, 23; The Captain's, 19

Cider, hot spiced, Hospitality Inn, 357

Cinnamon: butter, 287; rolls, peanut butter, 215

Clam spaghetti, Dr. Criscuolo's, 79

Cocoa: cloud cookies, 326; frosted, South American, 357

Coconut: brittle, 346; chocolate-, cake, 257; macaroons, 326; pineapple-rum, balls, 310; refrigerator dessert, 298; rum pie, Ethyl Furne's, 240; toffee, bars, 342; torte, White House, 299

Coffee: cream filling, 263; creamy, icing, 249; jelly, frosted, 300; lover's delight, 356; meringue pie, 228; old-fashioned egg, 359; -raspberry ribbon cake, 262; -rum crisps, 327; syrup, 289

Coffee cake, banana, 195

Coleslaw: bleu cheese, 48; -stuffed tomato, 61

Conserve(s): holiday, 366; plum, 367; rainbow, 367; rhubarb, 368. See also Jam; Preserves

Cookies: ammonia, 319; Bessie's gold bricks, 332; Blanche Eaves's pineapple cheesecake bars, 340; boozers, 321; candied cherry Christmas, 320; candy-bar, 322; Chinese chews, 322; chocolate-cherry, Mrs. Guenther's, 324; chocolate kisses, 325; chocolate pfeffernuesse, 325; chocolate, sandwiches, 319; cocoa cloud, 326; coconut macaroons, 326; coffee-rum crisps, 327; date-nut chews, 327; double-good peanut butter, 338; fig-nut squares, 328; Florentines, 328; forgotten, 329; fruit jewels, 330; Johanna Hall's very lemon, 333; Johnny Appleseed bars, 331; lemon diamonds, 333; mincemeat, 334; oatmeal crispies, 335; orange squares, 335; peanut balls, 336; peanut butterscotch bars, 337; pecan meringues, 336; pecan pie, 340; pink meringue clouds, 335; potato chip, 338; quick chocolate crisps, 323; raspberry walnut diamonds, 341; refrigerator, 330; Swedish nut ball, 334; toffee coconut bars, 342; whiskey snaps, 342. See also Brownies

Corn bread, molasses, 210

Corn: chicken-, soup, 21; chowder, Pennsylvania Dutch, 26; fresh, casserole, Perry County, 169; fritters, Grandma's, 171; muffins, supreme, Longfellow, 201; onion and, scallop, Anderson House, 175; relish, 368; soup with rivels, 26

Corned beef and dumplings, 107

Cornmeal ring, golden, with beef sauce, 99

Cottage cream dressing, 68

Crab: Alaskan King, gourmet sandwich, 80; Alaskan Snow, Monte Cristo decker, 90; casserole deluxe, 80; Mississippi scalloped, casserole, 83

Crabmeat: filling, 82; puffs, 82

Cranberry: burrs, skewered lamb with, 113; cream cheese frosting, 259; loaf, frozen, 300; -orange bread, 204; spice cake, 259

Cream cheese: orange-, bread, 212; -pecan pie, 236
Cream soup base, 27
Creamy pepper dressing, 69
Creole mustard dressing, 69
Cucumber(s): braised, 172; -carrot relish, 369; dressing, 68; escalloped, 173; fried, 172; frozen, 173; rings, stuffed, 50; sour cream-, sauce, 68
Custard sauce, alternate, 314

Daffodil cake, 264
Date(s): butter, 289; double, cake, 265; -nut chews, 327
Dessert(s): cheesy apple squares, 296; chocolate-filled snowballs, 296; chocolate-peppermint icebox, 297; coconut refrigerator, 298; Ellie Concidine's pineapple delight, 310; frosted coffee jelly, 300; frozen cranberry loaf, 300; Italian chocolate icebox, 302; lemon fluff squares, 304; maple frango, 306; maple-walnut tapioca, 308; melon balls Jon-Mar, 307; old fashioned apple, 293; pecan pie bars, 308; pineapple-rum-coconut balls, 310; pumpkin cake, 313; raspberry, 311; Vinarterta, 312. See also Cakes; Ice cream; Pies; Puddings; Soufflés; Tarts; Tortes
Dill: butter, 74; dressing, 70; pickles, 51
Dilled lasagne rollups, 104
Dilly beans, 369
Divinity fudge, 348
Dough: pot pie, 147; squares, 109
Doughnuts, fruit, Mahala's little, 210
Dressing(s): cottage cream, 68; creamy pepper, 69; Creole mustard, 69; cucumber, 68; dill, 70; green goddess, 72; herb, 73; honest-to-goodness dieters', 70; honey, 73; The Anderson House special French, 72. See also Salad dressings; Sauce
Dumplings, 22; chicken and, Grandma

Anderson's, 143; chicken, soup, 22; corned beef and, 107; Dutch chowder 'n', 23; egg, 107; Southern, 143

Easter eggs, onion, Pennsylvania Dutch, 370
Egg(s): beet and, salad, Nora Hoffman's, 42; Dutch pickled, 371; Easter, Pennsylvania Dutch onion, 370; pickled, 56, 370; ramp-and-, scramble, Loren's, 178
Eggnog: peach-brandy, 359; praline-, pie, 237; punchbowl, 360
Eggplant: Creole, Joyce's, 174; lamb-stuffed, 116

Fig: and fruit medley, Mississippi, 71; -honey, bread, whole wheat, 203; jam, Poplarville, Mississippi, 370; -nut squares, 328; pudding, steamed, 302; sauce, 328
Filling(s): cherry, 256; chocolate, 203; coffee-cream, 263; honey spread, 206
Fish: batter, secret, 84; mushroom-stuffed, 86. See also Red Snapper; Salmon; Trout; Tuna
Florentines, 328
French dressing, The Anderson House special, 72
Fritters, grandma's corn, 171
Frosting(s): brown sugar, 281; burnt-sugar, 253; buttercream, 257; caramel, 282; chocolate whipped cream, 283; cranberry cream cheese, 259; creamy white, 260; Kahlua, 284; lemon, 277; never-fail caramel chiffon, 282; never-fail delicate white, 283; no-cook marsh-mallow, 284; quick fudge, 251. See also Glazes; Icings; Toppings
Fruit: cake, double-chocolate, 266; cake, Ida's white, 276; fig and, medley, Mississippi, 71
Fudge: Alice Bruner's never-fail, 348; Belle Ebner's famous, 347; cake with fluffy peppermint icing, 267; divinity,

ter, 234; plantation peanut, 234; praline eggnog, 237; pumpkin meringue, 238; raspberry mousse meringue, 239; rhubarb, 238; sour cream-raisin, 242; strawberry-banana, 244; *See also* Tarts; Tortes

Pie crusts: chocolate petal crust, 226; mocha pie shell, 228

Pineapple: carrot circles and, 170; cheese and, salad, 49; cheesecake bars, Blanche Eaves's, 340; delight, Ellie Concidine's, 310; -rum-coconut balls, 310; squash, Johanna Hall's, 185; torte, 309

Plum: conserve, 367; -glazed chicken, 149

Polonaise sauce, 67

Pork: balls and sauerkraut, Ray Broadwater's, 124; chops, apple and onion, 126; chops, Hank's heavenly, 128; chops italiano, 126; chops with pears, 127; chop, Wrangler's, tin-plate special, 129; Nora's Pennsylvania Dutch scrapple, 132; pie, Mayor Latimer's Christmas, 125; tenderloin, Polish-style, 130. *See also* Ribs

Pot roast, Grandma's, 130

Potato(es): and bean soup, 33; and sauerkraut, Mahala's Pennsylvania Dutch, 178; bacon, salad, 58; carrot-, scallop, 170; chicken 'n', casserole, 150; chip cookies, 338; bacon and, chowder, Ann's, 17; country club, 177; creamed browned, with bacon, 181; green onion and, soup, 27; pudding, baked, 176; salad, old-fashioned, 58; sesame, spears, 177; soup, Basque, 32; why?, 181

Praline-eggnog pie, 237

Preserves, blue-ribbon strawberry, 373. *See also* Conserves; Jam

Pudding(s): baked potato, 176; caramel upside-down, 298; Kungsholm Swedish, with raspberry sauce, 314; New England Indian, 301; fig, steamed, 302

Pumpkin: cake dessert, 313; meringue pie, 238; soup, 33

Punch: anniversary, 355; banana, 355; Christmas Eve, 356

Raisin, sour cream-, pie, 242

Ramp-and-egg scramble, Loren's, 178

Raspberry(ies): chocolate-, cake supreme, 261; coffee-, ribbon cake, 262; dessert, 311; mousse meringue pie, 239; rolls, flaky, 213; salad, Katie Hall's, 59; tarts, Ann Polischtak's Ukrainian, 241; walnut diamonds, 341

Red beans and rice, Duke Ellington's, 160

Red cabbage: and sausage soup, 36; braised, with leg of lamb, 114; pickled, 162; sweet-and-sour, 165

Red snapper Creole, baked, 81

Relish(es): corn; 368; cucumber-carrot, 369

Reuben soup, 35

Rhubarb pie, 238

Ribs: and chicken, hoedown, 131; and kraut, 136; John Hall's moose hunter's beans and, 166; short, busy girl's great, 134

Rice, scalloped, 180

Rivels, corn soup with, 26

Rolls: blockbusters, 196; emergency caramel-nut, 199; flaky raspberry, 213; nut, never-fail holiday, 206; peanut butter cinnamon, 215; sixty-minute, 217

Roquefort mold, Madame's, 61

Rum: cake, 275; -coconut, pineapple-, balls, 310; -raisin sauce, 288

Rutabaga en casserole, 179

Salad(s): apricot, 42; bacon potato, 58; beet and apple, 43; Belle Ebner's special luncheon, 56; Bermuda, bowl, 46; Caesar, 47; cheese and pineapple, 49; chicken and sweetbread, 48; frozen banana, 41; Hospitality Inn, 52; jellied black cherry, 45; jellied cantaloupe, 46; Katie Hall's raspberry, 59; King's ransom, 53; mandarin orange sherbet, 54; Nora Hoffman's beet and egg, 42; old fashioned potato, 58; pasta primavera, 55; pear, with watermelon ice, 57; Pennsylvania Dutch wilted lettuce, 54; pickled eggs, 56; salmon, tropicale, 60; strawberry, 60; stuffed cucumber rings, 50; stuffed dill pickles, 51; summer ginger ale, 52; sweetbread, 62; vegetable-beef, 62. *See also* Coleslaw; Molds; Slaws

Salad dressing(s): apricot, 42; banana, 45; hot, 54; India relish, 46; island spice, 60; mayonnaise, 53; mint, 57; nut, 49; Polynesian, 75

Salmon: Imperial, 86; salad tropicale, 60

Salt pork cream gravy, 75

Salt, seasoned, 372

Sangria, summer, 360

Sauce(s): barbecue, 65, 136; beef, 99; dill butter, 74; Imperial, 87; fresh mushroom, 88; Mahala's mustard, 66; moutarde, 66; mushroom, 74, 91, 152; peanut, 74; polonaise, 67; sour cream-cucumber, 68; secret tartar, 85; verte, 67; white, basic, 72; white, thick, 76. *See also* Gravy

Sauce(s), dessert: Bing cherry, 285; blueberry, 286; brandied hard, 266; caramel rum, 247; elegant butterscotch, 287; fig, 328; Mississippi fig and fruit medley, 71; perfect chocolate fudge, 286; rum-raisin, 288; strawberry, 288; tutti-frutti sundae, 287. *See also* Dressings

Sauerkraut: and Polish sausage casserole, 125; balls, 183; casserole, Dutch, 182; ham-and-, balls, 111; pork balls and, Ray Broadwater's, 124; potatoes and, Mahala's Pennsylvania Dutch, 178; soup, Welcome Anderson's, 34

Sausage: Polish, sauerkraut and, casserole,

125; red cabbage and, soup, 36

Scallops: heavenly, 85; Rumaki, 87

Schweinkoteletten mit Birne, 127

Scrapple, Nora's Pennsylvania Dutch, 132

Seafood. *See* Clam; Crab; Scallops; Shrimp

Sesame potato spears, 177

Sherry wine jelly, 372

Short rib soup, 34

Shrimp squares with fresh mushroom sauce, 88

Slaw(s): Ann's cabbage, 45; beer cabbage, 44; hot, Pennsylvania Dutch go-to-meeting, 50

Soufflé(s): brandy Alexander, 294; cheese, with fresh mushroom sauce, 168; hot lemon, 305

Soup(s): Amsterdam tomato, 38; Anderson House beer and cheese, 20; Anderson House chicken noodle, 24; Anderson House pea, 31; Basque potato, 32; cabbage, San Juan, 18; cheese and spinach, 20; chicken-corn, 21; chicken dumpling, 22; corn, with rivels, 26; cream of broccoli, 18; cream of onion, 30; cream of peanut, 32; gazpacho, 28; green onion and potato, 27; Minnesota wild rice, 36; mushroom-barley, 28; oxtail, 30; potato and bean, 33; pumpkin, 33; red cabbage and sausage, 36; Reuben, 35; Senate bean, 17; short rib, 34; Shorty Piotter's chicken giblet, 22; split pea, 31; Welcome Anderson's country, 37; Welcome Anderson's sauerkraut, 34. *See also* Bisque; Chowders; Gumbo

Soup base, cream, 27

Sour cream: chocolate, buns, 202; cucumber sauce, 68; muffins, 217; -raisin pie, 242; topping, 285

Spaetzles, Hungarian, 105

Spinach: -and-cheese squares, 184; balls, 182; cheese and, soup, 20; filling, 168

Split pea soup, 31

Recipe Notes

Recipe Notes

Recipe Notes